After a career in advertising, Christopher Turner took a sabbatical to visit many European cities. Discovering that few guidebooks were 'user friendly', he decided to write one himself. His first book, *London Step by Step*, won the London Tourist Board's Guidebook of the Year award for 1985 and is now in its third edition. Five more London books followed in the series. In 1991 his first books on continental cities, *Paris Step by Step* and *Barcelona Step by Step*, were published, and he is now completing a guide to Amsterdam.

CHRISTOPHER TURNER

THE PENGUIN GUIDE TO
SEVILLE

PENGUIN BOOKS

PENGUIN BOOKS

Published by the Penguin Group
Penguin Books Ltd, 27 Wrights Lane, London w8 5tz, England
Penguin Books USA Inc., 375 Hudson Street, New York, New York 10014, USA
Penguin Books Australia Ltd, Ringwood, Victoria, Australia
Penguin Books Canada Ltd, 10 Alcorn Avenue, Toronto, Ontario, Canada m4v 3b2
Penguin Books (NZ) Ltd, 182–190 Wairau Road, Auckland 10, New Zealand

Penguin Books Ltd, Registered Offices: Harmondsworth, Middlesex, England

First published 1992
1 3 5 7 9 10 8 6 4 2

Printed in England by Clays Ltd, St Ives plc

CONTENTS

Excursions from Seville

INTRODUCTION

Seville is the only great European city with a large central area consisting almost entirely of narrow, winding streets that still follow their medieval pattern. This is an important component of its charm, of course, but it also creates a stumbling-block for the visitor who wants to discover the gems that are hidden within the maze. Partly for that reason, the emphasis in this book is on clear and precise directions, backed up by large-scale maps. The same principle is followed for major buildings – for example, Seville's cathedral is the world's largest and, unless every chapel is mentioned, it will be difficult for the visitor to follow a chosen route. Not all this detail makes for gripping bedside reading, of course, but it will prove indispensable when you are faced, for instance, with five interconnecting alleyways, most of which are unidentified, and know that a nearby building which you want to visit closes in twenty minutes.

The Penguin Guide to Seville is, therefore, essentially a guidebook, not a travel book, and I have kept literary purple passages and my own opinions to a minimum, bearing in mind that a visitor has limited reading time available 'on the hoof'. Typefaces throughout have been chosen with prime importance placed on adequate size and legibility, as not all readers will have perfect eyesight, and many church interiors are dark.

In conjunction with Expo '92, an enormous amount of money has been spent on restoring dilapidated buildings in the city, and the visitor will now be presented with a Seville more splendid than it has been for centuries. You may not have sufficient time to see it all, but such is the lure of this magical city that a return visit is a virtual certainty.

Christopher Turner

SEVILLE AND THE SEVILLANOS

The city

Seville is one of the few cities that, like Venice, immediately and completely fulfils the expectations of visitors. When describing it, a writer is hard put not to resort to clichés but, on the other hand, hyperbole is almost impossible. Seville is, in itself, a supreme cliché, reflecting everyone's first mental image of Spain – bullfights, *bodegas*, wrought-iron balconies, fountains, Moorish arabesques, ceramic tiles, *flamenco* . . . In fact, not only is Seville very untypical of Spain, it is also untypical of its province: the cities of Granada, Córdoba, Cádiz and Málaga might as well be 1,000 miles away for all that they have in common with Andalusia's capital. It is true that there are a few towns nearby that are somewhat reminiscent of Seville – Jerez, Huelva, Sanlúcar de Barrameda and Puerto de Santa María are prime examples – but these are spread over the relatively small 'sherry' region that hugs the Atlantic coast.

It is the blinding colours of Seville, more than anything else, that set it apart. The ever-present blue sky remains deep blue, rarely dissolving into the summer haziness of the Mediterranean coast. Much of the city is shaded by orange trees, their leaves remaining emerald green all year round. The oranges themselves provide additional speckles of colour during the cooler months, and towards the end of March the voluptuous scent of their blossom duels with, and defeats, the heavy perfumes favoured by wealthy tourists from Arabia.

Most towns and villages in southern Spain follow the 'Moorish tradition', which is interpreted as meaning that the exteriors of their buildings must be plain, and painted any colour – as long as it is white. To me, this 'white-out' quickly palls, for all its advantage of deflecting hot sunshine, and I become ravenous for colour. I have a theory that other northern Europeans possess this same latent need, which is why so many of them become dissatisfied with retirement in the whiter than white *pueblos* of Andalusia. Admittedly, the walls of most of the houses in Seville also have a white base but, possibly due to the existence of local pigments, various shades of yellow ochre and dusty pink enliven them. Multicoloured ceramic tiles are frequently applied with abandon, below eaves, around window and door openings and, most dramatically, within patios. Sometimes further colour is added by leaving quoins and architraves undecorated, so that the natural stone or brick of the fabric is revealed. Decorative wrought-iron work, painted black as it should always be, is used in a variety of ways, to form balconies, grilles, shutters, rails, lamps and window-frames.

Virtually all the buildings of interest in Seville lie within the area formerly bounded by its ancient wall, and it is supremely easy to see the city on foot, aided by the limited but efficient bus service. No stranger would be advised to attempt to use a car for sightseeing – even the local taxi-drivers get confused by the medieval street pattern and the ever-changing one-way systems. Only a fraction of the Moorish wall remains, but its route is outlined precisely by a ring road and, to the west, by the river Guadalquivir. From the southern wall of the Alcázar stretch a series of subtropical gardens, culminating in María Luisa Park and providing central Seville with a splendid coda of greenery.

As with all cities of enchantment, a typical walk through Seville is packed with visual excitement. This is achieved not by grand vistas as, for example, in Paris and Rome, or, with few exceptions, by architectural magnificence, but by winding streets, archways, quiet squares and the sudden, unexpected appearance of a portal or tower of a church, as in London. Lively bars, most of which are brimming with cornucopias of *tapas*, are found everywhere and are extremely hard to resist, particularly in summer, when their virtually mandatory air-conditioning provides an oasis in which to escape from the pulsating midday heat.

The three great 'sights' of the city, the cathedral, the Alcázar and the House of Pilate, remain open throughout the afternoon, but churches, museums and most shops close. In 1992, Expo will remain open for most of the day and night and it is probable that some other buildings of interest will forgo, at least temporarily, their normally obligatory siesta. My first visit to Seville was in mid-June 1972, and I found it impossible to remain outside for most of the afternoon – the dryness of the heat makes it less tolerable than in the Far East, where humidity takes some of the sting out of the sun. At midday I generally spent an hour in a *tapas* bar, then showered in my hotel and followed this with a siesta, from which I awoke around four – beware of sleeping *au naturel* in air-conditioning, as it is easy to catch a cold! After a reviving coffee, I would slowly continue exploring Seville. Those with hotel swimming-pools can mitigate the afternoon heat in a different way by impersonating a hippopotamus, with nostrils just above water level, and there are, of course, public swimming-pools (see page 25). By six, most churches are lethargically preparing for Mass and willing, at last, to admit visitors.

Readers will note that I rarely date vernacular buildings, very little reliable information about them being available. Although the fabric of some houses is known to go back to the Moorish period, most have been remodelled to provide what are regarded as 'typical' Seville dwellings. Unlike Barcelona, Romanesque and Gothic detailing is virtually non-existent. Balconies and roof terraces seem to have been established in the mid eighteenth century, but wrought-iron work did not replace timber until a century later and it can safely be said that the present appearance of the façades and patios of most buildings dates from this period. An obvious Moorish inheritance is the central patio, arcaded, tiled, provided with a fountain and brimming with flowers. In the summer months, this becomes the main 'living-room' of the house.

Few cities of similar size boast more churches of interest than Seville. Years of neglect had threatened the continued existence of many until recently, but immense government and provincial grants, in connection with the Expo '92 sprucing-up, have saved practically all of them – in the nick of time. Most of the churches to benefit are public ones, but a few monastic examples, mostly those open to visitors, have also received support. Churches were quickly established in the city after the 1248 Reconquest, initially in the form of consecrated mosques. New structures gradually took their place, but the brick-built minaret was frequently retained, as was the ablutions patio in the cases of El Salvador and the cathedral. Mudéjar (Muslims living under Christian rule) and Christian worked together building the churches, and a fairly rigid format of an aisled nave with bell-tower evolved. Equally stylized were the Mudéjar/Gothic façades, in particular their portals, which featured a pointed arch, its outer archivolts decorated with Moorish patterns. Corbels took the form of stylized lions' heads, and above them stood carved figures. Arches were frequently multi-lobed or horseshoe. Few minarets have survived in their entirety, due partly to earthquakes, and all are now surmounted by Baroque or Renaissance campaniles, most of which incorporate gleaming, ceramic-clad cupolas.

Important secular buildings range from the austere, Renaissance-style Archives of the Indies, through the Plateresque City Hall and the Baroque Fine Arts Museum, to the Revivalist pavilions built for the 1929 exhibition. These, like most buildings in the city, maintain the tradition of forsaking purity of style in favour of a Seville compromise, in which vivacity, colour and lightness of touch are the guiding principles. Many agree that the building that most typifies Seville, in its extraordinary but harmonious blend of Gothic, Mudéjar and Renaissance styles, is the House of Pilate, still the residence of the Dukes of Medinaceli, but fortunately open to the public.

The Sevillano

Sevillanos are alleged to possess a high degree of Moorish blood – thus accounting for their passionate, fiery, and narcissistic tendencies. Many, however, dispute this, pointing out that all Seville's Moors were replaced by Christians and Jews at the Reconquest and that Philip III banished those that had returned, early in the seventeenth century. Although some interbreeding has undoubtedly left a Moorish strain, it is more likely to be the vivacious gypsy population, arriving from Egypt in the fifteenth century, that has given Sevillanos some of their more notable traits. The gypsies were entirely responsible for *flamenco*.

The long afternoon siesta has given the Sevillano, and the Spanish in general, an unfair reputation for indolence; foreigners neglect to appreciate that work begins earlier and ends later than in most European countries. Only a few minutes spent outside on a torrid Andalusian afternoon will convince those from cooler climes of the urgent need for non-activity. In recent years, air-conditioning has made it possible for work to continue indoors, but the established time schedule is generally preferred.

Andalusians are still by far the poorest people in Spain. Just under 1.5 per cent of the landowners possess 50 per cent of the estates, and it is only this small minority that has really benefited from the tourist development boom along the coast. Most of the early contractors were foreign, and the experienced labour needed to run the new establishments initially came from other parts of Spain, there being no local hotel or restaurant tradition. The owners of the great sherry empires have for generations been primarily British, although intermarriage with Spaniards has gradually occurred. This unequal distribution of wealth has led to extreme poverty, rivalling parts of the third world. An elegant lady living in the ultra-fashionable Patio de las Banderas of the Alcázar remarked to me, as recently as 1990, 'True we are no longer in the third world – perhaps the two-and-a-half world would be more accurate.' She complained of inefficiency, conservatism, petty crime, excessive reliance on religion, drugs, corruption, pollution and male chauvinism. Only now, with the tremendous expenditure by the state on the infrastructure of western Andalusia, spurred on by Expo '92, are more general prosperity and a halt to emigration realistic prognostications.

One effect of all this is that the visitor needs to take extreme care with possessions. Relatively, Seville has the highest crime rate in Spain, therefore the minimum of cash and valuables should be carried, all covered by comprehensive insurance. Motorists should never park a car unguarded in the city or drive with windows open wide enough for a motorcyclist's snatch. The strict rule of Franco has been replaced by a soft glove – too soft in the view of many – and insufficient protection is provided against those who take advantage. Absurd lightning strikes can occur at any time, the complainants flailing around like spoilt children, intent on creating as much mayhem as possible. All ports in southern Spain were recently closed by fishermen because they had a dispute, not with their own country, but with Morocco! The inept and impotent authorities permitted them to barricade every harbour for three weeks, imprisoning cruise liners that were going nowhere near Morocco. Demented British tourists were suggesting that if the Almighty would not permit a brief return by Franco, at least Mrs Thatcher might be loaned for a short while to sort them out. Always be prepared for strikes and have plans ready to circumvent them, if at all possible.

Before long, it will become obvious to a stranger that the Roman Catholic religion plays a very important part in the life of the Sevillano. A succession of feast days devoted to saints and biblical events punctuates the calendar. Make sure you are aware of them, as virtually everything closes on those occasions (see page 22). Within the numerous churches, parishioners kneel in absolute devotion before statues and paintings of the Virgin Mary. The figures are frequently dressed in glamorous clothes of the most sumptuous materials – the results looking like dolls to many astonished foreigners; in addition, they are rarely left unpainted, thus amplifying their doll-like appearance. It should be remembered, however, that the common pre-Renaissance tradition of painting sculptures and carvings has been maintained.

Is it or is it not idolatry? No doubt the possibility of transubstantiation does exist for some, but most worshippers will claim that the figure, for them, is primarily a focusing aid for their prayers. My own theory is that the unusual popularity of representative religious figures in Andalusia arose as a conscious rebuttal of Islam's doctrinaire opposition to them. On occasions, it is not easy to separate genuine faith from mere observance of tradition; an enthusiastic current member of the *cofradía* (brotherhood) of the Macarena Virgin, for example, is a communist politician, who has openly professed atheism.

What will the foreigner's abiding impression of Sevillanos be? It depends on personal views and experiences, of course, but I found them in general more laid-back than most Spaniards, yet without ever losing a sense of formality and decorum. Andalusians are not to be compared with the exuberant Italians or Greeks. Always courteous and anxious to help, even though, as is generally the case, he understands no foreign languages, the Sevillano will do all he can to assist the stranger who is in difficulty.

Even the poorest young Sevillano manages to look elegant. Generally short in stature (presumably due to centuries of ill-nourishment), and with unbelievably narrow waists, the men wear jackets and ties when most would favour a tee-shirt. Drunkenness is a rarity in spite of high sherry consumption, the constant nibbling at *tapas* bars probably supplying a magic antidote to alcohol. Many of Spain's greatest painters, including Velázquez, Murillo and Picasso, first saw the light of day in Andalusia, and the artistry of the people is evident, examples of bad taste being rare, irrespective of wealth.

One suggestion – if the subject of Gibraltar's return to Spain comes up (and it often does), a good-humoured response is best. I usually point out how lucky the Spanish are to have somewhere as foreign and strange as Gibraltar on their doorstep, bemoaning the fact that Bexhill, for example, is not a Spanish enclave, where the English could pop over for an evening of proper *tapas*, cheap wine and drinkable coffee. This usually goes down well, and draft treaties are negotiated over another sherry.

THE HISTORY AND DEVELOPMENT OF SEVILLE

Seville's history fairly accurately reflects that of Spain itself, the city never having experienced long periods of independence like, for example, Granada and Catalonia. An existing settlement was razed by the Carthaginians shortly after 500 BC and they gave it the name of Hispalis, meaning flat land. The Roman general Scipio founded Itálica in 206 BC on a hill overlooking the west bank of the Guadalquivir, but it was not until 45 BC that Julius Caesar, immediately following his defeat of Pompey, named Seville, on the low-lying opposite bank of the river, Julia Romula Hispalis. Seville quickly developed as a trading city, primarily occupied by merchants, whereas Itálica was favoured by the aristocracy, politicians and administrators.

Little survives in Seville from the Roman period: above ground level only columns from a great temple remain, while below the Archbishop's Palace lie traces of baths and beneath the church of Santa Catalina, a section of the city wall. Roman mosaic pavements and sculptures exhibited in the Palace of the Countess of Lebrija, the House of Pilate and the Archaeological Museum come not from Seville but from Itálica, a much grander city.

During Diocletian's persecution of Christians in the third century, two female tile-makers from Triana, Justa and Rufina, were martyred and later became Seville's most popular saints, being featured in many paintings. Christianity was soon permitted, and it is probable that the city's first church was built on the site of the present El Salvador at the beginning of the fourth century.

The Vandals took Seville in 426, and some believe that their name for southern Spain was Vandalicia, which was gradually corrupted to Andalusia. The Visigoths, Germanic allies of Rome, swept through the peninsula, Seville falling to them early in the fifth century. In 589 they adopted Christianity as a unifying religion, and churches were built once more: the foundations of the basilica of their San Vicente lie beneath the Alcázar's Patio de las Banderas, and the great bowl of its font now stands in the cathedral's Patio de los Naranjos. Another Visigothic church is known to have stood on the site of the cathedral.

Only re-used features of Visigothic buildings survive, usually in the form of columns with distinctive capitals: there is an example embedded in a corner of Plaza de Santa Cruz, and several in the patio of El Salvador. Seville was the only true cultural centre to exist in Latin Christendom during the 300 years of Visigothic rule, which ended abruptly, due to internal feuding, early in the eighth century. One faction, supporting Akhila, sought help from North African Muslims against another faction led by Roderick, who was duly defeated and killed by the combined armies. Instead of returning to North Africa, however, the Muslims liked what they saw and within seven years had conquered the entire peninsula. Thus commenced 800 years of Moorish hegemony on Spanish soil, even though the Reconquest began within four years, when part of northern Spain was freed and the Christian kingdom of Astúrias was created.

All the Islamic conquerors of Spain are generally, but imprecisely, referred to as Moors, a word probably derived from Mauretania. In fact, their only unifying characteristics were the Arabic language and the Muslim religion, some ruling dynasties comprising Semitic Arabs from the Middle East, others Aryan Berbers from North Africa. Although there would almost certainly have been black people among the occupying forces, their leaders were fair-skinned: Shakespeare's depiction of the Moor, Othello, as a negro is historically implausible. It should not be assumed that as the Reconquest gradually gained momentum the Christian and Muslim states were perpetually opposed to each other on religious grounds, there being many instances of Christians assisting one Muslim leader against another and of Muslims assisting Christians against other Muslims. The Koran expressly tolerates Christianity and Judaism, and for most of Seville's period of Muslim rule, members of the three religions lived together in perfect harmony, with equal rights. Another misconception is that one style of 'Arab' art and architecture prevailed over the 800-year period. Although the contemporary Romanesque and Gothic styles of the Christians had virtually no influence, there is little in common between, for example, the buildings of the caliphate period, with their horseshoe arches and distinctive capitals, the Almohads' severe brick structures, decorated only with geometric panels, and the delicate columns and filigree plasterwork of the Nasrids.

Seville was taken by Moussa bin Nusayr in 712, but his excessive popularity rang alarm bells in Damascus and he was called back by the Caliph. Abdul Aziz then governed Seville from the Alcázar, his fortress probably being the first to be built on the site. Almost immediately, he married the widow of the defeated Visigothic leader, Roderick, probably regarding this as a shrewd political move to gain the co-operation of the Christians who had remained (Mozarabs). Seville now became known as Ishbilya, and this pronunciation of 'Sevilla' is still commonly heard. The city, an emirate of Damascus, was made the capital of al-Andalus, which then comprised the entire extent of Muslim Spain. Arabs, many of them from what is now Yemen, had the dominant position, Berbers being given inferior properties.

In 755, Abdul Rahman I, the only surviving member of the Umayyad dynasty, fled from Damascus, where the remainder of his family had been massacred, and set up an independent emirate in Córdoba. It appears that at this time Seville was unwalled, and an attack by marauding Vikings from the river Guadalquivir razed the city. Shortly afterwards, Abdul Rahman II built what may have been Seville's first defensive wall since the Roman period; he was also responsible for the earliest shipyards.

The Córdoba caliphate collapsed in 1031, when the last Umayyad was deposed, and, under the Abbasids, Seville outstripped Córdoba in importance. The city's first great mosque was built on the site of the church of El Salvador; most of this mosque's patio and the lower section of its minaret survive. Andalusia was now divided into several independent kingdoms, known as *taifas*, the most important of which was Seville.

Al Mutamid, Seville's 'poet king', was replaced by the Almoravids from the Sahara region in 1091. They had recently assisted Al Mutamid against the Christian Alfonso VI, victor at Toledo, but returned to depose him. The Almoravids were austere and deeply religious, but they were apparently quickly melted by the sybaritic atmosphere of Seville. Under Rachid, Seville's wall was expanded *c.* 1107, and the Almoravids' brick-built defences were to mark the final parameters of the city's enclosure; they remain the core of the few stretches that have survived, around the Alcázar and between the Córdoba and Macarena gates. Nothing else of importance from their rule survives.

In North Africa the Almoravids were defeated by the Almohads, who came from the mountains, and Seville fell to them in 1121. Yaqub Yasuf then governed Andalusia, residing in Seville's Alcázar and building a new palace there, from which the Patio del Yeso survives. In 1163 he inherited the caliphate, but remained in Seville, constructing its great mosque on the site of the present cathedral. Part of the ablutions patio remains, but more important is the minaret, now known as the Giralda.

As a defensive measure against the Christians, who now occupied half of Spain, the Tower of Gold was constructed in 1220, linked by a chain to a similar structure across the river. However, this did not stop Fernando III, fresh from his victory in Córdoba, and Seville fell to him in 1248: more than 500 years of Muslim dominion over the city were at an end. Fernando is known as the saint-king; he was canonized in 1671. Humanely, for the time, the Moors were given a month in which to vacate their properties, which were then distributed by the King among his followers. These included Jews, who expected, rightly, that in thanks for their support they would be treated better than they had been by the Almohads. Fernando was adamant that no buildings, including mosques, should be damaged in any way. Granada's first Nasrid ruler, Mohammed I, had assisted Fernando in his campaign, and was permitted to retain his kingdom, the King probably regarding it as a convenient settlement area for Spain's Muslim population. Nevertheless, from now on Granada was to be a vassal state of Castile, tribute being exacted.

Mosques were immediately consecrated as churches, but when Alfonso X inherited the throne four years later, he presented three of them to the Jewish community for use as synagogues, thus marking the high point in the relationship between Seville's Christians and Jews. Some Jews had lived in Seville before the Reconquest, and there was probably a ghetto in existence; by tradition, the key to the main gate in its wall was presented to Fernando when the city surrendered, and it is to be found among the possessions of the cathedral's treasury. After the Reconquest, most of the Jewish ghetto occupied what is now known as the Santa Cruz quarter, but it appears to have expanded to the north later. The fabric of one synagogue possibly exists beneath the superimposed shell of Santa María la Blanca, and its portal was re-used as a side entrance to the church. Apart from this, and some hidden wall remnants, no trace survives of the ghetto's 250-year existence.

Moors gradually returned to work in the city, still being permitted to follow their Islamic religion and assisting the Christians in their building work, including the replacement of mosques with churches. They were known as Mudéjars, and their Islamic architectural style was blended with Gothic, so that there are areas in some churches that appear to have strayed from mosques. Very few Reconquest buildings escaped Mudéjar influence, notable exceptions being the Tower of Don Fadrique, built in 1252, and Triana's great church of Santa Ana. Both of these, uniquely in Seville, combined the dying Romanesque style with Gothic, in a Transitional manner. Another early Gothic building to survive, in part, is the Palace of the Emperor Carlos V at the Alcázar, which represents a sixteenth-century remodelling of three rib-vaulted halls built for Alfonso X.

Pedro I (1334–69), known, perhaps somewhat unfairly, as 'Pedro the Cruel', was responsible for Spain's outstanding Mudéjar building, a veritable masterpiece, when he commissioned a new palace to be built at the Alcázar. Almost entirely Moorish in appearance, only the expert eye can discern that it was built for a Christian. Pedro had recently helped the Muslim leader of Granada regain his throne, and much of the work on the palace was executed by craftsmen responsible for recent work at the Alhambra, whom their grateful ruler had sent to assist.

Meanwhile, the wealth and skills of the Jewish community were creating, as elsewhere in Europe, anti-Semitic feeling, and a minor attack on the ghetto took place in 1354. Religious intolerance, led by Archbishop Fernán Martínez, was encouraged by the new dynasty that ruled Spain, and in 1391 the ghetto was sacked and many Jews were murdered. Soon afterwards, the Jewish religion was proscribed and synagogues were demolished; all Jews were forced to convert to Christianity or leave the city. By the fifteenth century the ghetto had disappeared, and in 1492 unconverted Jews were banished from all of Spain by decree of the Catholic Monarchs, Ferdinand and Isabella. The Inquisition had begun in Andalusia in 1482, and most of its early victims were baptized Jews convicted of heresy by officials of the Roman Catholic church.

Religious intolerance apart, the fifteenth century witnessed a great deal of creative activity, beginning with the building of the cathedral in 1402, now acknowledged as the largest in the world. Gothic in conception, it was one of the last great buildings to be designed in that style, although a series of Renaissance chapels was later to create an amalgam of styles. At the same time, the great monastery of Santa María de las Cuevas was begun on La Cartuja island. The end of the century saw the development of the Isabelline style, in which Gothic was given a great deal of sculptural embellishment. Maese Rodrigo founded what was to become Seville's first university, at Puerta de Jerez, and its small chapel, consecrated in 1506, survives. Another late Gothic building was the private chapel of the House of Pilate, probably completed c. 1490.

Two years later there occurred what would prove to be the most far-reaching event in the history of Spain, and particularly of Seville: the discovery of America by Christopher Columbus, though Columbus and the Catholic Monarchs died in ignorance of the great wealth of the Aztecs and the Incas that was soon to be discovered and plundered, paving the way for Spain's 'Age of Gold'. Isabella, with great prescience, in the middle of Columbus's last voyage and a year before her death in 1504, set up the Casa de la Contratación

within the Alcázar, in which the great explorers who followed Columbus planned their momentous voyages. Seville was given a complete
trading monopoly with the Americas and the city became the weal-
thiest in the world, attracting many foreigners, including Amerigo
Vespucci, who, like Columbus, was Italian-born, and the Portuguese
Magellan. The Spaniards Cortés, Pizarro and Diego de Amalgro,
three of the great *conquistadores*, also planned their colonizing voyages
in Seville.

Much of the loot was spent on beautifying existing buildings, in
particular the churches, and constructing new ones, such as the City
Hall and the rather severe Trade Exchange, now the Archives of the
Indies. The Isabelline style had gradually evolved into Plateresque,
which was basically Renaissance but with filigree decoration in the
manner of silversmiths (*plata* being silver). In 1568, Hernán Ruiz
the Younger replaced the top section of the cathedral's former minaret with a Renaissance campanile, creating the famous Giralda.
Wealthy Sevillanos also embellished or rebuilt their houses in the
Renaissance style, and existing examples are the House of Pilate, the
House of the Pinelo Family and the House of the Countess of Lebrija.
However, Mudéjar touches were not abandoned, particularly in the
application of coffered ceilings and ceramic tiles, although the latter
were supplied mostly by Nicolao Pisano's factory in Triana and bore
Italian rather than Arab designs. The city's first public gardens
were laid out in 1574, beside the Alameda de Hércules. Seville
survived the reign of the Holy Roman Emperor Carlos V (Carlos I
of Spain) without suffering too much damage from this iconoclast,
who built an unsuitable palace within the Alhambra and an equally
unsuitable cathedral within Córdoba's great mosque.

Having dealt with the Jews, Roman Catholic suspicions of heresy
now began to fall on the Moriscos (baptized Moors); use of the Arab
language was banned in 1556, and in 1567 all remaining Arab baths
were demolished (ritual ablutions play an important part in the
Islamic faith). Many converts were judged to be heretics by the
Inquisition and burnt at the stake. In 1610, Philip III expelled all
Moriscos from Spain. Thus, in a short period of time, Spain had lost
its entire Jewish and Moorish populations, representing a large

proportion of the country's most gifted and industrious citizens. Coming on top of the defeat of Philip II's *armada* by the English fleet in 1588, the seeds of Spain's imminent demise as a great power were sown. Too much money had been spent on pointless European wars, indulgences such as the great Escorial palace outside Madrid were a further waste of resources, and the supply of gold from the Americas had dried up. On the death of Philip II, who reigned over the greatest empire that the world has ever seen, Spain was virtually bankrupt.

In Seville, however, 'the band played on' and, as so often occurs, the city's wealth led to a cultural renaissance, virtually all the country's greatest artists of the period first achieving fame in the city. These include the painters Velázquez (who was immediately snapped up for the court in Madrid), Murillo, Zurbarán and Valdés Leal, and the sculptors Montañés, Roldán and Alonso Cano (from Granada) and Pedro de Mena. At the time of the *armada*'s defeat, Seville, with a population of 150,000, was the largest city in the western world.

From 1618 to 1648, Spain was crippled by the Thirty Years War, and in the year that it ended the Plague struck, killing half Seville's population. Major building activities in the city throughout most of the seventeenth century concentrated on religious and charitable institutions. Works to fill these and existing buildings were commissioned from the great artists, many inspired by the theory of the Immaculate Conception of Mary (see page 122) and taking the form of immense Baroque reredoses. Seville took to the Baroque style with great enthusiasm, its flourishes and curvilinear forms striking an empathetic chord in the city that had appreciated Moorish arabesques for so many centuries. Only with the coming of the Baroque style did Mudéjar work finally expire. Of the many examples that survive, the Hospital of the Venerable Priests and the Hospital of Charity, the Fine Arts Museum, the Palace of San Telmo and the churches of La Magdalene, El Salvador and San Luis are among the most impressive. Very few churches in the city do not have at least one Baroque reredos and a Baroque bell tower clad with ceramics.

In 1680 the silting up of the Guadalquivir made Seville's port

virtually unnavigable and the merchant fleet was transferred to
Cádiz. Seville finally lost its monopoly of trade with the Americas in
1717, when the Casa de la Contratación was also transferred to
Cádiz. The city declined abruptly, and injury was added to insult
when the great earthquake of 1755, centred on Lisbon, reduced
many of its houses to rubble. However, rebuilding established the
style of what is now thought of as the 'typical' Sevillian house, tiled,
with a roof terrace, internal patio and balcony. In spite of economic
problems throughout the eighteenth century, the city was able to
construct the Tobacco Factory (still Spain's second largest building
after the Escorial), the Royal Mint and the Maestranza bullring –
the first two buildings to provide work, the third entertainment. In
the same century, Carlos III, by giving the gypsies security, helped
to establish *flamenco*, possibly Andalusia's greatest gift to the entertainment world. Of great importance to the city centre was the laying
out of the Plaza de la Virgen de los Reyes, immediately south of the
cathedral.

Having been last to suffer from Spain's economic collapse, Seville
was also one of the last cities to benefit from the industrial revolution,
which progressed steadily southward through the peninsula from
Barcelona. Consequently, the usual nineteenth-century expansion
did not occur, neither were many new thoroughfares driven through
the ancient core. The Napoleonic occupation of 1810–12 deprived
the city of some of its finest works of art, the acquisitive Marshal
Soult purloining them for France; not all were returned after Water-
loo. Soult was also responsible for demolishing the Encarnación
Convent and the church of Santa Cruz, for the construction of
plazas.

As the century progressed, the ancient walls were demolished, a
subsidiary river, the Tagarete, was covered, the Plaza Nueva was
created and the Avenida de la Constitución was laid out in front of
the cathedral. After 700 years of pontoon bridges, new materials
and engineering techniques made it possible at last to build a permanent structure to span the river between Seville and Triana.

Of great benefit to the population in the 1890s were the twin gifts
of land for María Luisa Park and the Paseo de Catalina Ribera

promenade. A further recreational event of great moment took place when the Prado de San Sebastián was extended to accommodate Seville's first *feria* in April 1847. The great square's use as the Inquisition's 'burning place' had ended with the death there of the last victim in 1783, and in 1834 the Spanish Inquisition was finally suppressed. Also suppressed, by the following year's Disentailment, were the religious orders, all property belonging to them being confiscated. Because of this, vast tracts of monastic land came on the market and were bought at give-away prices by the rich, who thereby became even richer. Some remodelling took place in the Santa Cruz quarter, particularly around Plaza Doña Elvira, and wrought-iron balconies and oriel windows, such an important feature of Seville's urban scene, gradually replaced their timber predecessors.

Like the rest of Spain, Seville was fortunate enough to doze through both World Wars. Falling quickly to Franco's troops, its Civil War trauma was short. Unlike Barcelona, few church interiors were lost to arsonists. Partly for these reasons, the present century has left Seville relatively unscathed. Two railway stations were built *c.* 1900, and the Murillo Gardens were presented to the city by Alfonso XIII in 1911, thus improving access to the Santa Cruz quarter. At the same time, the Marqués de Vega-Inclán began the restoration of the Santa Cruz quarter, work which continued throughout the 1920s, marked by good taste and restraint. A plan to thrust two major roads through the ancient quarter was defeated, the widening of Calle Mateos Gago, in 1927, being the only development of consequence eventually permitted. Partly through good luck and partly through an innate conservatism, the city has managed to preserve the Barrio de Santa Cruz as representative of the quintessential Seville, a delightful tourist attraction of world-wide stature.

In 1929 a great exhibition, planned to serve as a showcase for Spain, Portugal and Latin American countries, was held in and around María Luisa Park. This made a tremendous impact on the southern part of the city – not only were new roads and the San Telmo bridge constructed, but many of the exhibition's pavilions were built as permanent structures and may still be seen. Those of note include Plaza de España, the pavilions in Plaza de la América and the Lope de Vega theatre. Revivalist styles sympathetic to the city's history were chosen, with Mudéjar pastiche-work dominant. Similar in appearance is the famous Hotel Alfonso XIII, built to coincide with the exhibition.

The Romantics had discovered the Andalusian cities in the mid nineteenth century, and Richard Ford, Washington Irving, Victor Hugo and Alexandre Dumas did much to encourage their restoration, incidentally promoting tourism. It was the 1950s, however, that saw tourism race ahead, with the development of the formerly desolate Mediterranean coastline of Andalusia. A percentage of the sun-worshippers penetrated inland in search of 'culture', and Seville gradually built up a tourist season in the scorching, previously neglected summer months.

Expo '92, on Seville's La Cartuja island, is one of the largest international exhibitions ever to be staged, and has encouraged the building of magnificent new bridges, a new airport and a new rail terminal. Of equal importance, a large proportion of the city's historic buildings, some almost in ruins and most in a dilapidated state, have been expertly restored, so that the city will be at its sparkling best for the great event. The Guadalquivir, diverted from its original course in the 1960s due to flooding problems, will once more be navigable to La Cartuja island, ferries providing an important means of access to the Expo '92 site. When the exhibition has ended, many of its buildings will serve as research and development centres. Just beside the bullring is the Palacio de la Cultura, Seville's opera house, the most important city-centre building to be opened in conjunction with Expo '92. New hotels have also been constructed and these will, of course, be a boon to the future generations of tourists who will be certain to descend on the city, following its worldwide publicity throughout 1992.

It must be hoped that Seville's renaissance will not threaten the preservation of this most human of cities, and that care will be taken to protect its riverside from any more buildings as trite as those recently built between the Maestranza bullring and the San Telmo bridge.

PRACTICAL INFORMATION

Timing a visit

Spring and autumn are best for sightseeing in Seville, as temperatures are then at their most equable. However, accommodation is at a premium during Holy Week and the *feria* that follows either one or two weeks later. Winters are generally mild and sunny, although surprisingly cold spells can occur in January and February. Mid-June to mid-September can see afternoon temperatures exceeding 100°F, and a *siesta*, or immersion in a swimming-pool, are obligatory. Most rainfall occurs between November and April, with downpours regularly spoiling the Holy Week processions. From April to October 1992, visitors should bear in mind that Expo '92 is expected to put a tremendous strain on hotel and restaurant resources within the city.

Arrival

As well as San Pablo airport, just nine miles east of the city centre, Seville can also be reached by air via Jerez, Gibraltar and Málaga. With the completion of the new bridge in 1991, Portugal's Faro airport provides another easy access point. Additionally, by 1992, a new 'bullet' train will entail a journey of no more than three hours between Seville and Madrid. Trains from the airport proceed to Seville's new Santa Justa station and also, during 1992, to the Expo site.

A new highway links Seville with the Costa de Sol and it is now possible to drive to the city from Málaga or Torremolinos in less than three hours. Until the motorway to Algeciras is completed (unlikely by 1992), journeys from the southern coastal resorts will remain surprisingly long for the distance involved. Local trains in Andalusia are now rarely as fast as buses.

Accommodation

During the period of Expo '92, accommodation of all grades may be booked through *Centro Oficial Reservas Alojamiento, Recinto de la Cartuja, 41010 Sevilla, Spain (Tel: 95 4290092; Fax: 95 4290206; Telex: 73213* CORALE*).* Reservations should be made as soon as possible, but it may be necessary to accept rooms sited some distance from the city centre, or in other Andalusian locations, in spite of the completion of twelve new hotels. All hotels in Seville, from one to five star, are air-conditioned and centrally heated. Those with outdoor swimming-pools, a great advantage in summer, do not open them until June or after September.

Hostals vary tremendously in the services offered, irrespective of whether they display one, two or three stars. Many of the cheap, one-star hostals lie in the narrow streets of the Santa Cruz quarter. Few in this category provide running hot water, stressing that in summer the sun warms the tank sufficiently! However, a search can reveal exceptions, where rooms are offered not only with hot water, but also with a shower and toilet en suite. Central heating and air-conditioning should never be expected in one-star hostals.

Transport

Buses Seville has no underground railway system, so buses or taxis must be relied on. Only a limited number of bus routes will be of use to tourists and these are simple to remember.

The city centre is traversed along a single north/south axis by **C3** (south to north direction) and **C4** (north to south direction), serving Avenida de la Constitución, the cathedral, Plaza Nueva, Calle Tetuán and Calle Amor de Dios, **C4** deviating along the Alameda de Hércules. Both buses then follow the eastern section of the ring road, **C3** clockwise and **C4** anti-clockwise, serving Ronda de Capuchinos, Avenida Menéndez y Pelayo and Avenida de María Luisa, returning to Avenida de la Constitución via Avenida de las Delícias.

Buses C1 clockwise, and **C2** anti-clockwise, follow most of the ring road, but cross the river to Triana between the Isabel II and San Telmo bridges.

Bus 43 also crosses the Isabel II bridge to Triana.

Buses 40 and 42 also cross the San Telmo bridge to Triana.

Bus 41 crosses the Generalísimo bridge to Los Remedios, passing Parque de los Príncipes, site of the Seville *feria*.

No buses serve Seville's riverside between the Isabel II and San Telmo bridges, nor is any straight, east/west route followed. Special services will be laid on for Expo '92.

A route (*red de lineas*) plan is available, free of charge, from Tussam or tourist offices.

Single tickets are purchased from the driver, but cheaper-rate *Bonobus* tickets are sold at tobacconists, newsagent kiosks and Tussam offices. These are valid for ten journeys, and routes may be changed within one hour of stamping the ticket. Monthly tickets are also available from Tussam offices.

Buses run from 06.00 until around 23.30.

Taxis As parts of the city centre lie some distance from a bus route, many will use taxis on occasions. Delays in obtaining one must be expected throughout Holy Week and the *feria* and, of course, during Expo '92, but long waits are rarely necessary at other times. The rank in Plaza de la Virgen de los Reyes, behind the cathedral, is particularly well served. Ranks in the city are indicated by a blue T or Taxi sign. Vehicles are distinguished by a stripe on the body of the vehicle. A *Libre* sign indicates that the cab is free and, during the hours of darkness, this is supplemented by a green roof light. Rates are displayed and indicate the supplements permitted for journeys beginning after 22.00, for Sundays, public holidays, and trips to the airport, and for luggage. A journey to the new railway station may also involve a small supplement.

Trains In 1991 the functions of Seville's two existing stations were combined at the completely new Santa Justa station, built east of the city centre in Avenida de Kansas City. Trains depart for destinations which include Barcelona, Málaga, Córdoba, Cádiz and Huelva. A high-speed 'bullet' train, providing a Seville/Madrid link in just three hours, will open during 1992.

Coaches Destinations throughout Spain are served from the main coach station, immediately east of the Prado de San Sebastián. The Huelva coast, however, is reached by coaches that leave from the Damas terminus, just north of the Isabel II bridge.

Public holidays

Most buildings, except churches, close on public holidays. These are: 1 January, 6 January, 28 February, 19 March, Maundy Thursday, Easter Friday, 1 May, 30 May, 15 August, 12 October, 1 November, 6 December, 7 December, 8 December and 25 December. During the Monday, Tuesday and Wednesday of Holy Week, and throughout the week of the *feria*, many establishments close in the afternoons.

Orientation

Most maps of Seville, including those in this book, are designed with the river Guadalquivir at the bottom and are therefore orientated east/west rather than the usual north/south.

Two almost straight north/south walking routes cover much of interest, as follows:

Centre Macarena, Calle Feria, Plaza de la Encarnación, El Salvador, Plaza de San Francisco, City Hall, cathedral, Santa Cruz quarter's western approach, Archives of the Indies, Alcázar, 'Carmen's' Tobacco Factory, María Luisa Park and Archaeological Museum.

West Fine Arts Museum (Bellas Artes), bullring, Palace of Culture (new opera house), Charity Hospital, Tower of Gold, San Telmo bridge and Triana riverside.

The omnipresent Giralda tower rises from the east end of the cathedral.

La Cartuja island, site of Expo '92, is approached from bridges to the north-west of the city.

Sin número (*s/n*) means that a location has no street number.

In alphabetical directories, *Ch* has a section to itself at the end of the *C*s and *ñ* is regarded as a separate letter from *n*.

Churches

All churches, apart from the cathedral, close in the afternoon, and many do not open at all until the evening. Admission is free, once more apart from the cathedral. Those attending services at the cathedral are also, of course, admitted free, although most chapels and sacristies of interest will then be closed.

Admission times indicated for churches throughout this book are subject to change, particularly during 1992, when it is expected that many of the more important places of worship will be open longer. See pages 29–31 for recommended interiors to visit.

Historic buildings, museums and art galleries

Seville's two best-known secular buildings, the Alcázar and the House of Pilate, remain open throughout the afternoon. All others close. Again, the situation may change in 1992. Buildings run by the state close on Mondays. Most buildings that are open to the public charge for admission, although municipally-run museums allow free entrance to Spanish nationals. No doubt the EC authorities will eventually stop this iniquitous discrimination, at least against visitors from other EC countries.

See pages 32–4 for a listing of the most important buildings that may be entered.

Shops

While department stores remain open throughout the afternoon, practically all other shops and markets close between 14.00 and 16.30. Some food shops, particularly bakers, open on Sunday.

Banks and currency exchange

Banks are open Monday to Friday 08.30–14.00, Saturday 08.30–12.00 or 13.00. All banks close on public holidays, although most exchange bureaux remain open, as do exchange desks at the larger hotels. Eurocheques, accepted by most banks, are convenient, but some currency or traveller's cheques should be kept in reserve for emergencies such as the unexpected closure of banks – few other exchange points accept Eurocheques. It cannot be said that Seville's banks are impressively efficient. At the south end of Avenida de la Constitución, for example, several banks have a habit of closing their exchange section either completely or until 12.00, and their clerks are prone to disappear for long discussions with colleagues, or to indulge in lengthy telephone conversations. Sometimes one queue must be joined for form-filling and another for obtaining the *pesetas*. An honourable exception is Banco Central, half-way down Avenida de la Constitución, on the cathedral side. During Expo, there will be exchange services on the site, but bear in mind earlier warnings of thieves. American Express traveller's cheques are recommended, as replacement is fast and uniquely quibble-free. They may be purchased in the United Kingdom by anyone, from branches of Lloyds and National Westminster banks and some building societies. Banco de Bilbao's overseas branches provide traveller's cheques in *peseta* values, at a slightly advantageous exchange rate, and cashing them involves no fees if this is done at the bank's many Spanish branches. Several cities in Britain now have a Banco de Bilbao office.

Tipping and taxes
Spanish bars, restaurants and hotels must include the service charge in their bills, and no additional amount is necessary or expected. Most also include the state tax, IVA, but not invariably – check first. It is usual to add a 10 per cent tip to a taxi fare. Porters have set charges, which are fully inclusive.

Telephones
Public telephone booths are painted grey. Hotels always charge a high rate for calls made from guests' rooms, and bars or restaurants with public telephones will also add a small supplement. Three five-*peseta* coins are sufficient for most local calls.

Calls at a standard rate may be made, with assistance in English, from Telefónica 3 Plaza Nueva. Lower rates apply from 22.00. Do not forget that Spanish time is normally one hour ahead of British. Direct dialling codes are 0744 for the United Kingdom, 071 for the United States and Canada, 0761 for Australia and 0764 for New Zealand.

Toilets
Public toilets are few, but hotels and bars must, by law, permit anyone to use their facilities even if not making a purchase. Not all bars possess a WC, and even those that do often run out of toilet paper; visitors are advised to make sure they always have some with them.

Food and drink
See pages 305–23.

Swimming-pools
Many Sevillanos seek relief from the intense summer heat by visiting public swimming-pools. Visitors whose hotel does not possess a private pool may wish to visit the centrally sited Club Natación Sevilla, 9 Trastamara (immediately north of Calle Reyes Católicos), or, at the west extremity of Triana, Mar del Plata, Calle Mar del Plata s/n.

Chemists
The word *farmacia*, often accompanied by a green cross, denotes a chemist. There is always one open twenty-four hours a day and the rota is indicated on every chemist's door when it is shut. Antibiotics may be bought without a prescription. *Droguerías* sell cosmetics but not medicines. The price of most items is now generally higher than in the United Kingdom.

Tobacconists
Known as *estancos*, tobacconists sell *Bonobus* tickets and postage stamps in addition to cigarettes (*cigarrillos*). American brands of cigarettes, such as Marlboro, Winston and Camel, are made in Spain under licence. The local Fortuna brand is also made from Virginia tobacco. Imported foreign brands are more expensive.

Electricity
The Spanish supply is now almost entirely AC 220–225v and British appliances can normally be used without much risk of damage; however, in some small or very ancient establishments it is safer to ask first. An adaptor will still be needed, however, as the British two-point plug just fails to fit Continental two-point sockets; most electrical shops stock them.

Bullfighting
Bullfights (*corridas*) in Seville take place exclusively in the historic

Maestranza bullring, situated beside the river. The season begins in Holy Week and continues until October. *Corridas* begin in the early evening, Sunday being the most popular day. Tickets are surprisingly expensive, but most foreigners are recommended to pay extra for a shaded position (*sombra*) and a cushion (*almohadilla*), as the seats are hard. Remember, it is the *picador* and *banderillero* who weaken the bull for the *matador* (not the mounted *toreador* – Bizet's mistake), who executes the *coup de grâce*. Whatever happens, the bull is always killed.

Flamenco

Flamenco music was developed by Triana gypsies, but the name was first recorded in 1837. It is believed to derive from a slang word for a boaster. *Flamenco* gained general popularity in Seville following Carlos III's edict in 1783 giving the gypsies protection. Before that, it had been performed exclusively in gypsies' homes, but it then moved to cafés as well. The gypsies, who hear it from an early age, are generally still the best performers of *flamenco*, perhaps because of its basic differences from western music.

The *cante jondo*, particularly the haunting *solea* songs of loneliness, are considered the most moving type of *flamenco*. Not all *flamenco* singing is accompanied by the guitar – clapping hands and tapping feet are often used instead. Costumes remain nineteenth-century gipsy dress, the women displaying large hair-combs, fringed shawls (*mantillas*) and frilly, polka-dot dresses.

It is now very difficult for a non-gypsy, particularly a foreigner, to be invited to a private *juerga*, the most enthralling form of *flamenco*, in which drink, drugs and sex play an important part. A *juerga* usually lasts for many hours, sometimes days, the performers gaining staying power from cocaine. It is hardly surprising that heart attacks are an occupational hazard.

Annual *flamenco* festivals have been held in Andalusia's towns since 1956, and some of the performers who take part are very good. Seville hosts the festival in even-numbered years. Staff at the La Carbonería bar sometimes hear of more intimate performances and, on Thursday evenings, *flamenco* is staged in the bar.

Most visitors will see *flamenco* at a permanent venue known as a *tablao*. Somewhat commercialized, *tablaos* are at least more genuine than the '*flamenco* shows' laid on in many Spanish tourist resorts. Non-*aficionados* may well find that their interest flags after an hour or so – there is always the bar! Best not to arrive before 22.00.

Recommended *tablaos* are: Los Gallos, 11 Plaza de Santa Cruz; Taberna Puerto de Triana, 137 Calle Castilla (not Sunday); Corazón de Triana, 118 Calle Pureza; and La Garrocha, 6 Calle Salado.

Useful addresses/telephone numbers

TOURIST INFORMATION OFFICE, 21 Avenida de la Constitución.

MUNICIPAL TOURIST OFFICE, 9 Paseo de las Delícias (south end).

EXPO '92 INFORMATION OFFICE, 10 Plaza de Cuba.

SAN PABLO AIRPORT, tel. 451 09 93.

LOST PROPERTY, 21 Calle Almansor.

POLICE EMERGENCY, tel. 091.

MUNICIPAL BUS OFFICE (TUSSAM), 2 Calle Diego de Riano.

UNITED KINGDOM CONSULATE, 8 Plaza Nueva, tel. 422 88 75.

UNITED STATES CONSULATE, 7 Paseo de las Delícias, tel. 423 18 85.

Spanish names

In general, Spanish names retain their original form throughout the book. A few have been anglicized, however, and in these instances I have used the English version to aid identification. These exceptions are: Christopher Columbus (Cristóbal Colón), Ferdinand (Fernando II of Aragón), Isabella (Isabel I of Castile) and Philip II (Felipe II of Spain).

Fernando III of Castile and León, although not canonized until 1671, is referred to throughout as St Fernando. All saints' names appear in their Spanish form preceded by Sant or Santa when a location such as a church or chapel has been dedicated to them. If referred to as a person, the saint's name is anglicized where such a version exists and is useful.

Addresses and the names of cities and towns in Spain are always shown in Spanish. Andalucía, however, appears throughout in its anglicized form, Andalusia. The names of major, i.e. numbered, locations appear in English, with the Spanish equivalent in brackets.

RELIGIOUS BUILDINGS

In addition to its great cathedral, Seville possesses many churches and chapels, both public and private. Few visitors will wish to or be able to enter all of them, though they may pass by a great many. The chief features of the majority are exuberant reredoses (altar-pieces), usually designed in Baroque style and featuring paintings and sculptures by Seville's masters of the seventeenth-century 'Golden Age'. It is not advisable to see too many of them in quick succession, as there is undoubtedly a repetitive element; and the restricted opening times would also mean rapid viewing and a great deal of travelling around the city in a short time.

It is preferable to make occasional forays to a limited number of buildings of exceptional interest, and the following brief summary of fourteen with outstanding internal features (a personal choice) is intended to aid selection. The page number in brackets after each refers to a fuller description elsewhere in the book.

Capillita San José (page 224)
Tiny, but jewel-like, the chapel is always illuminated within. Exuberantly Baroque, it should not be missed.

Charity Hospital (page 146)
The church of this seventeenth-century hospital is virtually an exhibition of religious paintings. Outstanding are the many *Murillos* and two gruesome works by *Valdés Leal*.

El Salvador (page 220)
After the cathedral, this is Seville's next largest church, built in Baroque style in the seventeenth century. Carvings include the famous *Jesus of the Passion* by **Montañés** and a *Transfiguration* by **Acosta**.

Hospital of the Venerable Priests (page 113)

Another Baroque seventeenth-century hospital. The walls and vaults of its church are covered with frescos by *Valdés Leal* and *Lucas Valdés*, and almost no area remains undecorated. There are superb carvings by *Pedro Roldán* and his daughter *Luisa*.

La Magdalena (page 153)

Again basically Baroque, a fourteenth-century Mudéjar chapel with three cupolas has been incorporated. Two paintings by *Zurbarán* and frescos by *Valdés* are of importance.

Macarena basilica (page 211)

Seville's most popular figure of the Virgin, *La Macarena*, is kept within this modern church. Also of interest is *Christ Sentenced to Death*, by *Morales*.

Madre de Dios de la Piedad Convent (page 177)

Built in the sixteenth century, the convent's church retains a Mudéjar ceiling. The tombs of the wife and daughter of the *conquistador* Cortés lie within the sanctuary. Carvings include works by *Jerónimo Hernández*.

San Esteban (page 180)

An outstanding Gothic/Mudéjar church, begun in the fourteenth century. A coffered ceiling and paintings of saints by *Zurbarán* are features of note.

San Isidoro (page 174)

Another Mudéjar/Gothic church, reputedly Seville's oldest, San Isidoro has been superbly restored. Its painted ceiling covers the entire nave. One of *Gijón*'s most important carvings, *Christ of the Three Falls*, stands in one of the chapels. The Milagrosa Chapel exhibits decorative Mudéjar brickwork.

San Pedro (page 195)

Velázquez, Spain's most famous old-master painter, was baptized here. The San Antonio Chapel possesses a lace-like Mudéjar vault, built in 1379. Among the many outstanding paintings are works by *Roelas* and *Valdés*.

Santa Ana (page 241)
Known as the 'cathedral' of Triana, Santa Ana, built in 1280, combines Romanesque and Gothic styles in a Transitional manner unique in Seville. A *Virgin of the Rosary* reredos, by *Alejo Fernández*, is an early work of the Seville School. Plateresque features give additional variety to the interior. Santa Ana is one of Seville's most interesting churches, and completely different from the others.

Santa Catalina (page 202)
A little-altered fourteenth-century church, Santa Catalina is entered through a horseshoe arch, the only one of its kind in the city. The ceiling of the nave is typically Mudéjar. Of prime importance is the Cristo de la Exaltación Chapel, with an unusual 'bow and ribbons' ceiling. Its reredos incorporates a figure of Christ by *Roldán* and a painting of St Peter by *Pedro de Campaña*.

Santa María la Blanca (page 105)
Filigree plasterwork on the vaults, and a *trompe l'œil* repeat of its design on the walls, are the features of this mid-seventeenth-century church, the most important in the Santa Cruz quarter. A sixteenth-century *Pietà* by *Luis de Vargas* is incorporated in a later reredos.

Santa Paula Convent (page 204)
Visitors are welcomed to this monastic church (and to the adjacent museum), completed around 1485, in Gothic/Mudéjar style. Carvings include *St John the Baptist* by *Montañés*, and *St John the Evangelist* by *Alonso Cano*. The Renaissance tomb of Leon Enríquez is decorated with heraldic tiles. Ceramics by *Pisano* decorate much of the sanctuary.

MUSEUMS AND HISTORIC SECULAR BUILDINGS

Seville possesses the second largest art gallery in Spain, the Fine Arts Museum, but it cannot otherwise be described as a 'museum city'. Seville has been described as a museum in itself, and this is true, more outstanding works of art being distributed among its many churches than are found in some of the world's finest museums. Although not classed as museums, buildings such as the Alcázar and the House of Pilate are open to the public and exhibit many items of great value. Each of the following brief descriptions of buildings in this category is accompanied by a page number referring to a fuller description elsewhere in the book.

Alcázar Palace (page 75)
Seville's most important residence since the first Islamic emirs settled there in 712. Few Moorish traces survive, apart from one small patio and the Almoravid fabric of its wall. However, Pedro the Cruel's fourteenth-century Mudéjar palace, within the complex, is built with the Moorish style dominant, and non-experts find much of it hard to differentiate from Granada's Alhambra. Isabella's Casa de la Contratación, where the *conquistadores* planned their colonizing expeditions, survives as a museum, although much altered. The subtropical gardens are the finest in the city.

Andalusian Parliament (page 209)
The great Renaissance complex, formerly a hospital (Hospital de la Sangre or de las Cinco Llagas), has been adapted to accommodate the provincial parliament.

Archives of the Indies (page 124)
Juan de Herrera, architect of Philip II's Escorial, designed this severe, late Renaissance building as a trade exchange. Since 1785, however, it has accommodated all state documents relating to the colonization of the Americas. Of greatest interest are the marble staircase and the Cuban wood bookcases on the first floor, where plans and copies of original letters are exhibited.

Archaeological Museum (page 135)
Finds throughout Andalusia are displayed here. Of outstanding interest are the sixth-century BC artefacts of gold from Carambolo and antiquities from the nearby Roman city of Itálica.

Bullring (Maestranza) Museum (page 151)
The prime exhibit is the bullring itself, where visitors can see the historic arena without witnessing a bullfight.

'Carmen's' Tobacco Factory (page 130)
Now Seville University's base, this is still the second largest building in Spain (after the Escorial). Visitors may enter the patios and ascend to the galleries, where tobacco products were formerly made.

City Hall (Ayuntamiento) (page 168)
The home of the municipal authority since 1568, the City Hall is the most exuberant example of Renaissance Plateresque work in Seville. Restoration of the interior is expected to be completed by 1992.

Contemporary Arts Museum (page 126)
Works by contemporary artists are changed at regular intervals.

Folk Arts and Customs Museum (page 136)
An eclectic museum, period room settings being the greatest attraction for most visitors.

House of Pilate (page 181)

This is the most sumptuous mansion in Seville, a successful blend of Gothic, Mudéjar and Renaissance elements.

House of the Pinelo Family (page 172)

This sixteenth-century house displays some of the finest Plateresque plasterwork in the city. It is now occupied by the Literary Academy, and only the patios may be entered.

Palace of the Countess of Lebrija (page 225)

Dating from the mid fifteenth century, the palace incorporates several Roman tessellated pavements brought from Itálica, together with coffered Mudéjar ceilings. Iberian and Roman artefacts are displayed.

Provincial Museum of Fine Arts (Bellas Artes) (page 155)

This vast art gallery specializes in paintings by the seventeenth-century Seville School, many of them confiscated from the monasteries at their dissolution in the nineteenth century. The museum itself occupies a former convent, and only here in Seville can works by *Velázquez* be seen.

Tower of Gold/Maritime Museum (page 144)

A rare survival from Seville's Moorish past, the tower houses a small maritime museum appertaining to the city's history as a major port.

SPECIAL EVENTS

In 1992 only, Seville's annual celebrations – Holy Week, the *feria* and Corpus Christi – will be augmented by Expo '92, which is expected to attract 36 million visitors during the six months that it is open.

Holy Week (*Semana Santa*)

Holy Week is celebrated throughout Spain, but nowhere as devoutly as in Seville. From Palm Sunday until the following Saturday, floats are paraded through the streets. Processions are organized by fifty-seven church brotherhoods (*cofradías*), most of them originating from sixteenth-century guilds; the oldest of these is the Cofradía del Silencio, established in 1564. Each guild adopts a church, its activities being social and charitable as well as religious; for some members, the traditional aspects are of prime importance. The object of the processions is to transport a venerated figure or figures from the *cofradía*'s adopted church to the cathedral and back.

Processional routes vary each year (see the daily newspaper *ABC* for details). The most popular processions occur between Maundy Thursday night and dawn on Good Friday, i.e. the very early hours, when the floats are lit by candles. There are eleven processions each day, all beginning at midday, apart from Good Friday. In the mornings, before the processions begin, it is customary to view the floats in their churches; visitors are given a *cofradía* badge.

On Palm Sunday, bars are set up in María Luisa Park and the La Paz *cofradía*'s procession passes through.

Monday is the most sober day, many of the processions being completely silent.

Maundy Thursday is a public holiday in Andalusia: the men wear dark suits and the women black hair-combs and *mantillas*. At midnight the Macarena Virgin leaves the basilica, supporters crying, '*Guapa, guapa*' ('Pretty, pretty'). Members of the *cofradía* are dressed as Roman soldiers.

The float of the Macarena's great rival, the Esperanza de Triana, also begins its journey on Thursday night, evoking equal fervour, particularly when the procession crosses the Isabel II bridge.

Jesús del Gran Poder leaves San Lorenzo at 02.00 and at dusk the Cachorro float crosses the Isabel II bridge.

Some tiered public seating is erected at vantage points, but this is all reserved by wealthy Seville families and, in any case, it is better from an atmospheric viewpoint to join the crowds in the streets. Fortunately for visitors, the Andalusians tend to be short, and foreigners of average height will have no viewing problems. Convention dictates the layout of each *cofradía*'s procession, which is usually focused on two floats (*pasos*), one displaying a figure of Christ, the other of the Virgin Mary.

A guiding cross (*cruz de guía*) leads the procession. Penitents wearing peaked hoods follow. They are known as *nazarenos*, and still bear crosses, although chains have been abandoned since the 1950s. Until the nineteenth century the penitents also flogged themselves, but this enthusiasm is no longer permitted. Anyone is eligible to be a penitent as long as the *cofradía*'s membership fee is paid; however, a place in the procession must be booked long in advance.

Standards herald the first float, which always displays a figure of Christ. Hidden from view beneath the structure are the *costaleros*, who transport it on their shoulders, guided by a *capataz*. Some of the *costaleros* are hired; their task requires a great deal of strength and stamina, and they are replaced at intervals (routes vary from two to nine miles).

More penitents follow, then church dignitaries and leading members of the *cofradía*.

A second float displays the Virgin Mary. Members of the crowd frequently shout their admiration and sing the plaintive *saeta* as it passes. Ending the procession is a band, perhaps followed by more penitents.

Feria

Seville's *feria* is held either one or two weeks after Easter week, depending on when the latter falls, but it always takes place during April. The event is a combination of fair, party, horse and carriage show, fashion parade and *flamenco* (at least, *flamenco*'s commercialized Sevillano version). Nobody seems to stop eating and drinking until they leave to enjoy the early evening bullfight, but excessive drunkenness is rare and greatly frowned on. Much of the enjoyment of the *feria* is the companionship of friends and family and most strangers, of course, miss out on this, few ever being invited to a private, or even a business, party.

The *feria* originated as a medieval market, evolving into a horse and cattle show. In 1847 the modern *feria* as we know it was first held in the Prado de San Sebastián; more space was needed eventually, and the Parque del Príncipe in Los Remedios, south of Triana, is now its venue.

Part of the site is a fairground, but most is laid out in streets named after Sevillano bullfighters. These are lined with rows of canvas marquees known as *casetas*, each one decorated with blue and red stripes. Within, furnishings, flowers and bunting create a festive atmosphere and there is, of course, the obligatory bar. All the *casetas* used to be hired privately by families, but the high cost now compels many to share. Businesses, as might be expected, hire more and more for entertaining their clients. Throughout the *feria*, it is customary for the ladies to wear *flamenco* costume, which is now very fashionable but until quite recently was regarded as vulgar. Officially the *feria* opens at midnight on Monday, but the *casetas* are prepared by Sunday and many private parties are already in full swing that evening. The event then continues until dawn the following Monday, some people having had little sleep for a week.

Mornings consist of a horseback parade, the men wearing tight suits and wide-brimmed hats, followed by a stroll around the fairground, pausing for sherry and *tapas* from time to time. After lunch, many vacate the site for the three-hour *corrida* at the Maestranza bullring, returning for wining, dining and *flamenco* in the *casetas* throughout most of the night. The *feria* is undoubtedly a splendid and picturesque event, but many non-Sevillanos find that the accent on private entertainment leaves them with a somewhat 'left-out' feeling.

Corpus Christi

Celebrated throughout Spain, Corpus Christi falls on the Thursday following Trinity Sunday, a variable date in June.

In the morning, the great silver monstrance made by Juan Arfe is taken from the cathedral and carried through the streets. Every afternoon during Corpus Christi week, ten young boys in sixteenth-century costume sing and dance the '*seises*' in the cathedral.

Romería del Rocío

On Whit Sunday and Monday, pilgrims congregate at the shrine of the Virgen del Rocío (Virgin of the Dew) near Almonte, beside the Doñana National Park in the province of Huelva. Processions follow three traditional routes, from Seville, Huelva and Sanlúcar de Barrameda. The majority of pilgrims, on foot, on horseback or in decorated wagons, spend one day on the road, but some, those from Seville for example, take four days.

Much of the enjoyment of the pilgrimage is gained from the camaraderie at the overnight halts, amplified by feasting and dancing. As at Seville's *feria*, traditional dress is worn, and the wagons are garlanded with flowers. Local brotherhoods (*hermandades*) organize the processions, which are led by a Virgin's banner known as the *simpecado*: two of the brotherhoods are based in Seville.

This event, popular since the early nineteenth century, celebrates a traditional story, dating from the fifteenth century, that the Virgin appeared in a tree to a hunter. Originally a hamlet, El Rocío has been greatly enlarged, and exorbitant amounts are demanded for renting its houses – and any other services required. Half a million people arrive at the shrine, where Mass is celebrated on Sunday and Monday mornings.

Anyone can join in, but the departure and return of the garlanded wagons is, in itself, a picturesque sight for those not able to make the journey.

Expo '92

From 20 April (Easter Monday) until 12 October 1992, Seville will be hosting Expo '92, the last exhibition classified as 'universal' to be held this century. Its closing day is the precise 500th anniversary of the discovery of America by Christopher Columbus. The theme of what the organizers prefer to call an 'exposition' will be 'The Age of Discovery', and a résumé of man's discoveries in all fields during the last 500 years will be recounted in the 100 pavilions. Taking part will be 110 countries – more than ever before – and 18 million visitors are expected over the six-month period, half of them non-Spaniards. The area of Expo '92 exceeds 2 million square metres.

Apart from the organizers, Spain has invested £7 billion in connection with the event, more than half the money being spent on improving the region's infrastructure. For example, seven bridges have been built over the Guadalquivir, two of them linking the old city with La Cartuja island, the site of Expo '92. Direct access will be by road, rail, boat and helicopter, but most visitors will simply walk across either of the bridges from the city centre.

On part of La Cartuja island stands Santa María de las Cuevas, the monastery in which Columbus lived when he came to Seville and where he was buried for thirty-seven years. Most of the former monastery has been restored and adapted, temporarily, to house the Fifteenth Century Pavilion, in which life during that period is described. There will also be a Columbus exhibition and a museum relating specifically to the monastery. An outer chapel is to serve as the Royal Pavilion, for the personal use of Juan Carlos I and his guests.

In order to create a microclimate and significantly reduce outdoor temperatures, a large lake and canals have been excavated and 350,000 trees planted. All the pavilions will be air-conditioned, at least in part, and other measures will be taken to minimize discomfort from the heat – the glass exterior of the British Pavilion, for example, will be cooled by a great cascade of water.

Six entrances will be open, and seven roads approach the site. Within Expo, an elevated monorail will follow a two-mile route, circling the main pavilions, a cable car with thirty-five cabins will follow the 'Way of Discovery', at a height of sixty feet, and there will be additional transport by boat, along the canals and lake.

More theme pavilions will deal with Navigation, Discoveries and the Future, while others will serve as showcases for individual countries, international organizations and multinational companies. There will also be a domed Space Theatre, an Olympic-standard athletics stadium and botanical gardens. Entertainment and cultural events will play a large part in Expo – 50,000 live performances in connection with this event are scheduled, many of which will be televised internationally via satellite. More than £80 million has been spent by the organizers on constructing twenty-one venues, most of them in the open air. These include an auditorium with one of the largest stages in the world, a cinema, and the Expo Theatre, specializing in avant-garde performances.

Cultural activities will take place from 18.00 to 02.00. A parade, led by the Expo mascot Curro, will open each day, and a one-hour procession will close it.

British Pavilion   The British Pavilion, comprising a great glass cube cooled by a huge cascade of water powered by solar energy, is one of the largest at Expo, its size matching that of Westminster Abbey. It has been designed by architect Nicholas Grimshaw, and the water engineering, including an internal lake, is the responsibility of William Pye (it is not, evidently, a reference to Britain's soggy climate!). 'Original Britain' is the theme of the presentation, stressing the inventiveness of the island race. Every participating country has been allotted a national day, when activities not only within Expo but also within the city of Seville are orientated to that country. Britain's national day is 21 May.

Monastery of Santa María de las Cuevas   The former monastery which provides the core of the Expo site was a ceramics factory for a long time, and has been restored for 1992 as authentically as possible, considering the dilapidated condition of its fabric. The island was used for ceramic manufacture from Moorish times, its base of clay proving ideal for the purpose, and caves (*cuevas*) were formed by the excavations. In the thirteenth century, according to tradition, a wooden image of the Virgin was discovered in one of the caves and a Franciscan hermitage was built. The present monastery was founded in 1400 by the Carthusians, and Gothic, Mudéjar and Baroque elements survive. A friar of the convent, Gaspar de Gorricio, who like Columbus was Italian-born, became a close friend of the explorer, who frequently stayed at La Cartuja. Columbus died at Valladolid in northern Spain in 1506, and probably requested in his will, although none exists, that he should be buried at La Cartuja. The Santa Ana Chapel was completed to receive his body in 1509 and it remained there until 1542 (for its future wanderings see page 56). Columbus's brother and son, both named Diego, and possibly his grandson Luis, were buried in the same chapel, but Hernando, his illegitimate son, was interred, at his own request, in Seville Cathedral. During the Napoleonic occupation of 1810–12, the monastery became the headquarters in southern Spain of Marshal Soult's garrison.

At the Disentailment, the monastery was purchased by a Liverpudlian, Charles Pickman, who, attracted by the quality of the clay, set up a factory to manufacture English-style flint china. The enterprise was a great success and Pickman was made a marquess. He died in 1883 at the age of seventy-five, still a British subject. In 1895, at its height, 1,200 were employed at the factory. No specific designs or style were maintained, the fame of La Cartuja's china being due to its high quality. In 1971 the factory was transferred to the outskirts of Seville, where it remains, and the site was purchased by the state. More than £25 million has been spent on restoring the historic complex, including the brick kilns, which are regarded as an important part of Seville's industrial history. After Expo '92 has ended, the former monastery will become a centre for art restoration and scientific research; some departments of Seville University are scheduled to move there as early as 1993.

ITINERARY 1

SEVILLE CATHEDRAL

Timing *Open Monday to Friday 11.00–17.00, Saturday 11.00–16.00, Sunday and public holidays 14.00–16.00 (access to the Giralda is then 11.00–13.00).*

Admission charge includes access to all chapels and sacristies.

Mass, held in the Sacristía Mayor (Main Sacristy), or, on Sunday, in the sanctuary, admission free.

LOCATIONS

1 Sagrario Chapel
2 San Gregorio Chapel
3 Virgen de la Estrella Chapel
4 Encarnación Chapel
5 Virgen Inmaculada Chapel
6 Virgen de los Dolores Chapel
7 Sacristía de los Cálices
8 Sagrado Corazón de Jesús Chapel
9 Sacristía Mayor
10 Santa Justa and Santa Rufina Altar
11 Mariscal Chapel
12 Antecabildo
13 Sala Capitular
14 Concepción Inmaculada Chapel
15 Santa Bárbara Altar
16 Capilla Real
17 San Pedro Chapel
18 Asunción Altar
19 Magdalena Altar
20 Virgen del Pilar Chapel
21 Evangelistas Chapel
22 Anunciación Chapel
23 Asunción Altar
24 Granada Chapel
25 Belén Altar
26 San Francisco de Asís Chapel
27 Santiago Apóstol Chapel
28 Scala Chapel
29 San Antonio Chapel (baptistery)
30 Angustias Chapel
31 Visitación Altar
32 Nuestra Señora de la Alcobilla Altar
33 San Leandro Chapel
34 Niño Jesús Altar
35 Nuestra Señora del Consuelo Chapel
36 Angel de la Guarda Chapel
37 Virgen del Madrono Chapel
38 San Isidoro Chapel
39 Nuestra Señora de la Cinta Altar
40 Nacimiento Chapel
41 San Laureano Chapel
42 Cristo de Maracaibo Chapel
43 San José Chapel
44 San Hermenegildo Chapel
45 Nuestra Señora de la Antigua Chapel
46 Concepción Altar

N

Calle Alemanes

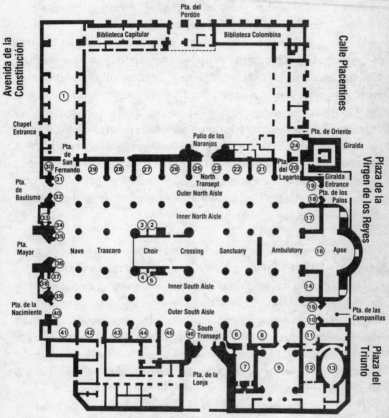

Pta. del
Perdón

Biblioteca Capitular

Biblioteca Colombina

Avenida de la Constitución

Calle Placentines

Chapel
Entrance

Pta. de Oriente

Pta.
de
San
Fernando

Patio de los
Naranjos

Giralda

Pta. de la Virgen de los Reyes

Pta.
del
Lagarto

Giralda
Entrance

North
Transept

Pta. de los
Palos

Pta.
de
Bautismo

Outer North Aisle

Inner North Aisle

Apse

Pta.
Mayor

Nave   Trascoro   Choir   Crossing   Sanctuary   Ambulatory

Inner South Aisle

Pta. de la
Nacimiento

Outer South Aisle

Pta. de las
Campanillas

South
Transept

Plaza del Triunfo

Pta. de la
Lonja

Calle Fray Ceferino González

The two most memorable aspects of Seville Cathedral are its enormous size and the famous Giralda tower, originally a Moorish minaret. Until quite recently this cathedral was rated second in size to St Peter's, Rome, but new calculations, based on cubic measurements, have given it the number one position. Collectors of superlatives will be happy to know that the *Guinness Book of Records* confirms this – 126.18m long, 82.6om wide, and 3048m high.

Although the projected cleaning will certainly help, the exterior of the cathedral is somewhat disappointing, apart from its west front and the façades of its transept. This is because at the lower, most visible level so much is repetitive Plateresque work, plain to the point of grimness.

Internally, the Gothic style dominates, with pointed arches rearing to a great height. Treasures, in a multiplicity of styles, include great paintings, an outstanding choir, a royal chapel and the world's largest reredos. Of great historic interest is the late nineteenth-century memorial to Christopher Columbus, incorporating what is said to be the explorer's tomb.

History Seville Cathedral is built on the site of the city's great mosque, which itself replaced a Visigothic Christian basilica.

The Almohad Sultan, Yacub Yusuf, when making Seville the new capital of al-Andalus, decided that the most important city mosque then in existence was too small, and commissioned architect **Ahmed ibn Baso** to design a much larger building. Work began in 1172 and the body of the mosque was completed within four years. Its minaret, now known as the Giralda, was not finished until much later, however.

The Almohads invariably built both structurally and decoratively in brick, and the Seville mosque was no exception. It is recorded that the mosque combined features from existing Almohad buildings in Morocco with the Caliphate architecture of the great mosque of Córdoba, which Seville's mosque attempted to rival. Seventeen parallel naves, orientated north to south, formed the bulk of the complex, which was approached from a large patio where worshippers performed their ritual ablutions (now the cathedral's Orange Tree Patio).

At the Reconquest of 1248, St Fernando, immediately dedicating the building to Santa María de la Sede, acquired the mosque for Christian worship. The Moorish architectural tradition was strongly established in southern Spain and, as at Córdoba, there seems to have been no pressure from Christians to replace Islamic decoration with their own iconography. Nevertheless, little seems to have been spent on its maintenance, for by the end of the fourteenth century the structure was in a dangerous condition. At the same time, Seville's expansion and religious fervour called for a building that could accommodate larger congregations and, in 1401, the decision was taken to rebuild. The civic pride of the cathedral's council must have attained euphoric proportions, as it was soon agreed not only that the new building must surpass the Almohad mosque in dimensions, but also that 'it should be one of the world's most wonderful churches'. A canon allegedly insisted that the cathedral should be 'so large that those who see it will think we were crazy'. In the event, the visitor to Seville, now Spain's fourth largest conurbation, may well have such thoughts: no other major city is so dominated by its cathedral, and the effect must have been even more extraordinary in the sixteenth century, when the great building towered over a much smaller community.

Beginning at the west end, in 1402, the bulk of the cathedral, one of the last great Gothic churches to be built, was finished by 1506, an extraordinarily short time for such a colossus.

Frustratingly, as with so much Gothic work, the identity of its designer is unknown. Undoubtedly the inspiration is northern French Gothic, and similarities with the church of St Ouen at Rouen have been noted. *Charles Galtes*, known in Spain as Carlí, worked on that church and it has been suggested that he may have been the master at Seville; Carlí certainly worked on the cathedral.

Other architects known to have been involved included *Isambret*, *Pedro García*, *Jean Norman*, *Alonso Martínez* and *Alonso Rodríguez*. In October 1506 the final stone was laid, marking the completion of the building's initial and most important stage. At lower level, apart from the west façade and the portals, most external features of this Gothic work have since been lost or concealed, due to the gradual addition of chapels and sacristies during the sixteenth and seventeenth centuries.

Exterior   The features of the cathedral are described as they are passed, in anti-clockwise order, commencing with the sections of the mosque that have been retained.

The Giralda

The finest overall view of the Giralda tower is without doubt obtained from Calle Mateos Gago, leading from Plaza de la Virgen de los Reyes.

Ever since it was built, the Giralda has symbolized the city. Originally the minaret of Seville's great mosque, this late twelfth-century tower is regarded, in spite of its eventual amalgamation of styles, as one of the world's most beautiful. The tower may be ascended without too much exertion, and views from its upper stages are unrivalled.

History   Although the body of Seville's new mosque was finished by 1176, work on its minaret did not begin until 1184. The site of the Visigothic church had been chosen for the mosque, and stone-work from that building that had been discovered, together with remnants of earlier Roman temples, was re-used to provide the minaret's 52-ft foundations. The mosque's architect, *Ahmed ibn Baso*, designed the tower, apparently influenced by the tenth-century minaret of Córdoba's great mosque, and by the Koutoubia in Marrakesh, begun twenty-five years earlier. In 1195 a similar minaret, the Tower of Hassan, was begun at Rabat, but it was never completed. Neither of the Moroccan towers, however, possess decorative *sebka* brickwork comparable with the Giralda's, and Córdoba's has long been hidden by its Baroque shell.

At the grand ceremony held on 10 March 1198 to celebrate the Almohad victory over Alfonso VIII at the battle of Alarcos, four gold spheres were raised at the top of the minaret. St Fernando remarked that the spheres, gleaming in the sunlight, could still be observed a day's journey from Seville. During an earthquake in 1395 the spheres fell to the ground, never to be replaced, and the tower itself suffered some structural damage. Today, similar spheres are to be seen on many mosques, an artistic feature, not obligatory on religious grounds.

A simple belfry, substituted in 1400, was replaced by a lantern in 1560. The present Renaissance belfry was begun eight years later by **Hernán Ruiz the Younger**, whose genius avoided a disastrous clash of architectural styles. Seville almost lost the minaret when the present cathedral was begun, as it was proposed to demolish it; fortunately, however, the great tower was so much a part of the city scene, and such an object of affection for Sevillanos, that the plan was overruled.

Exterior   The basement level comprises four courses of dressed stones, re-used from the Alcázar's walls. Elsewhere, brick was employed structurally throughout.

The white marble *Madonna and Child*, standing within a small niche inserted at low level in the nineteenth century, formerly surmounted the main entrance to the Corral de los Olmos, which occupied most of the present Plaza de la Virgen de los Reyes from the fifteenth to the nineteenth centuries.

From the half-way stage upward, each face of the Giralda is divided into three vertical panels of equal dimensions. The central panels, incorporating the windows, vary slightly in design, but the *sebka* fretwork of the side panels is identical.

Jasper colonettes are surmounted by tenth-century Omega capitals of stone, re-used from earlier buildings.

The balustrades, also of stone, are a Baroque replacement of the low brick walls which originally protected the windows.

Hernán Ruiz could so easily have ruined the Giralda in the sixteenth century with his four-stage Renaissance belfry. Instead, he achieved harmony by aligning the five-aperture layout of his lower stage with the existing three-panel composition, matching the brickwork and employing decoration which, although Classical, complemented the filigree effect of the towers. Originally the minaret matched similar ones, with a castellated roof-line and a smaller tower on top that also had a battlement but was surmounted by a cupola. This was decorated with a *sebka* pattern, repeating that of the main tower.

Twenty-four bells comprise the carillon: the oldest, cast in 1400, came from the cathedral's clock, the first public example in Spain.

Around the belfry, in Latin, is the dedication of the Giralda to Christianity.

Bartolomé Morel cast the bronze figure of *Faith* (*La Fé*), which surmounts the structure, to the design of **Diego de Pasquiera** in 1568. The banner serves as a weathervane and, because it spun in the wind, it gained the nickname *giradillo* (the little spinner). Eventually the entire structure became known as the Giralda (spinner). Close observation of *Faith* is now possible, as a full-size reproduction is displayed within the cathedral.

On approaching the north face of the Giralda, it will be seen that the windows do not align with those on the east face. This is because their purpose is to light the internal ramp; for the same reason, windows on the south and east faces are similarly out of alignment.

Only traces of plasterwork survive to record the sixteenth-century paintings by **Luis de Vargas** on this façade.

When visiting the cathedral, the Giralda is entered at a later stage and its interior will be described when this has been reached (page 67).

Stretching northward from the Giralda, facing Calle Placentines, is the east wall of the other important Moorish structure to survive from the mosque, the former ablutions patio now known as the **Patio de los Naranjos** (Orange Tree Patio). Its first entrance, the Puerta de Oriente (east doorway), adjoins the Giralda but is generally closed.

Not only the horseshoe arch but also the studded bronze doors are Almohad work.

The range is built entirely of brick, and retains two further horseshoe arches around entrances that are now blocked, together with roof-line castellation. Like the remainder of the patio, this has been restored over a very long period.

Facing Calle Alemanes, first left, the north façade of the patio continues. However, the brickwork here has been plastered and the apertures remodelled in Baroque style. Moorish stepped castellation is the only original feature to survive.

Inset above the corner window, in a later extension, is a Baroque cartouche.

Two paintings of the Giralda, in the spandrels of the doorway below, incorporate vases of lilies, the emblem of the Virgin and a theme that is frequently repeated in the city.

Looking down Calle Hernando Colón, the Puerta del Perdón may be entered, but access to the Patio de los Naranjos, to which it leads, may be gained only from the cathedral's interior.

The **Puerta del Perdón** (Doorway of Forgiveness) preserves its horseshoe archway, formerly the main entrance to the mosque. Also retained are blind side arches in the same style.

Terracotta Annunciation figures were added in 1519 by *Miguel Perrín*, who also inserted the relief of *The Casting out of the Merchants from the Temple* above the arch the following year. It has been suggested that the latter sardonically alluded to the dealing that took place on Las Gradas (the cathedral's steps) before the Lonja (market hall) was built in the sixteenth century.

Bartolomé López converted the overall appearance of the upper part of the portal from Moorish to Plateresque in 1522. Within the curve of the arch, outstanding Almohad plasterwork, recently restored, survives.

The doors themselves are among Spain's greatest treasures: made of larchwood faced with bronze, they are contemporary with the arch.

Buttons and minute Cufic lettering within lozenges, proclaiming 'the empire is Allah's', are the main elements in their sophisticated Almohad design.

Both door-knockers resemble examples to be found in the great mosque of Córdoba.

Within the next archway, less intricately designed, a small *Christ of Forgiveness Altar* has been inserted.

Facing this altar, the plastered Baroque doorway forms the entrance to the Chapter Library.

A third horseshoe arch, facing the courtyard, is decorated with a bold design in plasterwork.

From the railing may be seen the north façade of the cathedral, which, apart from its Flamboyant Gothic transept, is fronted by chapels.

The transept's entrance, known as the Puerta de los Naranjos (Orange Tree Portal), or, alternatively, Puerta de la Concepción (Conception Portal), is modern work, cast in concrete to the design of *Adolfo Fernández Casanova* in 1917. The figures are by *Joaquín Bilbao*. The portal is not a replacement – the proposed Gothic work was never executed.

Return to Calle Alemanes and continue anti-clockwise. Immediately to the right, a ceramic plaque, dated 1916, commemorates the mention by Cervantes of Las Gradas (the cathedral's steps) in *Rinconete y Cortadillo*.

The plastered north façade of the **Chapter Library** follows.

A three-bay loggia forms the north façade of the Tabernacle Chapel.

Tabernacle Chapel (Capilla del Sagrario)
Avenida de la Constitución.
   Open daily 11.00–13.00 and 18.30–21.00.
Built as the cathedral's largest chapel, the building now serves as the parish church and is entered only from Avenida de la Constitución. Its construction entailed the destruction of the entire west range of the mosque's patio.

In contrast to the plain exterior, the interior displays outstanding examples of the Plateresque style.

Begun by Miguel de Zumárraga in 1616, the building was completed by *Fernández de Iglesias* in 1662; other architects who worked on the project included *Alonso de Vandelvira* and *Cristóbal de Rojas*.

Exterior   The three-bay loggia is the only architectural feature of great interest externally.

Avenida de la Constitución, left, skirts the west façade, where Doric, Ionic and Corinthian orders have been superimposed. The effect is rather grim, only a balustrade and portal providing decorative relief of consequence.

Interior   The chapel's high altar is situated at the north end.

Surprisingly sumptuous, the interior of the building displays a wealth of Plateresque decoration, vaults throughout being exceptional.

Four colossal figures, the work of *José de Arce*, 1657, rest on both the east and west balustrades of the nave at **gallery** level, representing the Evangelists and doctors of the church.

The **transepts** contain matching Plateresque reredoses, carved by *Cornejo*, with figures by *Pereira*.

The high altar's reredos, designed by *Francisco Dionisio de Rivas*, incorporates figures by *Roldán*. It came from the demolished church of the San Francisco Convent.

Avenida de la Constitución now passes the west front of the cathedral, which is, as may be expected, its finest. One may regret, however, the lack of the usual *plaza* at this point, thus prohibiting an all-encompassing view. An overall French Flamboyant Gothic influence is apparent, although the central portal's figures are modern pastiche. Great churches were generally begun at their east end, so that the sanctuary might be completed quickly, enabling consecration and partial use as soon as possible. In this case, however, Enrique III refused to consent to the demolition of the ancient Chapel Royal, which stood at the east end of the former mosque, and construction therefore began at this, the west end, gradually proceeding eastward as the converted Islamic structure was demolished.

It will be noted that in spite of the great size of the cathedral, it possesses no towers or spires that rival the height of the Giralda.

The three portals are the chief features at lower level. All are fifteenth-century work, in the Flamboyant Gothic style.

North of the central portal is the **Puerta de Bautismo** (Baptistery Portal). Terracotta figures stand in the niches of the archivolts, representing the Evangelists, St Lawrence and St Hermenegildo. The work of *Lorenzo Mercadante*, 1467, and *Pedro Millán*, *c.* 1500, they are, together with similar figures on the Nativity Portal, some of the finest late Gothic statues in existence.

On the tympanum, the three canopied figures represent *The Baptism of Christ*.

Reserved for ceremonial use, the **Puerta Mayor** (Main Portal) is similarly decorated with figures, but these are modern, pastiche work, as the portal was not completed in the Gothic period.

The *Assumption of Mary* on the tympanum was carved by *Ricardo Bellver y Ramón* in 1885.

Above, flanked by flying buttresses, the rose window's tracery is bold in design.

The **Puerta del Nacimiento** (Nativity Portal) gains its name from the Nativity relief on its tympanum; an alternative name, **Puerta de San Miguel** (St Michael's Portal), is sometimes used.

This doorway is the usual entry point for those attending Mass when it is held in the sanctuary on Sundays and public holidays. Although much of the cathedral may then be seen free of charge, most of the areas of greatest interest, including the sacristies and the chapter house, will be closed.

Red terracotta figures on the archivolts and buttresses at lower level are by the same sculptors as the Baptistery Portal. These, however, were executed slightly earlier, 1453–67, as this was the first portal to be built, construction of the cathedral beginning at the south-west corner.

The south façade is best observed from the top of the steps that skirt the Archives of the Indies, as the upper-level Gothic work, including flying buttresses, pinnacles, balustrades and the tracery of the south aisle's windows, may then be appreciated.

Uninspired repetitive bays in Plateresque style are followed by the magnificent panel tracery of the transept's Flamboyant Gothic south façade.

Unusual tracery surrounds the rose window, which itself lacks decoration.

The south transept provides the entry point for visitors to the cathedral and its portal will be returned to shortly.

More repetitive Plateresque bays, unfortunately higher than those already seen, decorate the exterior of the **Sacristía Mayor** (Main Sacristy) of the cathedral. Its shallow dome incorporates a lantern.

Continue towards the Giralda, following the east façade of the cathedral. More Plateresque work continues, forming the east wall of the **Sala Capitular** (Chapter House). This is also roofed by a shallow dome with lantern.

Usually providing the exit from the cathedral, and the entrance for those attending Mass in the Chapel Royal, the **Puerta de las Campanillas** (Bells Portal) gained its name from the hand-bells that summoned workers in the cathedral to assemble at this point.

Its tympanum relief, *Christ's Entry into Jerusalem*, is by *Miguel Perrín*, and was carved in 1522. Terracotta figures were added the following year. This portal is one of a pair that flank the **Capilla Real** (Royal Chapel), which is enclosed by the elliptical apse of the cathedral.

Although basically Plateresque, with a series of great royal coats of arms carved at upper level, lion gargoyles in Gothic style are also incorporated.

The name of the next portal, **Puerta de los Palos** (Sticks Portal), commemorates the wooden sticks that once fenced it off.

More terracotta figures decorate the buttresses and archivolts.

The tympanum's *Adoration of the Magi* relief, also in terracotta and the work of *Perrín*, 1520, is reminiscent of similar work at Como, Italy.

Examination of the cathedral's exterior has now been completed and the visitor should return, clockwise, to the courtyard fronting the south transept, from where the cathedral is entered for 'Cultural Visits'.

Importuning gypsy flower-sellers usually gather at this point.

Tickets are sold from the kiosk, left, and should be retained.

The entrance has three alternative names: **Puerta de la Lonja**, as it faces the former Lonja (now the Archives of the Indies); **Puerta San Cristóbal**, referring to the mural of St Christopher immediately right of the doorway; or **Puerta de los Príncipes** (Princes' Portal).

Casanova completed the portal in 1895.

Interior The cathedral is best explored by proceeding immediately ahead to the centre and examining the sanctuary and the choir; then returning to the entrance to follow an anti-clockwise tour of areas such as the chapels, vestries, courtyards and Giralda, as they are approached from the outer aisles. In this way the most interesting part of the cathedral will be seen before fatigue reduces the visitor's enthusiasm.

Immediately right of the entrance, facing north, a painting of a *Pietà* forms the reredos of the altar. It is attributed to **Pedro Fernández de Guadalupe** and **Alejo Fernández**, 1527.

Adjacent to this, the huge St Christopher mural was painted by **Mateo Pérez** in the mid sixteenth century.

Standing with its back close to the entrance is the monument to Christopher Columbus by **Arturo Mélida**, 1901. This allegedly incorporates the explorer's tomb. Columbus died at Valladolid, northern Spain, in 1506, and his funeral took place there. However, his body was interned at the monastic church of Santa María de la Cuevas, on La Cartuja island, Seville's Expo '92 site.

In 1542 the remains were transported to the Caribbean island of Hispaniola (now Haiti and Dominica), where they were buried in Santo Domingo Cathedral. After this, the facts are disputed. Some claim that the remains of Columbus were transferred to Cuba in 1795, when the French took over Dominica, and that they were brought to Seville in 1899 when Cuba gained independence from Spain, as referred to in Gothic lettering around the pedestal of the monument. Others believe that Columbus still rests in a sarcophagus found in Santo Domingo Cathedral that bears inscriptions identifiable with the 'Admiral of the Seas'. Both the *Encyclopaedia Britannica* and the game 'Trivial Pursuit' support the Dominican faction. However, it was at one time common for Roman Catholics to distribute an illustrious person's remains among several locations, and it may be that both Seville and Santo Domingo are correct in claiming their possession of those of Columbus. This is only one of many events concerning the great explorer, as itinerant in death as in life, that are wrapped in conjecture and dispute.

The monument is one of the last major works to exhibit Spain's nineteenth-century Romantic style. The pages that bear the sarcophagus are dressed in tunics representing the four kingdoms that constituted the Spanish crown in 1492: Léon, Castile, Navarre and Aragón.

By continuing to the **crossing**, with the choir left and the sanctuary right, an overall impression of the immense building may best be gained. *Isambret* is credited with the design of most of the Gothic interior. The cathedral is rectangular, with only one apse; this forms the Chapel Royal at the east end (not visible from here).

Inner and outer aisles flank the **nave**, which is slightly wider but, at 120ft, significantly higher.

The **transept** matches the nave in width but is even higher at the crossing.

Vaults throughout were built of Jerez stone in the fifteenth century, but subsequent problems have led to some amendments.

In 1511 the crossing's vault collapsed and it was rebuilt in 1519 by *Juan Gil de Hontañón*, to a more elaborate and structurally sounder design. Above the choir, the most easterly bay of the nave now matches its appearance because, in 1888, the vault here also collapsed, due to weakening of the structure by earthquakes.

Elsewhere, the nave and its aisles retain their original, simple rib vaults. Interestingly, the nave has a long transverse rib, in the English style.

It is an unusual feature of Seville Cathedral that the normal blind triforium gallery has been replaced by false clerestory galleries; they are protected by Flamboyant Gothic balustrades.

The hot sunshine of Seville has been kept at bay by the designer of the cathedral, and much of the interior can be seen only with the aid of artificial illumination. Nevertheless, there are seventy-four examples of Gothic or Renaissance stained-glass windows, many of them outstanding. In general, the aisles and sanctuary are lit by Gothic stained glass from the late fifteenth and sixteenth centuries, the work of Flemish and Burgundian masters. The chapels and much of the eastern section of the cathedral are lit by Renaissance windows, added throughout the sixteenth century and considered to be of even greater artistic importance. Baroque examples from the seventeenth and eighteenth centuries are also to be found.

Originally the pavement of the cathedral was of brick, but this was replaced in 1793 by the present marble slabs.

The **sanctuary** (Capilla Mayor) lies immediately east of the crossing.

Gilded Renaissance rails, on three sides, were erected 1518–33.

Francisco de Salamanca was responsible for the central section and for the two gilded pulpits that extend from the rails.

Side rails were designed by *Sancho Muñoz* and *Diego de Idobro*.

The Gothic reredos, measuring approximately 60 × 40ft, the largest in the world, took almost a century to complete. The Flemish *Pieter Dancart* designed the piece, depicting the lives of Jesus and Mary, and worked on it for ten years, beginning in 1482. From then until 1526, *Marco Francisco*, *Bernardo de Ortega* and *Jorge Fernández Alemán*, who completed the upper reliefs, were responsible. More than 1,000 painted and gilded figures are incorporated in the reredos, and Gothic and Renaissance styles are both in evidence.

One of Seville's finest early Gothic works, the *Virgen de la Sede* (Virgin of the Chair), stands behind the central tabernacle; the figure, of silver-plated cedar, was made *c.* 1280.

Immediately right, a panel illustrates the Giralda as it appeared before alterations were made to its superstructure.

In the next panel but one to this, medieval Seville is depicted.

The top, overhanging section of the reredos, Renaissance work, illustrates groups of six apostles on either side of the *Pietà*: all were added in 1564.

Alejo Fernández was responsible for the outstanding painting and gilding of the reredos.

The two angled flanking panels were added by *Roque Balduque* and *Juan Bautista Vázquez* in 1550.

Facing the sanctuary is the **choir** (*coro*), which, unfortunately, may not be entered and is difficult to appreciate internally, due to poor illumination.

Its gilded Renaissance grille is the work of *Francisco de Salamanca*, 1519–23.

Choir stalls, on two levels, were made by *Nufro-Sánchez* in Flamboyant Gothic style. His completion of the work 'with God's help', in 1478, is confirmed by an inscription (not visible) on the back of the King's stall. Other craftsmen assisted with the decoration, *Alborique*, for example, being responsible for the carved Mudéjar work at upper level, which is illuminated. Additions were made from time to time and continued until the early sixteenth century, when the Renaissance style took over.

The centrally-sited lectern of wood and bronze, illuminated, fortunately, was made in 1565.

The organs flanking the choir were restored in 1901. It was above them that the vault had collapsed three years earlier, covering the instruments in rubble. Their cases were carved by *Cornejo* in 1741.

Proceed anti-clockwise around the choir.

The choir's exterior is rather more visible than its interior; the short, arcaded vestibule, with the north organ above it, was built in 1730.

Two of the choir's four Alabaster Chapels follow; all are designed in Plateresque style.

The mid eighteenth-century reredos of the **San Gregorio Chapel** is by *Manuel García de Santiago*, but its rail is earlier, Renaissance work. A late fifteenth-century *Virgin and Child* forms the centrepiece of the **Virgen de la Estrella** (Virgin of the Star) **Chapel**, which follows.

The west-facing end of the choir (*trascoro*) was carved from polychrome marble.

Its outstanding Classical reredos is dedicated to the Virgen de los Remedios, the subject of the early fifteenth-century *Virgin and Child* panel painting which is incorporated.

There may be conjecture about the whereabouts of the remains of Christopher Columbus, but there are none regarding those of his natural son Hernando (1483–1539). A tombstone in the centre of the pavement, towards the west door, indicates where they lie. Not easy to locate, it is a large stone, the second from the choir, and is flanked by smaller slabs depicting sailing ships. The second line of the Latin eulogy begins 'Colon' (Columbus in Spanish).

It was said of Hernando that 'he would be regarded as a great man had his father been less great'. When only fourteen, the boy sailed on his father's fourth voyage to America and eventually wrote an important biography of Columbus. The cathedral's Biblioteca Colombina incorporates a great collection of books that Hernando donated.

Christopher Columbus never married Hernando's mother, Beatriz

Enríquez, from Córdoba, but he did leave her money in his will, indicating an abiding affection.

Returning to the choir, and continuing anti-clockwise, two further Alabaster Chapels form its south side; both are by **Diego de Riaño**, dating from 1528, and combine Gothic and Renaissance styles. The first, the **Capilla de la Encarnación**, features an *Annunciation* reredos of 1635, from the school of *Montañés*.

Of Italian alabaster, the *Virgen de Genova* (Virgin of Genoa) stands against the column that separates the choir's south chapels.

The **Capilla de la Virgen Inmaculada** displays what is generally regarded as the most sensitive portrayal of the Virgin in Seville. Known as *La Cieguecita* (the little blind one), as the eyes are almost shut, its polychrome figure, carved from wood in 1630, is the *chef d'œuvre* of *Montañés*.

Below the south organ, the arcade is similar to that on the choir's north side.

The following anti-clockwise tour of the chapels begins at the St Christopher mural, immediately left of the cathedral's entrance.

First seen is the **Capilla de la Virgen de los Dolores** (Chapel of the Virgin of the Sorrows). Its late sixteenth-century *Crucifixion* reredos is by **Pedro de Mena**. This chapel now accommodates the tomb of Beato Marcelo, Cardinal Spinola y Maestre, much-loved archbishop of Seville, who was beatified in 1987.

The chapel also serves as the anteroom to the **Sacristía de los Cálices** (Chalices Sacristy). Mainly Gothic in style, the sacristy was completed by **Martín de Gainza** in 1537. Now, like the Sacristía Mayor, the main function of the room is to display a selection of the cathedral's great collection of paintings, together with the outstanding figure of Christ carved by *Montañés* in 1603 for Las Cuevas monastery.

Although the cathedral charges an admission fee for the 'Cultural Visit', virtually no attempt is made, at the time of writing, to identify the paintings displayed, many of which are of great importance. Accepting that a church is not a museum, it would surely be possible to provide some discreet identification for visitors, at least within the two great sacristies. A half-hearted attempt has been made with a small sheet on one wall, but even this manages to get the information muddled! A selection of some of the most important is therefore given below; bear in mind that their positions may change.

Paintings flanking the *Montañés Crucifixion* on the south wall, from left to right and top to bottom, are: *Crucifixion* by **Juan Sánchez**, *Pietà* by **Juan Núñez**, *Christ in the Arms of God* by **Luis Tristán**, *Virgin and Child* by **Zurbarán**.

On the east wall, left, the outstanding work is the centrally placed *Death of the Virgin* by **Van Eyck**. *The Adoration of the Magi*, the first painting on this wall, is by **Algo Fernández**.

On the west wall, nearest the south (*Crucifixion*) wall, is *St Jerome* by **Zurbarán**. In the centre is *Saints Justa and Rufina* by **Goya**.

On the north, entrance wall, the painting left of the door is *St John the Baptist* by **Zurbarán**.

Returning to the cathedral's outer south aisle, the next chapel eastward, now dedicated to the **Sagrado Corazón de Jesús** (Sacred Heart of Jesus), accommodates, right, mid fourteenth-century tombs of the Pérez de Guzmán y Ayala family. Two large paintings by **Lucas Jordán** are exhibited.

The **anteroom** to the **Sacristía Mayor** (Main Sacristy) displays two large eighteenth-century cupboards carved by **Cornejo**; they house the sections of silver that make up the portable altar.

Within the Plateresque doorway, ahead, the doors were carved by **Guillén** in 1548.

The **Sacristía Mayor** was apparently designed by **Diego de Riaño** in 1528, although it has been said that **Diego de Siloé** also had some responsibility for it. Philip II is reported to have observed to members of the Chapter, 'Your sacristy is finer than my Chapel Royal.'

A rectangular shape, together with the form of the vault, reveals the essentially Gothic nature of the sacristy, in spite of its Plateresque detailing by **Martín de Gaínza** and **Rodrigo Gil de Hontañón**.

In the corner, left of the entrance, stands the great monstrance, a processional tabernacle of silver by **Juan de Arfe**, 1580–87. Extensive embellishments were made in 1688.

The figure of *Faith*, surmounting the 600-lb piece, is similar to the Giralda's.

As in the Chalices Sacristy, paintings are not identified and a selection therefore follows.

On the east wall (left of the entrance wall), the first painting is *The Appearance of Christ to St Ignatius of Loyola*, by **Murillo**. Also by **Murillo**, above the partition's door, is a painting of the mitred St Leandro.

Wooden partitions fronting both side walls screen the cathedral's relics and treasures.

Of greatest importance, against the wall facing the entrance to the enclosed area, left, is the early Gothic triptych reliquary of 1280, presented by Alfonso X and known as the Alfonsine tablets. Precious stones are inset in the gilded silver. The last painting on the east wall, at low level, is *St Jerome* by **Ribera**.

Dominating the south wall is probably the sacristy's most renowned painting, *The Descent from the Cross* by **Pedro de Campaña**, 1548.

To its right is a portrait of St Teresa, attributed to **Zurbarán**.

A portrait of the mitred St Isidoro by **Murillo**, above the west partition's entrance, matches the same artist's work directly opposite. *St Francis with Christ and the Virgin*, right, is by **Sánchez Cotán**.

In front of this painting stands the *tenebrio*, a candelabra of wood and bronze that plays an important part in the Easter processions. It was designed by **Hernán Ruiz** and made by **Bartolomé Morel** and **Pedro Delgado** in 1562. The piece is 25ft high and incorporates fifteen small statues.

From the Main Sacristy turn right; directly ahead stands the **Altar of St Justa and St Rufina**, by **Cornejo**, transferred from the church of El Salvador.

Between the saints, a model of the Giralda clearly depicts its paintings on plaster; these were added in the sixteenth century but have now faded.

The **Capilla del Mariscal**, entered right, was named to commemorate its founder, Diego Caballero, Marshal of Hispaniola.

Its reredos, depicting *The Purification of the Virgin*, is from the School of **Campaña**, 1555; flanking panels are by **Antonio de Alfán**. Portraits of the Caballero family are painted below.

Facing the reredos is the vestibule, with its coffered ceiling.

Ancient altar frontals of silk are exhibited, together with vestments.

Of particular interest are the costumes of the '*seises*'. During Corpus Christi week, on the Feast of the Assumption and 8 December, after Mass, a group of young boys, in sixteenth-century pages' costumes, sing and dance in the cathedral before high dignitaries of the church. The name *seises* (sixes) refers to the number of boys who originally sang in the cathedral choir, but ten now take part. Religious dancing, always popular in Spain, was frowned on in some quarters, and Pope Eugenius IV decreed that the Dance of the Seises would have to stop once the traditional garments had worn out. As may be expected, continuous patching ensured that the costumes never did wear out, and performances seem likely to continue for the foreseeable future.

The origins of the dance, probably secular, are lost in antiquity; however, there is a reference to it in 1503, the same year that the Feast of Corpus Christi was inaugurated. Performances, accompanied by a small orchestra, take place either before the portable altar or within the sanctuary, depending on the occasion. Songs written in the eighteenth century praise Christ and the Virgin.

Return to the Capilla del Mariscal and proceed left, via either door from the Plateresque vestibule, to the **Antecabildo**, the anteroom to the Chapter House. *Hernán Ruiz the Younger* designed the room in 1564, but it was completed by *Juan de Minjares*.

Plateresque bas-reliefs on the walls, by *Diego de Pesquera* and *Marcus Cabrera*, were all completed by 1590.

Illuminated choir books, dating from the fifteenth to the nineteenth centuries, are displayed in cases.

From the Antecabildo, a curved passage leads to the Sala Capitular.

Diego de Riaño prepared a plaster model of the oval **Sala Capitular** (Chapter House), and work on the room, in Renaissance style, began in 1530. However, due to subsequent amendments, little of his original concept remains. It has been suggested that *Hernán Ruiz* may have been involved in the scheme. *Martín de Gaínza* and *Juan de Orca* continued work on the project, which was completed only in 1592, by *Juan de Minjares*.

The geometric marble floor is outstanding.

Stone benches provide seats for members of the Chapter.

Diego Velasco carved the marble bas-reliefs of *St John and the Angel*, and the *Expulsion of the Merchants*, while *Juan Bautista Vázquez* was responsible for the other reliefs, very Italian in style. All this work, on the theme of the life of the Virgin, was executed between 1587 and 1590.

The eight strip paintings between the bases of the pillars, in *trompe l'œil* style, by *Pablo de Céspedes*, 1592, are believed to have been restored by *Murillo*.

Painted medallions in the segments of the cupola, depicting Seville saints, are by *Murillo*, 1688.

The painting of *The Immaculate Conception* over the bishop's throne is also by *Murillo*.

On returning to the Altar of St Justa and St Rufina, a left turn may have to be made because of the barrier that is erected when Mass is being held in the Chapel Royal. Pass through the barrier's first entrance and proceed to the **Capilla de la Concepción Inmaculada** (Chapel of the Immaculate Conception), which adjoins the Chapel Royal to its south. Formerly the Capilla de San Pablo (St Paul's Chapel), the chapel has been subdivided to form a clerical office.

The seventeenth-century Baroque reredos is by *Francisco de Rivas*, and its figure of the Virgin is by *Alonso Martínez*.

Above is the revered figure of *Christ Crucified* (Cristo de San Pablo).

A recess in the wall, right, was made in the nineteenth century for the tomb of Cardinal Cienfuegos; its arch was brought here from the Chalices Sacristy.

South of the chapel, beside the Puerta de las Campanillas, stands the **Altar de Santa Bárbara**.

Its reredos incorporates paintings in the Italian style by *Antón Ruiz*, 1544.

Return northward and proceed to the Capilla Real (unless Mass is being held, when a later return will be preferable).

The Baroque grille, donated by Carlos III in 1771, depicts in its crest St Fernando receiving the keys of Seville, the work of *Sebastián van der Borcht*. The **Capilla Real** (Royal Chapel) was designed by **Martín de Gaínza** in 1552 as a royal mausoleum. Earlier, the projected chapel was to have been polygonal and Gothic in style, but permission could not then be obtained from the King to demolish the existing royal burial chamber, which it was to replace. Eventually Juan II did give permission but, Gothic then being out of fashion, a Renaissance design was commissioned.

On the death of **Martín de Gaínza** in 1555, **Hernán Ruiz the Younger** continued the work, and it was completed by **Juan de Mesa** in 1575.

Baroque holy water stoups flank the entrance.

In both side wall niches stand the modern sepulchres of, left, Alfonso X (d. 1284), son of St Fernando, and right, his mother Beatriz of Swabia.

Plateresque decoration on the walls includes figures of Old Testament kings within niches in the ceiling of the apse.

Spanish kings, in bas-relief, cover the entire cupola.

The seventeenth-century reredos at the east end, by **Luis Ortiz**, incorporates Seville's patron saint, a thirteenth-century Gothic Virgin and Child, *La Virgen de los Reyes* (Virgin of the Kings); little of the figure may now be seen, due to its sumptuous clothing. According to tradition, St Louis of France gave the sculpture to St Fernando, his cousin, and it was presented to the cathedral by Alfonso X.

The Baroque sepulchre of silver gilt was made by **Juan Laureano de Pina** and donated by Felipe V in 1717. Within are the embalmed remains of St Fernando, which are exhibited publicly in the cathedral on 14 and 30 May and 23 November.

Side panels at the base of the altar come from an earlier sarcophagus of the King; they bear inscriptions in Arabic, Latin, Hebrew and Spanish.

St Fernando had strong English connections – his great-grandfather was Henry II and his daughter Eleanor married Edward I, 'the hammer of the Scots'. Their son, the first Prince of Wales, was later crowned Edward II. On Eleanor's death, her grieving husband instructed that a stone cross should be erected wherever the catafalque had rested on its journey to Westminster – hence the Eleanor crosses, three of which survive.

Busts of St Justa and St Rufina, at the sides of the reredos, are by *Diego de Pesquera*. According to tradition, the Romans intended that the ladies should be martyred together in a lions' den, but the beasts miraculously refused to harm them.

Kept within the Chapel Royal are the remains of the 'New Kings' of Spain, from St Fernando to Pedro the Cruel. Most lie in its crypt, approached by steps (not open to the public). Here also are the original coffins of St Fernando, Pedro the Cruel and his mistress María de Padilla, together with an ivory Virgen de los Batallos (Virgin of the Battles), said to have been attached to St Fernando's saddle.

In the chapel's choir, right of the altar, are eighteenth-century choir stalls; the door leads to its small sacristy.

If Mass is being held, it may be necessary to return through the barrier (showing entry ticket) and proceed between the choir and the sanctuary to the chapel adjoining the north side of the Chapel Royal. If there is no barrier, simply exit right to the next chapel.

An eighteenth-century Baroque grille, the work of *Fray José Cordero*, protects the **Capilla de San Pedro**, dedicated in 1525. Its reredos, by *Diego López Bueno*, 1625, incorporates scenes from the life of St Peter, painted by *Zurbarán* in 1625.

The upper painting, depicting God, is a seventeenth-century replacement, presumably for another *Zurbarán* work.

Inset within a niche is the tomb of Columbus's mentor from La Rábida, Archbishop Fray Diego de Deza.

Paintings, right, include works by *Zurbarán*, *Reina* and *Valdés Leal*.

The **Puerta de los Palos**, immediately left of the chapel, is flanked by altars.

The **Altar de la Asunción**, right, has an unexceptional bas-relief of the Virgin accompanied by angels and saints between St Ildefonso and St Diego of Alcalá. Other paintings are by *Vázquez* (1593).

Left of the portal, the reredos of the **Altar de la Magdalena** features a painting of *The Risen Christ before Mary Magdalene* by *Gonzalo Díaz*, 1499.

The Puerta de los Palos leads to a small courtyard, with access, left, to the **Giralda** (no additional entry charge). A description of the Giralda's history and exterior has been given on pages 48–50.

Access to the viewing platform, at 230 feet, is by a ramp of thirty-five gently inclining sections. It is believed that a ramp was chosen rather than steps so that animals transporting building materials could reach the top. According to tradition, St Fernando rode his horse to the tower's summit.

Seven rooms are passed, one on each level.

As may be expected, the views from the platform of the city and its surrounding countryside are all-embracing.

Return to the cathedral and proceed to its north-east corner, where a Baroque grille of 1717 protects the **Capilla de la Virgen del Pilar** (Chapel of the Virgin of the Pillar).

The fifteenth-century terracotta *Virgin and Child*, supported by the top of a pillar, is by *Pedro Millán* and forms part of a Baroque reredos, standing within a Gothic niche.

Pass the Puerta del Lagarto (Alligator Portal) to the **Capilla de los Evangelistas** (Chapel of the Evangelists).

This chapel's picture-frame reredos features a *Mass of St Gregory* theme, painted by *Hernando de Esturmio* in 1555.

St Justa and St Rufina are painted on the low side panels. Although these ladies lived in the third century, long before the Giralda was built, the tower is incorporated in many paintings of them, allegorically representing Seville. Here, the Giralda is usefully depicted in its original minaret form.

Paintings elsewhere in the chapel are replicas of work by *Andrea del Sarto* and *Murillo*.

The stained-glass window, by *Arnao de Flandres* is dated 1553.

The next chapel, now the **Capilla de la Anunciación** (Annunciation Chapel), was known until fairly recently as the **Capilla de las Doncellas** (Chapel of the Maidens), to commemorate its foundation by a brotherhood founded to provide poor maidens with dowries so that they could marry.

A Renaissance rail of 1579 faces the aisle, and another smaller rail the reredos.

The reredos is an eighteenth-century piece incorporating

sixteenth-century paintings, based on the maiden's dowry theme; some are by *Cristóbal de Morales*.

Ceramics from Cuenca decorate the platform facing the reredos.

An outstanding late sixteenth-century stained-glass window features *The Virgin with Two Maidens*, by *Arnao de Flandres*, and below, *Christ with Fishermen*, by *de Vergara*.

Immediately before the Puerta de los Naranjos, to its right, is the **Altar de la Asunción** (Ascension Altar), its painted scene attributed to the Italian *Carlos Maratta*.

The **Patio de los Naranjos** (Orange Tree Patio) originally served as the ablutions courtyard common to all mosques, where worshippers cleansed themselves before prayer. However, none of the fountains that now stand in the patio were used for these ritual ablutions.

The large example incorporates a marble sixth-century Visigothic font, discovered in the Patio de las Banderas; it is the oldest font in Spain.

Although some Moorish work remains, and more is gradually being revealed, the patio bears little relation to its former appearance. All four sides were originally colonnaded, with horseshoe arches, but this homogeneity was lost in the sixteenth century when two libraries were created, the **Biblioteca Capitular** (Chapter Library), built with Roman and Visigothic stones, immediately left of the Puerta del Perdón, ahead, and the **Biblioteca Colombina**, which occupies the remainder of the north range and the entire east range. The latter was donated by Hernando, the natural son of Christopher Columbus, and accommodates 3,000 works, including a manuscript in the explorer's hand, explaining that his adventures were vindicated by the Bible.

Collapse of the roof in 1985 has prevented visitors from entering the building until restoration is complete. Within may be seen sixteenth-century décor by *Luis Vargas*, and paintings that include an important *St Fernando* by *Murillo*.

Most damage to the patio took place in 1618, when the Capilla del Sagrario (Tabernacle Chapel) was built, all Moorish work forming the west side being demolished because of it. Now the parish church, the former chapel cannot be entered from the patio (see page 52).

Approached from the east arcade of the patio, where it joins the cathedral, the small foyer is early sixteenth-century Mudéjar work, incorporating a carved wooden ceiling. The entire foyer was transferred here from the College of St Thomas.

In the north-east corner is the cathedral's **Puerta del Lagarto** (Alligator Portal), so named because of the stuffed reptile, presented to Alfonso X in 1260 by the Sultan of Egypt, which was hung above the door: the present 'beast' is a wooden replica.

Also displayed (before restoration began) are an elephant's tusk, discovered in the Roman amphitheatre at Itálica, a horse's bridle and a rod of justice.

Immediately left of the Mudéjar vestibule is the **Capilla de la Granada** (Granada Chapel). Its entrance arch is decorated with Mudéjar plasterwork, but the chapel itself is a survivor from the mosque.

Two Visigothic capitals are incorporated in the entrance arch and four more examples in the altarpiece, dedicated to Cristo de los Escobones (Christ of the Bones), a further allusion to Christ clearing the Temple of merchants.

From the stone pulpit preached St John of Avila, St Francis of Borja and Vincent Ferrer, whose eloquence inspired the brotherhoods of flagellants which may have been the source of Seville's Holy Week ceremonies.

Immediately north of this chapel is the Puerta de Oriente, already described from the other side.

At one time the patio was planted with many varieties of trees, including palms and ancient cedars, but in the sixteenth century these were removed and the greenery restricted to orange trees, more suited to the formal appearance in vogue at the time of the Renaissance.

Royal funeral ceremonies took place in the patio after the Reconquest, and in 1504 *Antonio de Nebrija*, author of the first Spanish grammar book, taught the humanities here.

The cathedral's north façade has already been described (page 52).

Return to the interior of the cathedral and turn right.

Beside the doorway is the **Altar de la Virgen de Belén** (Virgin of Bethlehem Altar). Its painting, one of the finest works of *Alonso Cano*, was presented to the cathedral in 1691.

On the adjacent wall is a painting of *The Slaughter of the Innocents*.

Within the **Capilla de San Francisco de Asís**, a large *Apotheosis of St Francis of Assisi* by *Herrera the Younger*, 1657, right, is framed by its reredos, the work of *Simón de Pineda*.

Above, the painting of *The Virgin Presenting a Chasuble to St Ildefonso*, by *Valdés Leal*, 1661, illustrates the miracle that is alleged to have occurred at Toledo.

Stained glass is again by *Arnao de Flandres* and dated 1556.

The chapel that follows is dedicated to **Santiago Apóstol** (St James of Compostela).

On the east wall, its reredos exhibits the well-known painting of *St James Slaying the Moors* by *Juan de Roelas*, 1609.

Above this, the painting of *St Lawrence* is by *Valdés Leal*.

The Gothic tomb of Archbishop Gonzalo de Mena, founder of the monastery of La Cartuja, dates from the early part of the fifteenth century.

Above the entrance, the stained glass, also from the Gothic period, is by *Enrique Alemán*, 1478. Over the tomb is a Virgin and Child figure, known as *The Virgin of the Pillow* (*La Virgen del Cojín*). Of terracotta, its style and blue and white glazing proclaim the hand of the fifteenth-century Florentine master, *Andrea della Robbia*.

Other paintings in the chapel, hard to see, include: *Sybils and Prophets*, and *Creation*, by *Simón de Vos*; Old Testament scenes by *Valdés Leal*, and *St Anthony*, attributed to *Zurbarán*.

The Renaissance window is by *Vicente Menardo*, 1560.

The **Capilla de la Scala** commemorates its founder, a canon of the cathedral, Baltasar del Río, Bishop of Scala in Turkey. Its white marble sarcophagus, by the Genoese *Gazini de Bissone*, remains empty, as the bishop (*d.* 1540) was buried in Rome.

On a platform above, also of white marble, and of Italian workmanship, are the **Altar del Espíritu Santo** and its reredos, 1539.

Below the main scene, a Renaissance bas-relief illustrates *The Feeding of the Five Thousand*, from the studio of *Gazini*.

The glazed terracotta relief on the west wall, of the Virgin of Granada, depicts *Mary Crowned by Cherubs*. She is accompanied by St Francis of Assisi, St Sebastian and St Elizabeth.

The **Capilla de San Antonio** serves as the cathedral's baptistery. Within its reredos is a painting of *The Vision of St Anthony of Padua*, 1656, one of *Murillo*'s most famous works. A long tear above the saint's head, painted over, is a reminder that part of the work was ripped out of the reredos by thieves in 1874. It was eventually traced to New York and returned.

Another *Murillo*, *Christ's Baptism*, forms the upper painting of the same reredos.

Other paintings in the baptistery include a *Life of St Peter* series by *Valdés Leal*, an *Immaculate Conception* by *Roelas*, a *Circumcision* and a *Nativity* by *Jordán*, biblical scenes by *Simón de Vos*, a *Conception* by *Pacheco*, and *St Justa and St Rufina* by *Zurbarán*.

The stained-glass window depicting St Justa and St Rufina, by *Juan Bautista de León*, is dated 1685.

Outside the **Puerta de San Fernando**, which leads, when unlocked, to the Tabernacle Chapel, stands the full size replica of *La Fé*, the original of which surmounts the Giralda.

Against the west wall is the **Capilla de las Angustias** (Chapel of the Anguishes), or alternatively, **Capilla de los Jácomes**, commemorating the Flemish family who donated the reredos.

Its *Pietà*, by *Roelas*, 1609, has been poorly restored.

A Plateresque reredos serves as a frame for paintings by *Pedro Villegas Marmilejo*, in the **Altar de la Visitación**. Portraits of its donors appear below.

Within a niche stands an exceptional carving of St Jerome, by *Hernández*.

On the south side of the Baptistery Portal, the **Altar de Nuestra Señora de la Alcobilla** incorporates a fifteenth-century Flemish group.

The **Capilla de San Leandro** was designed by *Matías de Figueroa* in 1733, and its carving executed by *Diego de Castillejo*.

Manuel de Escobar designed the reredos, carved by *Cornejo* in 1733.

The rail, by **Francisco de Guzmán** and **Ocampo the Younger**, is contemporary with it.

A 'mute child' (*mudo*) figure, carved in the seventeenth century, is featured in the **Altar del Niño Jesús** (Altar of the Child Jesus).

The **Capilla de Nuestra Señora del Consuelo** (Chapel of Our Lady of Consolation) displays a *Virgin and Child* painting by **Alonso Miguel de Tobar**, 1720.

Left of the main door, the **Capilla del Angel de la Guarda** (Chapel of the Guardian Angel) features, in its reredos, *Murillo*'s painting *The Guardian Angel*, originally painted for the Capuchin Convent's church and presented to the cathedral by the order in 1814.

The **Altar de la Virgen del Madroño** incorporates a polychrome *Virgin and* (less than appealing) *Child*, the work of *Lorenzo Mercadante de Bretaña*, 1454.

Currently poorly illuminated, the Baroque **Capilla de San Isidoro** is chiefly remarkable for its grille, which incorporates an ornate gate.

A terracotta figure of a crowned *Virgin with Child*, in the style of *Mercadante*, 1470, stands in the reredos of the **Altar de Nuestra Señora de la Cinta** (Altar of Our Lady of the Sash).

South of the Nativity Portal, the **Capilla del Nacimiento** (Nativity Chapel) has a Plateresque reredos, with panels painted by *Luis de Vargas* in 1555. An *Adoration of the Shepherds* is featured.

The chapel's rail is Renaissance work.

Construction of the cathedral began at its south-west corner in 1403, with the **Capilla San Laureano**.

Its window was made by *Vicente Menardo* in 1572.

The Neo-classical tomb of Cardinal Lluch, by *Agapito Valmitllana*, was made in 1885.

Paintings are by *Martín de Arteaga*.

On the south wall of the **Capilla de Cristo de Maracaibo** is a modern altar by *Joaquín Bilbao*; its mid-nineteenth-century painting of *Christ* is by an unknown artist, but allegedly came from Maracaibo in Venezuela.

The Gothic reredos was presented in 1504. It incorporates fourteen contemporary paintings in the Flemish style.

Two works by *Zurbarán* are displayed.

The Neo-classical reredos of marble and bronze was made for the **Capilla de San José** by *Pedro Arnal* in the late eighteenth century. Its figure of *Jesus with a Child* is attributed to *La Roldana*.

Stained glass is by *Enrique Alemán*, 1478.

The impressive Flamboyant Gothic tomb of Cardinal Juan de Cervantes (d. 1453) stands in the centre of the **Capilla de San Hermenegildo**. In alabaster, it is the work of *Lorenzo Mercadante de Bretaña*, 1458.

Within the eighteenth-century Baroque reredos by *Manuel García de Santiago*, St Hermenegildo was carved by his father, *Bartolomé*.

The figures of St James the Great and St James the Less have been attributed to *Pedro Millán*.

Apart from the Chapel Royal, the **Capilla de Nuestra Señora de la Antigua** (Chapel of Our Lady of Ancient Times) is the largest and most sumptuous in the cathedral; it was restored in 1991.

The chapel was founded by Cardinal Archbishop Diego Huertado de Mendoza for his own eventual interment but, although its rib vault had been raised by 1504, the chapel was not completed until 1568.

A section of wall was then brought from elsewhere, bearing a fresco of *The Virgin* which, at the time, was thought to be extremely ancient. French, Italian and Spanish influences have been noted in the fresco, now believed to be fourteenth-century work, although overpainted in part. The fresco was incorporated in the Baroque marble reredos when it was made by *Juan Fernando Iglesias* in 1734. Mendoza's Plateresque sepulchre, by *Micer Domenico Alessandro Fancelli*, was made in Genoa in 1510. Flanking marble figures of St Joachim and St Anne are by *Cornejo*.

In the wall niche, left, is the Baroque tomb of Cardinal Archbishop Luis de Salcedo, who presented the reredos.

Wall paintings are the eighteenth-century work of *Domingo Martínez*.

The rail and silver balustrade of the altar were also made in the eighteenth century.

Just before the entrance to the cathedral stands the **Altar de la Concepción**, nicknamed '*de la Gamba*'. It allegedly gained the latter name when the Italian *Mateo Pérez de Alesio*, who painted the great St Christopher fresco opposite, admiringly proclaimed to *Luis de Vargas*, the painter of the altar's reredos, that Adam's leg (*gamba* in Italian) was of greater value than his entire St Christopher. *Vargas* painted the allegory in 1561, including a portrait of Juan de Medina, the chapel's donor.

The sixteenth-century Renaissance rail, designed by *Juan Méndez*, was completed by *Pedro Delgado* in 1562.

It is often possible to leave the cathedral by its entrance ahead, the **Puerta de los Príncipes**, but when crowds are great, the **Puerta de las Campanillas** exit, at the east end (approached through the barrier), will prove more accessible.

ITINERARY 2

THE ALCÁZAR PALACE

Timing *Open Tuesday to Saturday 10.30–18.00, Sunday and public holidays 10.00–14.00.*

The Alcázar is occasionally closed for public functions and when the King is in residence.

An admission charge covers all sections of the palace.

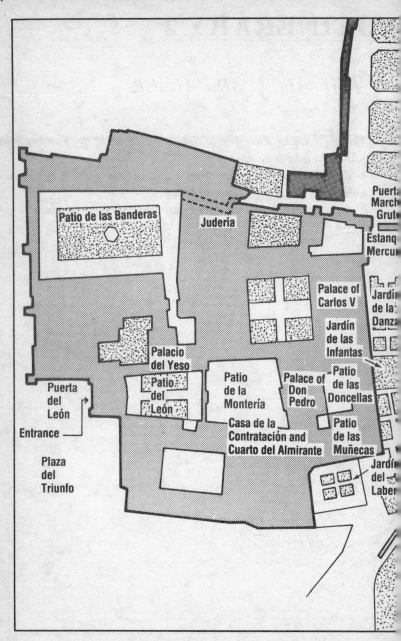

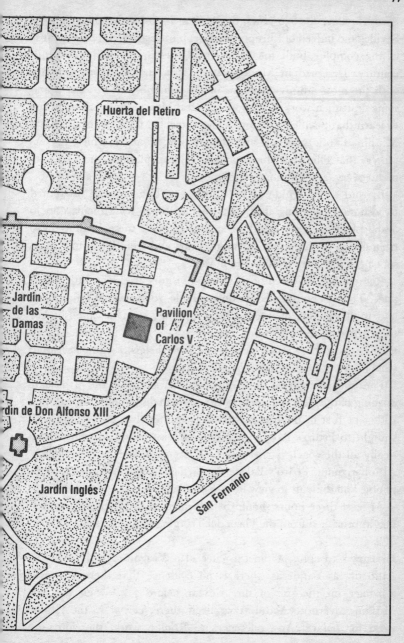

Huerta del Retiro

Jardín
de las
Damas

Pavilion
of
Carlos V

dín de Don Alfonso XIII

Jardín Inglés

San Fernando

A royal palace for 650 years, the Alcázar is one of the great sights of Seville, and indeed of Europe. Most people are attracted to it because of the complex built for Pedro the Cruel in the mid fourteenth century. Designed in Mudéjar style, it is virtually contemporary with the most admired sections of the Alhambra at Granada, and some craftsmen worked on both palaces. Most visitors are surprised to learn that Seville's building was constructed for a Christian, not a Muslim. Exotic gardens, and the suite of rooms in which the explorers that followed Christopher Columbus planned their voyages of discovery, are additional attractions.

In 1991 a 'miniguide' to the Alcázar, in English, was distributed to visitors, explaining that visits to the Royal Apartments and to archaeological areas could be made. In fact, these sections have been closed to the public for many years and seem likely to remain so. Check the current situation, however.

Regrettably, at the time of writing, visitors are given little assistance. There is no detailed guide available, rooms are not identified, and most exhibits of interest lack captions, even in Spanish. For these reasons, the directions that follow are given in greater detail than would otherwise be necessary. Nevertheless, a compass would still be a great boon in Pedro's Palace!

For much of the year, long queues of tourists await the rather late opening of the Alcázar, the majority of them disgorged from coaches. Either be first in the queue (arriving no later than 09.15) and rush straight to Pedro's Palace, or time your visit for 13.30, when practically all the coach parties will have been whisked away for lunch. At other times, Pedro's Palace, in particular, can become claustrophobic and difficult to view in comfort.

At least three hours should be allocated to the Alcázar, which is best approached from the Plaza del Triunfo (see page 122).

History In spite of the existence of a Visigothic basilica in the Patio de las Banderas, there is no evidence that there was ever a palace on the site of the Alcázar before 712, when the first Muslim governor, Abdul Aziz, lived there: *al-ksar* is the Arabic word for palace. Any references to Roman work, therefore, are purely speculative. During most of the period of the Córdoba caliphate (mid eighth century to 1031), Seville lost its importance, being occupied only by the Caliph's delegate. Nevertheless, the Syrian architect **Abdullah Ben Sinán** built a new palace on the site for Emir Abdul Rahman II in the ninth century.

In 1091 the Almoravids conquered Seville and the Alcázar became the headquarters of Ali Ben Yusuf, viceroy of Spain. It was his son Rachid who expanded Seville's wall in 1107, the core of which still survives; however, there are no known remnants of Almoravid buildings in the Alcázar.

The Almohads were responsible for the oldest fragments within the complex that can be seen today. Remaining from their twelfth-century Palacio de Yeso (Palace of Plaster) is a patio which has been under restoration for some years. A short stretch of wall from the Almohads' time also exists, separating the Patio del León from the Patio de la Montería. It has also been suggested that further examples of Almohad work may survive elsewhere, covered over by later construction.

In the mid thirteenth century Alfonso X built three Gothic halls, which were later remodelled in the sixteenth century and still exist as the Palacio de Carlos V.

The chief glory of the Alcázar, however, is the Mudéjar Palacio del Rey Pedro (Palace of Pedro I). Work probably began shortly after Pedro's accession to the throne in 1350, and it is known to have continued at least until 1366. The palace remains basically in its fourteenth-century form although, not unexpectedly, many succeeding monarchs made changes of a minor nature.

Ferdinand and Isabella spent a great deal of time at the Alcázar, particularly after the subjugation of Granada, replacing several Mudéjar ceilings with Plateresque work. Their chief addition, however, was the Casa de la Contratación, built in 1503 as offices for navigators to plan their epic voyages.

Carlos V, the arch-vandal responsible for building his unsuitable Renaissance palace within the Alhambra and constructing the cathedral within the mosque at Córdoba, did relatively little harm at the Alcázar. Most of his work here involved the creation of domestic accommodation above the Casa de la Contratación and the conversion of Alfonso X's Gothic halls to form his own palace. Perhaps his greatest architectural misdemeanour was to rebuild the gallery of the Patio de las Doncellas, in Pedro's Palace, in Plateresque style, greatly altering its appearance. Carlos V also remodelled the gardens in a formal, Renaissance manner, and one of his pavilions is the only structure in the gardens to survive.

Subsequent monarchs made limited alterations, the most important being the construction of the present Apeadero and the façade of the Palace of Carlos V, both in the eighteenth century.

The nineteenth century witnessed the usual well-meaning but unfortunate 'restoration' that took place throughout Europe, generally involving reconstruction in pastiche style. Pedro's Palace was most affected by this unwarranted attention and some areas were spoiled. The upper storey of the exquisite Patio de las Doncellas, for example, is entirely a nineteenth-century addition.

The Alcázar is still a royal palace and becomes the Seville residence of the King when he stays in Seville.

Those who have already visited the Alhambra at Granada will undoubtedly miss its dramatic setting beneath snow-capped mountains, the ethereal delicacy of its architecture and, perhaps most important, the fountains and ponds in its patios. In spite of this, however, the Alcázar will still delight and should not be missed by any visitor to Andalusia.

The Alcázar is entered from the **Puerta del León** (Lion's Gate), at the southern extremity of the Plaza del Triunfo.

Glazed tiles from the fourteenth century form the heraldic lion on the lintel.

After tickets have been purchased, the **Patio del León** is entered immediately. It is alleged that from 1248 to 1364 a lion was kept chained in the patio to symbolize the regal nature of the Alcázar's occupants – hence the name of the patio and entrance. However, the lion emblem on the gate may have been its more prosaic origin.

Closing the east side of the patio, left, is the **Salón de Justicia**, built by Alfonso XI c. 1345. Within is plasterwork in the Grenadine style, and the oldest example of Mudéjar panelling in Seville. Unfortunately, the building may no longer be visited.

Behind this (not visible) lies the **Patio del Yeso** (Palace of Plaster). Discovered in 1890, its chief interest is an arcade with re-used caliphate capitals. It is the only important part that can be said with certainty to remain of the Almohads' Alcázar, although it is possible that other examples may survive, covered over, within Pedro's Palace. Restoration has been continuing for many years. Once again, visitors are no longer welcome.

Ahead, the wall is also Almohad work; two blocked horseshoe arches and arabesques may be observed.

Proceeding through the arch, the **Patio de la Montería** (Hunting Patio) is reached. This was an assembly point for those accompanying the King on hunting expeditions. A theatre was apparently built in the patio in 1626 so that the King could watch entertainments without leaving the complex. According to tradition, the first *flamenco* singer, Juan del Arenal, performed here during the reign of Philip IV.

The present format of the patio was established in the seventeenth century by the Count-Dukes of Olivares.

Immediately right, forming the west side of the courtyard, is a two-storey building, the ground floor of which was built as the **Casa de la Contratación de Indias** in 1503. The upper floor evolved in various stages, incorporating the early sixteenth-century private chapel of Isabella I, and linking with the bedroom of Pedro I, *c.* 1356, and the same King's Audience Chamber, together with its Anteroom. Most of the rooms, however, were created in the sixteenth century for the wedding of the Emperor Carlos V.

The Casa de la Contratacíon de Indias was created by Isabella I to provide offices for leaders of expeditions to the New World, from where personnel could be hired (*contratación*) and materials, including ships, requisitioned. With the exception of the chapel, the rooms retain little of their original appearance, although most of the beamed ceilings, doors and windows date from the early sixteenth century.

Christopher Columbus had begun his last mission when the

building was under construction, but later explorers planned their voyages in the first room seen, the **Cuarto del Almirante** (Admiral's Room), the name of which commemorates the appointment of Columbus as Gran Almirante del Mar Océano (Grand Admiral of the Ocean). Apart from its historic associations, the room is of little interest.

Ahead, the second room is now an exhibition area, which includes fans and paintings belonging to the royal family; little identification of the exhibits is provided.

Of greatest interest is the fifteenth-century city flag depicting St Francis, which is displayed in a cabinet. A copy, made recently, may be seen in the City Hall.

At the end of this room, a reproduction of Isabel II's Baroque bedroom has been created, incorporating original furniture and fittings. Originally, the room was sited on the upper floor.

Returning to the Cuarto del Almirante, the doorway on the right leads to the chapel.

The **Capilla de los Navegantes** (Navigators' Chapel) is the most interesting section of the complex, its seventeenth-century coffered ceiling being one of the last works in Spain to exhibit Muslim influence in its design.

On the wall fabric are displayed the arms of Castilian admirals from 1248.

A model of Columbus's first flagship, the *Santa María*, stands beside the reredos. *Alejo Fernández* was commissioned to paint the reredos specifically for this room, and completed the work in 1537. To the left, clothed in gold, stands Christopher Columbus, together with the Pinzón brothers, who sailed with him on his first voyage to the New World. Carlos V is depicted on the other side of the Virgin. Contemporary vessels are illustrated below.

It is necessary to return to the Patio de la Montería, as for security reasons the upper storey of the building is no longer open to the public. When the royal family stays in Seville, this floor provides their residence.

Occupying the south side of the patio is Seville's greatest attraction apart from its cathedral.

Palacio del Rey Don Pedro (Palace of Pedro I)

This is the most important and extensive building ever to have been constructed in the Mudéjar style, although Muslim craftsmen were also employed to complete the project. It was commissioned by Pedro I (1334–69), who inherited the Crown of Castile and León from his father Alfonso XI in 1350.

Don Pedro was known as Pedro the Cruel but also as Pedro the Just; the former because he executed members of his own family, the latter because many considered that their actions had been treasonable. In addition, Pedro gave protection to the proletariat against abuse by the aristocracy and reduced the privileges of church officers. Pedro was a fifth-generation descendant of St Fernando and, through the latter's grandmother, Eleanor, a blood relative of the English Crown. The Black Prince supported Pedro against his half-brother Enrique, who was assisted by the French, an Anglo/Castilian army winning a decisive battle against them in 1367. The grateful Pedro presented the Black Prince with an uncut ruby that he had stolen from Abu Said of Granada after having him murdered. Worn by the Black Prince and Henry V in battle, the great ruby now glows in the Imperial State Crown of the United Kingdom.

In spite of his gift, Pedro soon fell out with the Black Prince and, lacking English support, became prey to further attacks from Enrique. Having lost the battle of Montiel in 1369, Pedro took refuge, but was tricked into meeting his half-brother in the French battle tent, for 'negotiations'. Enrique stabbed him and took the Crown of Castile, thus founding the Trastámara dynasty.

Allegedly a womanizer, Pedro remained devoted to María de Padilla, returning to her immediately after his political marriage to Blanche, daughter of the Duc de Bourbon, had been solemnized in 1353. After María's death in 1362, Pedro convened the Cortes in Madrid and declared that he had married her (albeit bigamously). Witnesses were produced and the Archbishop of Toledo legitimized the offspring, thereby granting Pedro's wish that their eldest child should be permitted to inherit the throne. One of Pedro's daughters married John of Gaunt, and another Edmund of Langley, thereby strengthening the King's English connections.

It seems likely that the structural work on the palace was begun by local Mudéjar and Christian craftsmen, carpenters from Toledo being added as work progressed. However, after having regained his Granada throne with Pedro's help in 1362, Mohammed V sent Moorish workers to assist in the completion of the building. Some of the craftsmen would certainly have participated in his recently completed palace at the Alhambra, which included the famous Lions Patio. Their appearance was probably too late to influence much more than the façade and some decorative elements, which may be one reason why Don Pedro's Palace fails quite to match the exquisite delicacy of the Alhambra.

Although classified as Mudéjar, the palace is therefore a combination of the efforts of Mudéjar, Muslim and Christian. It is believed that much of the Alcázar was in ruins when Pedro began his palace and that some Almohad work may remain behind its walls.

Façade Similarities between the façade of Don Pedro's Palace and that of the Comares Palace at the Alhambra, also the work of Muhammad V, have been noted, and this part of the building, due to its late construction, probably owes more to Muslim architects than any other.

The ground floor's design is attributed to local Christian workers, who added decorative *sebka* work above the blank side doors, in the manner of the Giralda.

Below the upper side windows are carved castles, lions and other Christian heraldic devices, thus emphasizing that Pedro was king of both Christians and Muslims.

Cufic lettering proclaims that 'There is no God but Allah' and 'God alone conquers', the latter being the motto of Muhammad V.

The building is dated 1402, which we now compute as 1364, a date that undoubtedly commemorates the completion of the façade. It is known, however, that the decoration of other sections of the palace continued at least until 1366, just three years before Pedro's death.

The roof is the work of Toledo carpenters.

As recently as the early seventeenth century, Rodrigo Caro records that the façade was completely gilded, but no trace of this remains.

Interior The layout of the palace follows the usual labyrinthine format favoured by Muslim architects in order to protect occupants from surprise attacks. As the rooms and patios are not identified and no plan is available, each section is mentioned here and precise directions given – it is easy to lose one's bearings. No records survive of the rooms' original names and they have changed throughout the years. It cannot be certain exactly what function most of them served during the long history of the palace; the names given are based on the latest suggestions.

Vestíbulo (Vestibule) Here visitors deposited their outer clothing. The work is Mudéjar but the door has been restored and the columns probably re-used from elsewhere.

Turn right and follow the corridor ahead.

Patio de las Muñecas (Patio of the Dolls) The domestic, as opposed to the official, part of the palace, was concentrated around this small patio, which was initially, of course, unglazed.

Only the ground floor is original, the upper storey being a mid nineteenth-century addition.

Columns, with their capitals, are in the tenth-century Caliphate style and may have been re-used from the ruined city of Medina Zahara.

According to tradition, the patio was commissioned by Pedro for his daughters to play in. On entering the patio, the first arch, left, displays on both sides, at the bottom of the first inward-facing lobe, a minute doll's head set within a circle. These presumably gave the patio its name, which was recorded in the sixteenth century and may be original.

Turn right, and enter the long Cuarto del Príncipe, which lies off the patio. Most rooms would almost certainly have been fitted with tapestries and carpets, particularly in the winter, to add warmth. Cushions scattered on the floors provided the seating.

Cuarto del Príncipe (Prince's Quarters) Isabella I assigned this room to her son, Prince Juan of Spain, following his birth at the Alcázar, possibly in this room, in 1478. It was heavily restored in 1854.

The coffered ceiling in the alcove, left, was made in 1543 by *Juan de Simancas*.

Return to the Patio de las Muñecas and enter the room left.

Sala de los Pasos Perdidos (Room of the Lost Steps) retains its original ceiling and floor. According to Pedro López de Ayala it was here, in 1358, that Don Pedro's illegitimate half-brother, Fadrique, Maestre de Santiago, met his death. When Pedro learned that Fadrique had seduced his consort Blanche, he lured him to the Alcázar and instructed his armourers to stab him. Blanche was incarcerated in a tower for the rest of her life.

Proceed via the **Camara Regia** (Regal Chamber) to the Dormitorio Real, via a triple arch, left.

The **Dormitorio Real** (Royal Bedroom) was known for a long time as the Dormitorio de los Reyes Moros (Bedroom of the Moorish Kings), when the origins of Pedro's palace had been forgotten and were believed to have been Moorish. In fact, although there is an alcove which is likely to have accommodated a bed, there is no proof that this room was ever used as a royal bedroom.

The Mudéjar doors are outstanding.

Return to the adjoining Camara Regia and continue ahead.

Patio de las Doncellas (Patio of the Maids of Honour) This two-storey patio was the centre of the public, as opposed to the private, activities of the monarch in the palace. Formerly known as the Patio Principal, its present name traditionally derives from the young ladies who observed the ambassadorial processions in the patio from the gallery above.

Ferdinand and Isabella replaced many of the ground floor ceilings with Plateresque work.

Columns, in Italian Renaissance style, are by *Francisco Martínez*, 1559.

Lobed arches survive from the fourteenth century, and their *sebka* decoration suggests that they were made by Seville Christians.

Also remaining from Pedro's time are the ceramic dado and plaster frieze, the finest in the palace.

Luis de Vargas rebuilt the gallery for Charles V in the mid sixteenth century, and the colonettes are by *Martínez*.

Medallions set between its arches emphasize the Plateresque nature of the work, although the wall behind is still Mudéjar.

Lying west of the patio is the Salón de Embajadores. The position of the sun should aid orientation here; however, through the entrance can be observed a triple horseshoe arch with window behind. On the north side, a similar triple arch indicates the Dormitorio Real, already seen, but there is no window. Confusion between the two rooms will be avoided by bearing this in mind.

Salón de Embajadores, or **Salón de la Media Naranja** (Hall of the Ambassadors, or of the Half-Orange) The alternative names refer respectively to the function of the hall and its domed ceiling. This is the most splendid of the Alcázar's rooms, an inscription in Arabic confirming that it was built by Toledo craftsmen and completed in 1366.

Carlos V married Isabel of Portugal here in 1526. It is said that the Emperor fell in love with Isabel after seeing her portrait, and was not disappointed with the reality. (England's Henry VIII had less luck with Anne of Cleves, 'the Mare of Flanders', whose beauty fell far short of that depicted in the painting shown to him.)

Three sets of horseshoe arches are in the Córdoba Caliphate style found at Medina Zahara.

The Mudéjar tiles are original.

A sixteenth-century frieze around the four walls, immediately beneath the dome, depicts the heads of Spanish kings up to Philip II.

Busts were made by *Diego de Esquivel* in 1529.

Small wrought-iron balconies which interrupt the frieze were constructed by *Francisco López*, in 1592; their incongruity is regarded as unfortunate.

The great ceiling is not the hall's first, but was added in 1427 by *Diego Ruiz*. It consists of lacelike wooden sections, some of the spaces between them being filled with enamels that reflect the light.

The two rooms flanking the hall are without exceptional interest.

Return to the Patio de las Doncellas and enter the room right.

Sala de Techo de Carlos V (Hall of the Ceiling of Carlos V) The Emperor commissioned the coffered Renaissance ceiling to replace the original. Of the twelve carved busts, those in the centre are alleged to represent Carlos V and his consort. Leading from the room are the three **Habitaciones de los Infantes**, or **Habitaciones de María Padilla** (Rooms of the Children, or Rooms of María Padilla). It seems unlikely that these rooms were ever occupied by María Padilla, as was once believed, because she died in 1362; however, they may have been intended for her.

A wall plaque in the central room confirms one of the few certainties that can be applied to the palace without question, recording, as it does, the birth here on 21 September 1848, to the Infanta Luisa Fernández, of Princess María Isabel de Orléans y Borbón.

The last of these three rooms connects with the long **Sala del Techo del Felipe II**, or **Comedor** (Hall of the Ceiling of Philip II, or Dining Hall). Philip II changed the appearance of the room in the sixteenth century, principally by means of its coffered ceiling, which was made by *Juan de Simancas*.

At the centre of the hall, the triple horseshoe arch, which connects with the Salón de Embajadores, is decorated with peacocks on its spandrels. This Persian theme has given rise to speculation that Persian artists were employed, but there is no direct evidence and Toledo craftsmen seem more likely.

Continue through the hall to the room at its end.

Sala del Techo de los Reyes Católicos (Room of the Ceiling of the Catholic Monarchs) This room's appearance dates from the late fifteenth century. It is said that Isabella I spent much of her spare time here, due to its proximity to her son's quarters.

Exit to the Patio de las Muñecas and, from the corner ahead, follow the corridor to the Vestíbulo and exit left from the palace to the Patio de la Montería. Turn right and follow the passage beneath the arch. A sign, 'Capilla y Salones de Carlos V', indicates the Patio del Crucero, right.

Patio del Crucero (Patio of the Crossing) is so named because formerly it was a sunken winter garden divided by arcades in the form of a cross.

Palacio de Carlos V This building occupies the south side of the patio, also providing public access to the Alcázar's gardens.

Carlos V remodelled Gothic buildings that had been constructed for Alfonso X in the thirteenth century. However, the Classical façade is the eighteenth-century work of Sebastián van der Borcht, architect of Seville's great Tobacco Factory.

First visited is the **Salón de los Tapices de la Conquista de Túnez** (Hall of the Conquest of Tunis Tapestries), in which hang copies of tapestries made to commemorate Carlos V's defeat of the Moors at Tunis in 1535. Mary of Hungary, sister of the Emperor, commissioned the Flemish *Jan Vermayer*, a leading contemporary painter of battle scenes, to accompany the Spanish army and prepare a series of frescos. Eventually, however, it was decided to turn his sketches into tapestries, and these were made by *Willem Pannemaker* of Brussels, who completed them in 1554. Twelve tapestries were made, and they were exhibited in London to mark the marriage of Mary I and Philip II.

The six exhibited here are copies made in 1740; the originals are in Madrid. Of particular interest is the tapestry at the end of the hall, illustrating the western Mediterranean with north and south transposed, as was usual in Arab maps.

Behind this hall, the **Salón del Emperador** (Emperor's Hall) retains its Gothic rib vault.

The ceramic dado was made at Triana by *Cristóbal de Augusta*, in 1579.

At the end of the hall, right, is the chapel.

The **Alcázar's Gardens** are reached from the opposite end of the hall. These are without doubt the most beautiful gardens in Seville, and it is hard to think of many others that approach their combination of variety, colour and perfume. Although created by the Moors, the layout is now a mixture of Renaissance, Baroque and Romantic styles. Approximately four-fifths of the Alcázar's area is covered by them, and they used to be even more extensive before much of the orchard and vegetable garden was lost for the creation of the Paseo de Caterina Ribera and the Murillo Gardens.

Immediately ahead is the **Estanque de Mercurio** (Pool of Mercury), created for Philip II.

The bronze figure of *Mercury* was designed by *García de Pesquera*, and made by *Bartolomé Morel* in 1576.

Backing the pool is the rusticated **Galería del Grutesco**

(Grotesque Gallery), fronting the city wall, which bisects the Alcázar at this point. It originally continued to the end of the gardens before doubling back westward to the Torre del Oro.

The stonework, niches and gallery were added in the seventeenth and eighteenth centuries.

Caliphate capitals have been re-used in the arcade of the gallery.

An eighteenth-century staircase descends to the **Jardín de la Danza** (Garden of the Dance), prepared for the wedding of Carlos V and Isabel of Portugal in the sixteenth century but restored and altered somewhat in 1802. The eighteenth-century nymph and satyr, in dancing poses, have given the garden its name, and it is alleged that they were placed here to commemorate a great ball held at the Alcázar in 1350 in honour of the Black Prince. As part of the festivities, girls performed Moorish dances, and English morris dancing is believed to have derived from them.

Immediately right, at the basement level of the Palacio de Carlos V, a passage leads to the '**Baths of María Padilla**', in reality an auxiliary water supply for the palace.

The gardens lead southward, each section bearing a different name, e.g. **Jardín del Príncipe** (Prince's Garden, the Prince being Prince Juan, who was born in the Alcázar to the Catholic Monarchs and died there in 1497 aged nineteen), **Jardín de las Infantes** (Children's Garden), **Jardín Grande** (Great Garden), and **Jardín de las Damas** (Ladies' Garden), which lies immediately behind the Estanque de Mercurio.

Carlos V built several pavilions in the gardens, but only one survives, in neo-Moorish style, designed by *Juan Hernández* and completed in 1543. Its interior can be seen through the doorway but cannot be entered.

The gateway in the wall is the **Puerta del Privilegio**; it leads to relatively new sections of the gardens, once part of the fruit and vegetable section. The last tower in the wall is known as the **Torre de la Cita** (Meeting Tower). By following the wall back towards the palace it will be noted that there is no grotesque decoration on this side.

At its end, attached to the **Torre del Enlace** (Link Tower), is the blocked gateway that was made *c.* 1500 for the Palace of the Duke of Arcos in Marchena and transferred here for Alfonso XIII in 1913. Its Gothic detailing survives.

Return, via the Palacio de Carlos V, to the Patio del Crucero. At the passageway on its north side, turn right towards the exit from the Alcázar.

Immediately left runs the **Apeadero**, a large coach hall built for Philip V *c.* 1733. A double row of marble columns divides the hall into aisles. At one time this was the main entrance to the Alcázar, and still is for some who inadvertently wander in, not understanding the Spanish signs. Occasionally a visitor who is obviously a tourist will be stopped, but others are frequently not, part of Seville's *laissez-faire* charm.

Fronting the Apeadero is the **Patio de las Banderas**, which lies within the Alcázar's wall, confirming that it once formed part of the complex. Banderas refers to the flags of the army that assembled here prior to battle.

An Almoravid vault has been discovered within **No. 2** Patio de las Banderas, and other survivals from the Muslim period exist. Part of the patio was once occupied by the fifth-century paleo-Christian basilica dedicated to St Vincent, where St Isidoro was buried. Excavations discovered its baptismal font, the oldest known example in Spain and now standing in the cathedral's Patio de los Naranjos; the church had been converted to a mosque.

Christopher Columbus, according to tradition, prayed at a small chapel set in the patio's outer gateway immediately prior to leaving the city on his first voyage of discovery.

ITINERARY 3

SANTA CRUZ QUARTER

To enter the area of the former Jewish ghetto of Seville, now known as the Barrio de Santa Cruz, is a unique experience. It has been likened to going backstage on the set of *Carmen* and discovering that the streets and plazas spread out for half a square mile. Churches, palaces and monastic establishments of interest lie within, but it is the winding streets themselves that are the chief attraction.

Tinkling fountains, ceramic tiles, wrought-iron balconies, orange trees, bougainvillaea and walls painted white, ochre and dusky pink – the street colours of Seville – provide an enchantment, at all seasons, that few other cities in the world can match.

A brief history of the Santa Cruz quarter is given on pages 13 and 17 and, for convenience, some of its peripheral sections are dealt with elsewhere.

Timing *Santa Cruz should be seen by night as well as by day, moonlight and the traditional-style street lamps casting a soft, white light that adds another dimension to its charm.*

Following restoration, opening details for the Hospital of the Venerable Priests should be checked locally.

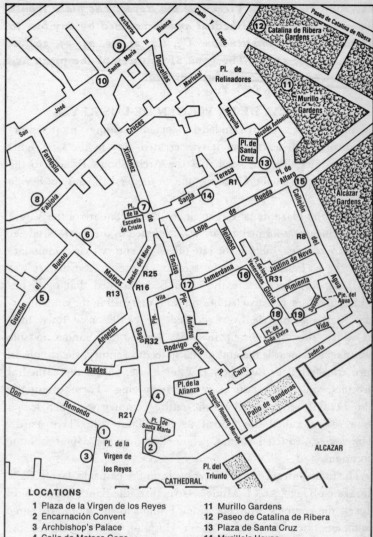

LOCATIONS

1 Plaza de la Virgen de los Reyes
2 Encarnación Convent
3 Archbishop's Palace
4 Calle de Mateos Gago
5 Convent of San José de la Montaña
6 Santa Cruz Church
7 Patio de la Escuela de Cristo
8 Birthplace of Cardinal Wiseman
9 Santa María la Blanca
10 Calle de Santa María la Blanca

11 Murillo Gardens
12 Paseo de Catalina de Ribera
13 Plaza de Santa Cruz
14 Murillo's House
15 Callejón del Agua
16 Hospital of the Venerable Priests
17 Calle Jamerdana
18 Plaza de Doña Elvira
19 Calle Susona

START *Plaza de la Virgen de los Reyes. The plaza fronts the apse of Seville Cathedral and is reached by any bus to Avenida de la Constitución: C3, C4, 21, 22, 23, 25, 26, 30, 31, 33, 34, 40, 41, 42.* **The general features of the plaza are best viewed from the central fountain.**

Location 1 PLAZA DE LA VIRGEN DE LOS REYES

Because the *plaza* is surrounded by ancient buildings, most visitors are surprised to learn that it was created only in the late eighteenth century. To the north lies the Archbishop's Palace, to the south the Encarnación Convent, and to the west the apse of Seville Cathedral.

Before the Plaza de la Virgen de los Reyes (Square of the Virgin of the Kings) was formed, its site was occupied by an ornate Mudéjar structure of brick, built in the late fifteenth century to accommodate both the ecclesiastical and the secular chapters of Seville. It was not long, however, before the latter body decided that more imposing premises, constructed of stone and designed in the contemporary Renaissance style, were needed: hence the new town hall, to which they transferred in 1568, leaving the canons in sole occupancy. Towards the end of the sixteenth century, the canons in turn transferred to their new chapter house, within the cathedral precinct, only ecclesiastical offices remaining. These eventually also became redundant and the entire complex was then leased as a *bodega*, called the Corral de los Olmos (Elm Tree Yard). The *bodega* attracted rogues, whose licentious behaviour became notorious.

The main entrance to the *bodega* was on the east side, facing Calle de Mateos Gago, and a Mudéjar structure, the Santa Marta arch, linked the complex with Plaza del Triunfo to the south. Its name commemorated the Santa Marta Hospital, which occupied the premises of what is now the Encarnación Convent.

The Corral de los Olmos was demolished when the *plaza* was laid out in the late eighteenth century, the only trace of it to survive being the white marble *Madonna and Child* sculpture, which had surmounted its main entrance and now stands within a small low-level niche, specially created for it in the Giralda tower, facing the *plaza*.

A monumental lamp-post/fountain, designed by *José Lafita*, was erected in the centre of the *plaza* early in the present century.

The grotesque heads, from which water spouts, are based on Roman originals, discovered nearby at Itálica and now displayed within the House of Pilate (page 181).

José Moquer, whose forge stood nearby, in Calle de Mateos Gago, was responsible for the decorative ironwork supporting the lamps.

Stationed in front of the Encarnación Convent are the horse-drawn carriages (*coches de caballo*), long-established Seville favourites. These will take visitors wherever they wish to go, but are hired chiefly for short, 'city highlight' trips, in the manner of Venetian gondolas; to regard them as public transport is an expensive proposition. A further staging point for the carriages is at the entrance to María Luisa Park, for trips around these former grounds of San Telmo Palace.

Location 2 ENCARNACIÓN CONVENT (CONVENT DE LA ENCARNACIÓN)
Plaza de la Virgen de los Reyes.

Fronted by orange trees, the white façade of the convent's church, relieved by distinctive brick arches, is the most typically 'Andalusian' feature of the *plaza*. It originated as the mosque 'de los Ossos' and was given to the church by Alfonso X, becoming part of the monastic Hospital de Santa Marta at its foundation, when Archdeacon Fernán Martínez purchased the building for the Chapter in the late fourteenth century. Monks of the Encarnación Convent acquired the premises in 1819, as their original convent had been destroyed by Napoleon's occupying forces in order to create the Plaza de la Encarnación, now one of the least beguiling of the city's central plazas. A small part of the brick-built mosque was retained, but most was rebuilt in the late fourteenth century, in Mudéjar style. The detail of this building is better appreciated from close quarters.

Two ceramic plaques have been inserted in the side of the nave of the Convent's church, facing the *plaza*. That to the left records the existence of the Corral de los Olmos, the other commemorates Cervantes's reference to it in his *El Rufián Dichoso*. The latter plaque is one of a group made in 1916, the 300th anniversary of Cervantes's death, indicating the Seville locations referred to by the great writer in his novels. So many were put up that they were caustically described by some Sevillanos as marking 'the way of the Cervantino crosses'.

It is believed that the bell-tower may incorporate Muslim fabric in its structure. The belfry, however, is a Baroque, seventeenth-century addition.

Although built in the late fourteenth century, the interior of the church is decorated with Classical features. It is generally closed to the public.

To the east, the square protruding sanctuary of the church originally formed part of the mosque.

Its panel of exposed brickwork incorporates a multi-lobed window, now blocked.

Another blocked lobed window is seen from Calle Santa Marta, first right, which continues ahead, beneath the arch, to **Plaza de Santa Marta**.

This *plaza*, one of the smallest and most charming in Seville, is missed by many visitors. It is a cul-de-sac, as were many of those that were formed in the city during the Muslim period. They echo the numerous 'dead-end' squares of minute proportions still to be found in North African cities such as Fez and Marrakesh, and form an important part of the labyrinthine town planning that probably evolved as a defensive measure.

Orange trees surround the cobbled *plaza*, in which stands a Renaissance cross. This comprises a crucifix and a *Pietà*, the work of **Hernán Ruiz the Younger**, which originally stood towards the edge of the city, near the ancient wall.

There is no exit from this *plaza* and a return must be made to Plaza de la Virgen de los Reyes. Immediately ahead, the Archbishop's Palace occupies all the north side.

Location 3 ARCHBISHOP'S PALACE (PALACIO ARZOBISPAL)

Plaza de la Virgen de los Reyes.

Patio and staircase open. To visit the Hall and Throne Room it is necessary to join a group. Admission free.

This Baroque palace displays one of the finest staircases in the city, made entirely of jasper.

History At the Reconquest, St Fernando presented the site for the palace to Remondo, first Archbishop of Seville, and construction began immediately. Nothing visible survives of the thirteenth-century building, however, as it was completely remodelled in the second half of the seventeenth century. Marshal Soult, Napoleon's commander, occupied the palace as his headquarters following the French conquest of Seville in 1810. On his departure, many of its works of art were taken to France.

Exterior The façade, of rose brick and stone, in high Baroque style, was completed by *Lorenzo Fernández de Iglesias* in 1717, although the elaborate main entrance was ready by 1704.

The gate leads to a patio, behind which lies the garden. From the vestibule in the far right-hand corner rises the great staircase.

Interior *Friar Manuel Ramos* designed this outstanding staircase, made of salmon-pink jasper. It was apparently even more impressive until Soult removed the paintings that hung from the walls.

The **cupola**, above the stairwell, is decorated with paintings by the eighteenth-century Sevillano artist *Juan de Espinal*.

From the top of the staircase, the door, right, leads to the anteroom of the **Hall** (Salón de Sinodus), but this is open only to groups of visitors. However, it is usually possible to join one. Early seventeenth-century paintings include a set of biblical scenes by *Juan de Zamora*.

The **Throne Room** (Salón del Trono) is linked directly with the Hall. Facing the archbishop's throne is a painting of San Isidoro, by *Valdés Leal*.

Other works include copies of paintings by Murillo.

On leaving the palace, return clockwise to the second turning left, Calle de Mateos Gago, the main artery of the Santa Cruz quarter.

Location 4 CALLE DE MATEOS GAGO

This gently curving thoroughfare, the only major street in the Santa Cruz quarter to have been widened, boasts numerous *tapas* bars and restaurants. Rather dominated at the cathedral end by tourists during the day, young Sevillanos take over at night, spilling on to the pavements from the more popular taverns. Good nature always seems to prevail, even after football matches, and visitors need have no fear of drunken hooliganism.

History Until it was widened in 1927, this was a narrow thorough-fare formerly named Calle Borceguinería, due to the *borceguíes* (laced-shoe-makers) who once held premises there. Steam baths appear to have been popular around this street during the Muslim period, and some vestiges remain. Other buildings of interest that once stood in Calle de Mateos Gago include the Carnicería de los Dolentes (Butcher for the Suffering), the trader permitted exclusively to sell meat during Lent, but only to the sick; the mid-sixteenth-century palace of the counts of Gelves; and a confectioner's that specialized in 'marshal meringues', so named due to their popularity with Marshal Soult, the French governor of Seville, who lived in the Archbishop's Palace nearby. Nineteenth-century houses now pre-dominate, the ground floors of most of them having been converted to commercial premises.

All buildings on the south side, at the cathedral end of the street, date from the 1927 widening; both rows of orange trees were planted at the same time.

Immediately left, **Bar Giralda,** No. 2 incorporates part of the structure of a Moorish steam bath (*hammam*). Vaults are supported by four columns. The Mudéjar-style bar is popular with tourists and locals alike.

From the other side of the road at this point, one of the clearest, and therefore most photographed views of the Giralda may be gained.

Calle Abades, the first street passed, left, follows the approximate line of the Roman main thoroughfare, Cardus, which was retained during the Moorish period under the name of Hara Mayur. The street then led in a straight line northward to the Macarena Gate.

On the opposite side of Calle de Mateos Gago, forming the east corner of Calle de Rodrigo Caro, is the arcaded **Bodega Santa Cruz,** No. 1. It is of no particular appeal décor-wise, but is, however, very reasonably priced and serves larger than normal portions of *tapas*. The space outside permits great crowds of youngsters to gather at night until the early hours.

Continue following Calle de Mateos Gago eastward. The tiny *bodega*, **Juan García Aviles**, at No. 20, is matched by many similar premises in Seville, but it has one extraordinary feature: a shimmering wooden bar top, one of the last examples remaining in the city, made of Spanish mahogany and installed in the nineteenth century. After every glass has been removed, the owner, or his assistant, unfailingly wipes the surface with a damp cloth, as though part of a religious rite. As if this wasn't enough, the wood is French-polished annually; the result matches any specimen admired on *The Antiques Roadshow*. After two or three of the patron's *manzanillas*, the glow appears to deepen in a miraculous way.

Facing the bar is **Calle de los Angeles**, to which is attached a Sevillian legend, almost certainly apocryphal. It appears that a Jewess was passionately in love with King Pedro, but he would not forsake his mistress, María de Padilla. Mad with jealousy, she hid one night beneath the ghetto wall, which passed the Mateos Gago end of the street, waiting for the King to pass. As he did so, she attempted to stab him, but Pedro managed to grasp her wrist, and proceeded on his way unharmed. Rather untypically of Pedro the Cruel, it is said that the King magnanimously took no proceedings against his assailant.

Vertice Libros, No. 24 Calle de Mateos Gago, is a well-known Seville bookshop: many English editions are stocked and advice, in perfect English, will be given by the charming sisters who run the establishment.

It is known that a gate in the ghetto wall was formerly approached from Calle Mesón del Moro, first right.

On the corner, at **No. 1**, the Baroque house incorporates a terra-cotta model of the Giralda in a niche at upper level. Remains of Moorish baths are incorporated within the bar **Mesón del Moro**, at No. 4 (open evenings only). Some eleventh-century horseshoe arches and star-shaped windows are visible, and it seems probable that it was this building that gave the street its name (House of the Moor).

Returning to Calle de Mateos Gago and continuing eastward, carved Baroque arms, probably seventeenth-century, are passed, an embellishment to the doorway of **No. 21**.

Retained in the next street left, Calle Guzmán el Bueno, formerly Calle de la Botica de las Aguas (Apothecary's Shop), are fifteenth- and sixteenth-century houses, although all have since been re-modelled. Many possess attractive patios that may be glimpsed.

Location 5 CONVENT OF SAN JOSÉ DE LA MONTAÑA
No. 10 Calle Guzmán el Bueno
Open only if convenient.
(Ring the bell in the patio and request to see the *Capilla*.)

Built in the fourteenth century as the Casa de Olea, a private palace, the former salon, now adapted as the convent's chapel, retains the finest Mudéjar decor in the city after the Alcázar. Other Mudéjar work that the building once possessed has been lost, due to remodelling.

The Grenadine taste of the period is followed, plasterwork with Cufic inscriptions being reminiscent of the Alhambra. Doors and doorways are exceptional.

A deep wooden frieze, at upper level, incorporates square pierced windows.

On returning to Calle Guzmán el Bueno, the Gothic balustrade of a watchtower may be seen left. This is part of the former Casa de Los Pinelo, described on page 172.

On returning to Calle de Mateos Gago, the façade of Santa Cruz church stands immediately ahead.

Location 6 SANTA CRUZ
Calle de Mateos Gago
Open 09.30–10.00 and 19.00–21.30 (Winter 20.00–21.30)

Painted white, but with darker, exposed stone features, Santa Cruz superficially appears to be typical of Seville's many Baroque churches. However, its façade was completely remodelled in the present century.

History   Originally, the church was monastic, being commissioned in 1665 for the Clérigos Menores (Minor Clerics) to the design of *José Tirado*. In 1810 the original parish church of Santa Cruz was demolished and its function transferred here.

Exterior   The façade, including its iron cross, is the work of *Juan de Talavera*, 1929. Its remodelling formed part of the extensive restoration and beautification of the quarter carried out by the same architect for the Marqués de Vega-Inclan.

Interior   The barrel-vaulted **nave** is aisled, with galleries, above.
   Each bay forms a chapel incorporating a large, gilded reredos.
   The first two **north chapels** are dedicated, respectively, to St Anne and the Virgin. Their reredoses incorporate principal figures in central niches by *Pedro Roldán*.
   A deep cupola roofs the crossing.
   The **north transept** is dedicated to St Francisco Caracciolo, founder of the Clérigos Menores.
   Its reredos was designed by *Duque Cornejo*.
   The **sanctuary**, in Classical style, is the work of *Blas Molner*, 1792.
   The *baldacchino* above the high altar was designed by *Bernard Simón de Pineda* in 1678.
   The *Virgin and Child*, attributed to *Jerónimo Hernández*, came from the lost St Pablo Convent.
   From the east end of the south aisle, a door leads to a corridor from which another door, left, opens on to a delightful patio.

Location 7 PATIO DE LA ESCUELA DE CRISTO

Tiny, and filled with plants and trees, this easily missed patio is one of the most tranquil in Seville.

The building to the right is the former chapel of the Escuela de Cristo (School of Christ), built in 1793; it is the only one of this institution of flagellants' three eighteenth-century chapels to survive.

A ceramic plaque above the water trough reproduces a seventeenth-century painting, *The Adoration of the Shepherds*, now in Mexico. The young shepherd is a portrait of the co-founder of the institution, Juan de Palafox y Mendoza (1600–1659).

Leaving the church and continuing eastward along Calle de Mateos Gago, No. 5 Calle de Fabiola stands immediately ahead.

Location 8 BIRTHPLACE OF CARDINAL WISEMAN
5 Calle de Fabiola.

The plaque, made in 1869, records the birth in this house on 2 August 1802 of Cardinal Wiseman, Archbishop of Westminster.

Nicholas Wiseman, 1802–65, was born of Irish parents who had emigrated to Spain. After the death of his father, he returned with the family to Ireland. Nicholas preached on Catholicism in London, 1835–6, and founded the *Dublin Review*, a religious quarterly which sympathized with the Oxford Movement. Made a bishop in 1840, Wiseman served in the Midlands before transferring to London. Pius IX appointed him cardinal in 1850 and Wiseman was soon to become the first Archbishop of Westminster. His novel, *Fabiola*, written in 1854, gave the present name to the street.

Calle Fabiola stretches south-eastward, some of its houses incorporating the only surviving part of the medieval wall of the ghetto.

After passing two private passages, follow, to the right, Calle Ximénez de Encisco. The base of the wall of its first house incorporates eighteen great millstones. This narrow, winding thoroughfare is one of the longest in Santa Cruz. Its name commemorates a sixteenth-century poet, much praised by Cervantes. During the Jewish period, butchers operated at the far end.

Immediately left, Calle Cruces leads to a small *plaza*.

Now, popularly, but apparently unofficially, known as **Plaza de**

las Cruces (Square of the Crosses), in the nineteenth century this small *plaza* was called Plaza de las Cuatros Vientos (Square of the Four Winds), as the four roads that lead into it came from the cardinal points of the compass. In the middle of the present century, the *plaza* was enlarged by demolishing a small pen, where farm animals were kept. An iron cross on a marble column was then erected in the centre: it has since been joined by two others.

First left, Calle Doncellas, leads to first left again, Calle de Santa María la Blanca. Cross the road.

Location 9 SANTA MARÍA LA BLANCA
5 Calle de Santa María la Blanca.

It is believed that beneath the Baroque shell of this church lies the structure of a thirteenth-century synagogue, only the portal of which is now visible (at the side of the building). Unusually deeply sculpted plasterwork on the vaults is a distinctive feature of the interior.

History On the site of Santa María la Blanca stood one of the three mosques presented to the Jews by Alfonso X for adaptation to synagogues in 1252. The mosque was probably rebuilt completely, but it is likely that the thirteenth-century structure survives. Remodelling as a church, in Gothic/Mudéjar style, took place in 1391 and again, in Baroque style, in 1659.

Exterior As is common among Seville's Baroque churches, the main façade retains an earlier Gothic/Mudéjar portal. This came from the fourteenth-century remodelling of the synagogue and is the only feature to survive from this period.

The side entrance in Calle de los Archeros is formed by the portal of the original synagogue. It is the only decorative feature of architecture from the ghetto period that can now be seen in the city. The doorway is flanked by columns with Visigothic capitals; these certainly pre-date the Moorish occupation of Seville and may have come from a very early Christian church on the site.

Enter the church from Calle de Santa María la Blanca.

Interior   The nave is aisled and the interior probably follows the plan of the fourteenth-century building.

Barrel-vaulted throughout, the ceiling is entirely covered with filigree plasterwork, the design of which is extended over the walls in *trompe l'œil* style. **Pedro** and **Miguel de Borja** were responsible for the work, which features scrolls, urns, flora, cherubs' heads and, beneath the cupola, a representation of the Giralda.

A dado of blue ceramics runs throughout at lower level.

Immediately past the north aisle's side door, an engaging sculpture of St Joseph holding the infant Jesus stands on a bracket, typical of the seventeenth-century Seville style.

The Baroque reredos in the centre of the north wall, remodelled in 1774, incorporates a *Pietà*, painted by **Luis de Vargas** in 1564 for an earlier reredos.

It is flanked by painted figures of St John the Baptist and St Francis of Assisi.

Hanging adjacent to this is a foreboding *Last Supper* painting, attributed to **Murillo** but more likely the work of **Sebastián Gomez**, one of his followers.

Facing down the aisle, the **north-east chapel**'s reredos is dedicated to St John Nepomuceno. Its sixteenth-century *Ecce Homo* is from the school of **Morales**.

The high altar's reredos incorporates a Virgin dressed in white (La Blanca), holding the infant Jesus, the work of *Juan de Astorga*.

Below, on side pedestals, stand figures, of St Justa and St Rufina, *c.* 1720.

The west chapel, at the end of the south aisle, displays a Holy Trinity reredos on the wall to the left; it is a Baroque eighteenth-century work by *Blas Molner*.

Immediately fronting the church, a small *plaza* extends from Calle de Santa María la Blanca.

Location 10 CALLE DE SANTA MARÍA LA BLANCA

Calle de Santa María la Blanca formed part of the chief commercial thoroughfare of the ghetto, leading from the Puerta de Minjoar gate northward to the gate beside what is now St Nicolás Church.

The small square, facing the church, was known as Plaza de la Azueycal (temporary market) during the Jewish period. At this point, moneychangers profited from strangers entering the city via the nearby gate in the wall. Bars and restaurants now proliferate.

Immediately right, occupying the block between Calle Dos Hermanos and Calle Céspedes, stands the once-more imposing façade of the **Altamira Palace**, restored in 1992 from its ruined condition to become local government offices. Built as the seat of the aristocratic Altamira family early in the seventeenth century, the palace is one of Seville's finest examples of Mannerism.

Return south-eastward along Calle Santa María la Blanca to the junction with Calle Cano y Cueto (second right).

Still known as **Puerta de la Carne** (Meat Gate), the name given to this, the east end of Calle de Santa María la Blanca, commemorates the ancient gateway in the city wall which formerly stood here. The Moors called it Bab Yahwar (Gateway of Pearls), but the name became corrupted to Puerta de Minjoar by the Jews. Eventually, the erroneous belief became widespread that Minjoar had been a wealthy Jew, who lived nearby. In the sixteenth century the gate was rebuilt as a Renaissance stone archway, and the structure survived until demolished, together with the wall, in the nineteenth century. At one time this was a red-light district, but the new name of the gateway reflected a different kind of meat trade: the butchers that operated beside it.

Follow the Calle Cano y Cueto westward to **No. 7**, where a ceramic panel at upper level represents St Fernando. By tradition, the King spent the first night after his Reconquest in a palace that stood on the site.

Ahead, **Plaza de los Refinadores** has retained its name and dimensions unchanged for centuries, unusual in Santa Cruz. Refinadores refers to the metal refiners who once had premises here.

The central statue of **Don Juan Tenorio**, by *Nicomedes*, 1974, commemorates the mythical, libidinous hero created, allegedly, by Tirso de Molina in the tragic drama *El Burlador* (seducer) *de Sevilla*, published in 1630. 'Don Juan' became virtually synonymous with great lovers and appeared as the leading character in works by Molière, Mozart (*Don Giovanni*), Byron, Shaw and Richard Strauss, among others. The *plaza* was originally bounded to the south-east by the city wall, but this section was demolished in 1911 and the Murillo Gardens were then laid out.

Location 11 MURILLO GARDENS (JARDINES DE MURILLO)

These wedge-shaped gardens are considered by many to be the most enchanting in this city of outstandingly beautiful open spaces. Winding paths, a variety of trees and tranquil arbours help to disguise the relatively small area covered.

Alfonso XIII presented part of the Alcázar's Huerta del Retiro (Orchard of Seclusion) to the city in 1911, so that more access points to Santa Cruz would become available. *Juan Talavera* laid out the gardens between 1911–17. José Laguillo, director of the journal *El Liberal*, suggested their name, to commemorate the great painter.

A stroll through the centre of the gardens, in the direction of the Alcázar wall, passes arbours decorated with ceramic tiles from Triana, their designs based on folk scenes painted by *José García Ramos*.

By turning left, when the Alcázar wall is reached, and continuing ahead, the much larger Catalina de Ribera gardens are entered.

Location 12 PASEO DE CATALINA DE RIBERA

The *paseo* (walkway) bisects gardens that are formal in style and flanked by straight paths. At their north end the gardens adjoin the Murillo Gardens, with which they are often confused. Most Sevillanos generally refer to the whole, incorrectly, as the Murillo Gardens. Monuments to Columbus and to Catalina de Ribera are incorporated.

Like the Murillo Gardens, the area once formed part of the Alcázar's vegetable and fruit garden. The walk was created in 1898, and palm trees were planted. Various alterations were made in 1920, all under the direction of *Talavera*. At one time the walk became so popular with bereaved families that it was known as the Paseo de los Lutos (Walkway of the Mourners).

In the centre, rising from a circular pool, is Seville's monument to **Christopher Columbus**, who set sail in 1492 on his epic voyage of discovery from Palos, a small Atlantic port on a tributary of the Guadalquivir, forty miles from the city. The explorer intended to return to Seville, but a storm diverted his vessel to Lisbon. *Talavera* designed the monument, which was sculpted by *Coullaut-Valera*. It consists of two Corinthian columns, set on a pedestal and supporting a carved lion; his paw rests on a sphere, representing the world.

Set half-way up and linking the columns, a bronze represents Columbus's caravel, the *Santa María*. Medallions set on either side of the ship bear the names of the sponsors of the voyage, Fernando (Ferdinand) and Isabel (Isabella).

A bust of Columbus is set in the base on the south side. Half way along the relatively modern wall of the Alcázar Gardens, the **Caterina de Ribera fountain** pays tribute to the sixteenth-century founder of the Hospital de la Sangre, whose name is commemorated by the walkway.

A structure of stone, in the form of a Classical, rusticated portal, acts as a backing to the fountain and this, once more, was designed by *Talavera*, *c.* 1911.

The central ceramic portrait represents Caterina de Ribera.

The sixteenth-century marble fountain was brought here from Plaza del Pumarejo.

Return north-eastward, skirting the wall, and then take the first path left. The path at the rear of the Murillo Gardens leads to Calle Nicolás Antonio, first left.

A plaque above the entrance to **No. 2** Calle Nicolás Antonio records that land was 'freely given' by its owner in 1911, so that the street could be laid out. A section of the ancient city wall also had to be removed before access to the Murillo Gardens could be obtained.

Immediately ahead lies Plaza de Santa Cruz.

Location 13 PLAZA DE SANTA CRUZ

Although small, this is still one of the three largest *plazas* within the Santa Cruz quarter and, albeit a nineteenth-century creation, one of the most picturesque.

The largest of Seville's former synagogues stood on its site until demolished by Marshal Soult in 1810, during the Napoleonic occupation. It had been converted to Santa Cruz Church in 1391, giving its name to the parish.

Talavera remodelled the *plaza* in 1918, transferring to it the central iron cross, **Cruz de la Cerrajería**, made by *Sebastián Conde* in 1692. This had originally stood in Calle Cerrajería, on the corner with Calle Sierpes, but because the cross obstructed processions and, so it is said, the carriage of Pedro V, it was moved (originally to the Minimas Convent). In summer the cross is surrounded by an attractive display of roses.

La Albahaca restaurant, at No. 12, is renowned for its innovative food (see page 312). It occupies an ancient house that has been sympathetically converted and furnished with antiques. The architect *Juan Talavera* lived here in the 1920s and his *tertulia* (cultural discussion groups) were renowned.

On the corner, a column with a Visigothic capital has been incorporated in the wall.

Tablao los Gallos, No. 11, is regarded as one of the most authentic *flamenco* theatres in Seville. Performances are from 21.30 (see page 27).

A large marble plaque on the wall of **No. 10** commemorates the painter *Bartolomé Esteban Murillo*, who was buried in the lost Santa Cruz Church, allegedly below its bell tower. It is believed that his remains still lie somewhere beneath the pavement of the *plaza*, but their precise location is unknown. Murillo, among others, founded Seville's Academía de Bellas Artes, and that body erected the plaque as 'a modest monument, but the first'.

Calle Santa Teresa leads to the long white building which accommodates the Convent of San José, founded by St Teresa in 1596. It was designed by *Vermondo Resta*.

A ceramic portrait of St Teresa is displayed on the wall ahead. It is based on the painting of her, from life, by *Friar Juan de la Misería*, which is kept within the convent together with personal items belonging to the saint.

The church is open only for Mass at 08.45 (Sunday 09.00).

Great gilded Baroque reredoses, mostly late seventeenth-century, line both lateral walls up to cornice height.

The high altar's reredos, a tremendous Classical example by *Jerome Velázquez*, 1630, incorporates paintings and figures. A cupola roofs the crossing.

Right of the sanctuary, behind the grille, the nuns of the convent participate in the Mass, unseen by the congregation.

Location 14 MURILLO'S HOUSE
8 Calle Santa Teresa.

Murillo lived in this house immediately prior to his death in 1682. Opened as a museum in 1982, the building has been restored recently but seems unlikely to be reopened to the public.

The painter had several addresses in Seville, moving here from the adjacent San Bartolomé quarter following the death of his close friends, Justino de Neve and Miguel Mañara, who had lived close by. In 1682, when Murillo was painting the reredos of the high altar in the Capuchinos church at Cádiz, he fell from the scaffolding and was fatally injured. Brought back to Seville, he spent his last days in the San José Convent opposite, cared for by the nuns.

The two-storey building is constructed around an arcaded patio. Sadly, virtually nothing survives internally from the seventeenth century.

Calle de Lope de Rueda, first left, displays, set in the wall at the first bend in the road, a Baroque carving of musicians, flanking a coat of arms supported by a marble column.

Continue ahead until Calle Reinoso is joined. The name of Calle de Lope de Rueda commemorates a sixteenth-century Sevillano playwright, but the street was formerly called Calle de Barrabás and a romantic tale is related in connection with it. Barrabás, a Jew, was enamoured of Esther, a Jewess who lived in the present Calle Reinoso. A Moor from Granada was similarly enraptured with her and won the lady's heart. One morning his dead body was discovered outside her house, presumably murdered by Barrabás. The street was then renamed Calle de Moro Muerto (Street of the Dead Moor). Its present name, Reinoso, commemorates an eighteenth-century Sevillano poet.

No. 21 Calle de Lope de Rueda, the residence of the Marqués de Pickman (the Englishman Charles Pickman founded the La Cartuja ceramics factory), exhibits an outstanding portal in Plater-esque style. This was brought here from the Renaissance palace of Ubeda; other features from the same source are incorporated within (it is not open to the public).

The street leads ahead to **Plaza de Alfaro**, where a former palace occupies the east side.

Its portal is a good example of Baroque work. According to tradition, the corner balcony inspired the scene where Figaro serenades Rosina in *The Barber of Seville*.

Callejón del Agua skirts the wall of the Alcázar Gardens.

Location 15 CALLEJÓN DEL AGUA

Water (*agua*) to the Alcázar was conducted along the wall that flanks this street, hence its name.

No. 2, Casa de Peñaranda, formerly established as the Residencia de América, where notable American visitors to the city were accommodated, displays a bronze plaque commemorating **Washington Irving**'s love of Spain. This was made by **Mariano Benlliure** in 1925 and sited here by Vega-Inclán. Irving (1783–1859) was known as the First American Man of Letters; he was great lover of folktales and his most famous work, *The Sketch Book of Geoffrey Crayon, Gent*, included *The Legend of Sleepy Hollow* and *Rip van Winkle*. In 1826 Washington Irving was attached to the American legation in Spain and three years later published *Tales of the Alhambra*. He served as minister to Spain, 1842–6. The large patio is exceptional.

At **No. 4**, on the corner with Calle de Justino de Neve, a plaque records the rejuvenation of the Santa Cruz quarter by the Marqués de Vega-Inclán.

One of Seville's loveliest patios may be visited at No. 6, as it forms part of the **Corral del Agua** restaurant, situated on the Calle Pimienta corner. The restaurant is under the same management as La Albahaca and its food is as delightful as the setting (see page 313).

A very narrow thoroughfare, **Calle Pimienta**, follows, with its balconies dripping foliage in the manner of Córdoba. Another Santa Cruz legend is attached to its name (Pepper Street). According to this, a Jewish spice-merchant who lived here was unable to obtain pepper in the city, but a Christian acquaintance told him that God would provide some. The next day the merchant awoke to find a pepper tree growing outside his house, and was thereby converted to Christianity.

On the Callejón del Agua corner, **No. 14a** displays, at first floor level, a *Virgin and Child* terracotta plaque, in the style of the Della Robbias.

A stone, inserted below, records that a famous Spanish actress, María Guerrero, lived here.

Calle Gloria, first right, leads to Plaza de los Venerables.

Facing, as it does, the famous Hospital of the Venerable Priests, the *plaza* is dominated by bars and restaurants that are obviously aimed at tourists. Prices are, therefore, relatively high for Seville, with supplements charged for sitting outside.

Leading south-eastward from the *plaza*, **Calle de Justino de Neve** commemorates the seventeenth-century founder of the Hospital of the Venerable Priests. It was previously called Calle de Chorro (Street of the Jet), as the pipe carrying the water supply to the Alcázar once broke here and water gushed into the street.

Location 16 HOSPITAL OF THE VENERABLE PRIESTS (HOSPITAL DE LOS VENERABLE SACERDOTES) *1687*
Plaza de los Venerables/Calle Jamerdana.
Opening times to be established after restoration. Concerts will be given in the church and exhibitions held in the refectory of the former hospital.

Undoubtedly one of the city's most important Baroque buildings, the church of what was recently a home for retired priests is a veritable art gallery, displaying works by many of Seville's most gifted artists: **Roelas**, **Pedro** and **Luisa Roldán**, and possibly, **Montañés**. Particularly important are the frescos by **Valdés Leal** and **Lucas Valdés**, which cover the walls and vaults.

History A canon of Seville Cathedral, *Justino de Neve*, founded this home for elderly and infirm priests (Sacerdotes) in 1675. His close friend, *Murillo*, painted a magnificent full-length portrait of him which can be seen in London's National Gallery. The Duke of Veraguas presented the site, on which the Corral de Comedias, the sixteenth-century playhouse of Doña Elvira de Ayala, had previously stood.

Square in plan, the hospital is built around a two-storey patio. Work was begun by *Juan Domínguez*, but *Leonardo de Figueroa* soon took over, completing the church in 1687.

Archbishop Palafox consecrated the building the following year. It was the first to be dedicated to St Fernando, the recently canonized King. Living accommodation for the priests was not yet completed, but in 1697 they were brought in procession to their new home.

Antonio, the internationally renowned *flamenco* artist, is said to have danced professionally for the first time in the hospital complex.

Fronting Calle Jamerdana is the Baroque façade of the church, entirely the work of *Figueroa*.

Interior Frescos painted in the vestibule by *Lucas Valdés* have now faded, but restoration is planned.

Magnificently Baroque, virtually no surface of the aisleless interior has escaped decoration. It is chiefly the work of *Juan Valdés Leal*, who concentrated on the vaults of the sanctuary and sacristy, and his son, *Lucas Valdés*, who was responsible for the walls.

The church is orientated with the high altar at the west end, presumably to permit direct access from the street. Outstanding carvings of St Peter and St Fernando, by *Pedro Roldán*, flank the east door.

Upper-level frescos by *Lucas Valdés*, in the style of tapestries, illustrate *The Triumph of the Pontificate*. The St Jerome reredos, at the east end of the south wall, is attributed to *Herrera the Elder*.

A doorway leads to the patio (return later).

In the third bay, a reredos of *The Immaculate Conception*, mid eighteenth-century Florentine work, was presented by Admiral

Colbert. This incorporates a small figure of St Stephen, attributed to *Montañés*.

The Baroque pulpit is followed by a reredos incorporating an early seventeenth-century painting of *The Crucifixion*. Its altar frontal is of Neapolitan marble. Eight *trompe l'œil* paintings, designed as bronze busts, by *Valdés Leal*, decorate the **cupola**: they depict Spanish bishops who have been canonized.

Private pews at gallery level on both sides have Baroque gilded screens. Paintings on either side of the sanctuary are by *Lucas Valdés*: *St Fernando Presenting the Mosque of Seville to Don Remondo*, and *St Fernando with an Opponent before the Virgin*.

In the late nineteenth century the entire **west wall** was remodelled to form the reredos of the high altar.

At its upper level, a painting of *St Fernando Crowned by the Church*, by *Valdés Leal*, is flanked by *St Clement* and *St Isidora*, painted by *Virgilio Mattoni* in 1891. The large painting of *The Last Supper* that dominates the reredos is a seventeenth-century work by *Roelas*.

Below, the two polychrome, alabaster bas-reliefs of the Virgin and Child were made in the first half of the sixteenth century.

Figures of St John the Evangelist and St John the Baptist, attributed to *Montañés*, flank the **sanctuary**.

The north door leads to the **sacristy**. Its outstanding ceiling fresco, by *Lucas Valdés*, depicts the Triumph of the Cross.

Of chief interest on the **north side** of the church is the figure of St Joseph, by *Luisa Roldán*, in the central bay. In side niches are two unusual examples of pink coral Baroque work, carved to depict a carriage and a tree.

The arcaded two-storey **patio** is filled with trees and plants; unusually, circular steps descend to a central fountain.

A Baroque **staircase** leads to the first floor. Extravagant plasterwork decorates its **cupola**.

Return from the church to Calle Jamerdana and turn left.

Location 17 CALLE JAMERDANA
During the ghetto period, abattoirs operated at the far end of this street, dumping waste for collection. Jamerdana (slaughterhouse

sewage) is, therefore, a name of ancient lineage which undoubtedly shares a Latin source with the English word 'shambles', given to many butchers' streets in the Middle Ages and still surviving, for example, at Manchester and York.

At Calle de Ximénez de Encisco (first right), a plaque on the corner records that **Blanco White** was born in the street in 1775. Of Spanish parentage, José María Blanco y Crespo was a Roman Catholic priest who became a freethinker, writing poetry and prose. When the French invaded Spain in 1808, he took to journalism, fleeing to England two years later, after Seville had fallen to Napoleon. Blanco's opposition to the French, particularly through his journal *El Español*, earned him a pension from the British Government in 1815. He then took Anglican orders, changed his name to White (the English translation of Blanco), and settled in Liverpool, where he died, a staunch Unitarian, in 1841.

Return to Plaza de los Venerables and follow Calle Gloria, first right, to Plaza de Doña Elvira.

Location 18 PLAZA DE DOÑA ELVIRA

The name of this small *plaza* commemorates Doña Elvira de Agula, daughter of a sixteenth-century Chancellor. In addition to possessing the Corral de Comedias theatre, which stood nearby on the site of the Hospital of the Venerable Priests, she owned most of the properties in the tiny streets that then occupied the present square.

Two of them, Calleja de los Caballos (Passage of the Horses) and Plazuela de los Caballos (Little Square of the Horses), gained these names when they became part of the riding school of the Counts of Gelves. Both were demolished in the eighteenth century for the creation of the *plaza*. Remodelling and extension by **Talavera** took place in 1924 when Calle del Ataúd was incorporated, and the *plaza* is now one of the most picturesque in the city, possessing, as it does, views of a Mudéjar tower of the Alcázar. From the *plaza* follow, first left, Calle Susona and continue ahead to **No. 10a.**

Location 19 CALLE SUSONA

The small ceramic skull on the wall, right, commemorates a Santa

Cruz legend that has more of a ring of truth to it than most. Susona, the lovely daughter of a Jew, Diego Susón, lived with her family in Calle del Ataúd. Unknown to them, she was secretly in love with a Christian knight, even though he had been involved in the 1391 sacking of the ghetto. Discovering that her father was planning to kill him, she warned her lover, who promptly organized a further raid on the Jews in which Susona's father and brother died. The knight then refused to have any more to do with the girl. In remorse, she converted to Christianity and became a nun, decreeing that when she died her skull should be nailed above the door of her late father's house as a reminder of her treachery. It is said that the skull remained there until the eighteenth century.

To commemorate the legend, this street was renamed Susona in the nineteenth century having previously been called, successively, Calle de la Muerta (Street of Death) and Calle de la Guadana (Street of the Scythe). It was apparently felt that the area was overburdened with grimly named streets, which then also included Calle del Ataúd (Street of the Coffin), so Calle de las Venerables (Street of the Ancients) was changed at the same time to Calle Gloria (Street of Glory) as part of the cheering-up process.

Follow Pasaje del Agua beneath the arch and ahead and turn right at the end. Callejón del Agua leads to Calle Vida, right. An unnamed passage, left, leads to Calle Judería.

In the corner, immediately left, is a Baroque fountain.

Follow the passage, which continues beneath one of the Alcázar's towers, to the Patio de las Banderas (page 91). Proceed clockwise to the exit from the patio in its south-west corner to Plaza del Triunfo (page 122).

Nearest buses are again those that pass Avenida de la Constitución.

ITINERARY 4

'CARMEN'S' TOBACCO FACTORY, ARCHIVES OF THE INDIES AND MARÍA LUISA PARK

Seville's two most theatrical *plazas* and three of its ancient postern gateways are visited. The Archives of the Indies, designed in the sixteenth century by the architect of Madrid's Escorial, is where all documents relating to the early years of the New World are kept.

Bizet set much of his opera *Carmen* in the former Tobacco Factory, now occupied by Seville University.

At the south end of María Luisa Park is the Archaeological Museum, where the most important Roman finds from nearby Itálica are displayed.

Timing *The Archives of the Indies is open weekdays until 13.00. The Archaeological Museum and the Folk Arts and Customs Museum are both open Tuesday to Saturday 10.00–14.00.*

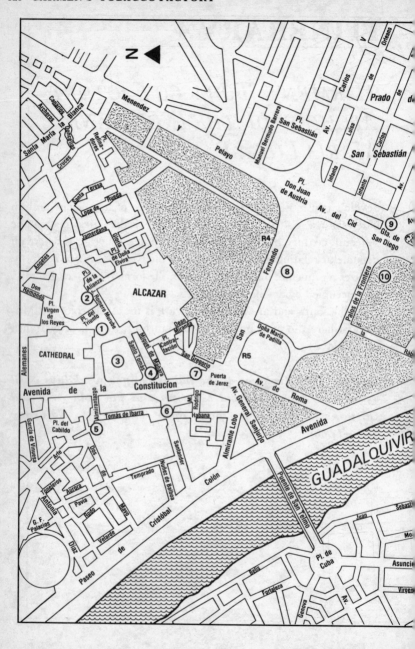

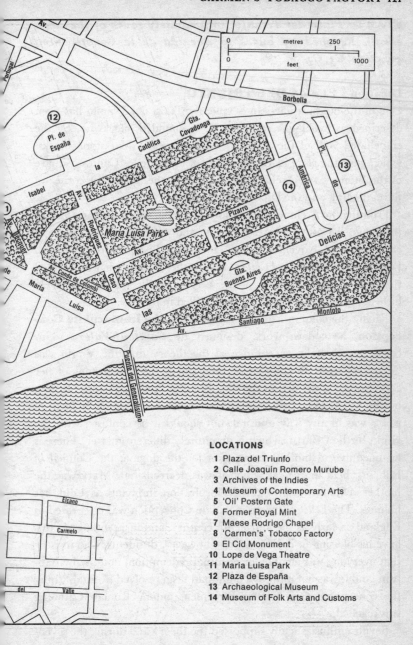

LOCATIONS

1 Plaza del Triunfo
2 Calle Joaquín Romero Murube
3 Archives of the Indies
4 Museum of Contemporary Arts
5 'Oil' Postern Gate
6 Former Royal Mint
7 Maese Rodrigo Chapel
8 'Carmen's' Tobacco Factory
9 El Cid Monument
10 Lope de Vega Theatre
11 María Luisa Park
12 Plaza de España
13 Archaeological Museum
14 Museum of Folk Arts and Customs

START *Plaza del Triunfo (immediately south of the cathedral). Reached by buses to Avenida de la Constitución: 40, 41, 42, C3, C4*

Location 1 PLAZA DEL TRIUNFO

One of the oldest squares in Seville, the Plaza del Triunfo has been described as evoking a stage set. It is bounded, clockwise, by the crenellated wall of the Alcázar, built of great ashlar stone blocks, which gave the *plaza* its earlier name of Plaza de los Cantos (Square of the Stones), the Archives of the Indies, the south-east corner of the cathedral, and the Diputación Provincial.

Fronting the Archives of the Indies is the Baroque **column** (*triunfo*) that gave the *plaza* its present name and commemorates the great earthquake of November 1755, in which Lisbon was destroyed. Figures of the *Virgin and Child* stand on the column – it was claimed that due to the patronage of the Virgin, Seville suffered relatively little damage. Nevertheless, six were killed in the city.

Facing the column is the **Monument to the Immaculate Conception**, a modern work, designed by *Coullaut-Valera*. This celebrates Catholic acceptance of the theory that the Virgin was 'preserved from all stain of original sin in the first instant of her conception', as defined in the papal bull of Pius IX in 1854. It does not imply, as some believe, that the physical conception or birth of Mary was in any way unusual; nor should it be confused with the virgin birth of Christ, which is an entirely different matter. There is no unequivocal biblical foundation for the dogma; the Council of Ephesus, held in 431, at which it was decreed that 'Mary was the mother of God', was probably its inspiration, implying, as it did, her holiness. The Feast of the Immaculate Conception was celebrated in England as early as the fourteenth century, and in 1476 Pope Sixtus gave his blessing to it. There were, however, dissidents, who insisted that everyone was eligible for eventual redemption, notably by baptism, and it was not until this point had been resolved by establishing the conception element that agreement among Roman Catholics was reached.

Seville enthusiastically supported the theory and during the seventeenth century many churches and convents commissioned works of art in its honour. A full-length solitary figure of the Virgin, often standing on a crescent moon, is the most popular form adopted.

Figures at the monument's pedestal represent two of the most important artists involved, **Murillo** and **Montañés**, the poet **Miguel Cid** and the theologian *Juan de Pineda*.

The Baroque building closing the north-east side of the *plaza* houses the Diputación Provincial, the local government of the Seville region. Its site was formerly occupied by the Hospital del Rey (King's Hospital).

Skirting the south façade of the Diputación building is Calle Joaquín Romero Murube.

Location 2 CALLE JOAQUÍN ROMERO MURUBE

This street was laid out in 1965, linking two of the oldest Santa Cruz *plazas*, Plaza del Triunfo and Plaza de la Alianza. It was originally called Calle de la Alcazaba, as it followed the line of the Alcázar's wall, but recently the street was renamed to commemorate the modern poet who had performed its opening ceremony.

Immediately right can be seen a rare surviving feature of the Alcázar from the Muslim period, probably eleventh-century work: a blocked, horseshoe arch, formerly a minor exit from the palace. At this point the crenellated wall of the Alcázar also served as the city wall, following the line established by the Almoravids in the eleventh century. Most of the fabric is original, but the great stone slabs were probably added after the Reconquest, as part of the Christian restoration work.

Immediately left, on reaching the Plaza de la Alianza, the wall is decorated with a ceramic Calvary scene known as *The Christ of Mercy of the Brotherhood of Santa Cruz*.

In the centre of the *plaza* stands a fountain; this must have dried up at one time, as the former name of the *plaza* was Plaza del Pozo Seco (Square of the Dry Well). Its present name refers not to a political alliance but, much more prosaically, to a grocer's shop that once stood here.

The section of Calle Rodrigo Caro that runs north-eastward from the *plaza* was formerly called Calle del Tambor (Street of the Drum). Two conflicting sources for the name have been suggested: that Africans lived here and played their drums, or that a guardian of the ghetto gate that stood in the street played a drum to denote the nightly curfew. Rodrigo Caro, a poet, allegedly died in one of the houses in 1647.

Return to Plaza del Triunfo and continue ahead to the Archives of the Indies building, occupying the west side of the *plaza*. On the way, the entrance to the Patio de las Banderas is passed (described on page 91).

Location 3 ARCHIVES OF THE INDIES (ARCHIVO GENERAL DE LAS INDIAS) *Juan de Herrera 1584–98*
Avenida de la Constitución.
Open Monday to Saturday 10.00–13.00.
Admission free.

A late-Renaissance building, designed by *Juan de Herrera*, architect of the Escorial palace near Madrid, the Archives of the Indies houses the world's most extensive documentation of early American history. Its 38,000 files are in the process of being computerized.

History In 1572, Seville's Archbishop Sandoral y Rojas convinced Philip II that a *lonja* (market hall) should be built as a merchants' commodity exchange. At that time, dealing took place in the arcades of the Patio de los Naranjos of the cathedral and on Las Gradas (the cathedral's steps), but during inclement weather, merchants continued their transactions within the cathedral itself, much to the annoyance of the clergy.

Due to the silting up of the Guadalquivir, Seville's monopoly of the American trade was transferred to Cádiz in 1717 and the exchange became redundant. In 1785 Carlos III decided that the papers relating to the New World, then dispersed among various buildings, should be united to form the General Archives of the Indies, and the former exchange was adapted to receive them.

Exterior   Like the Escorial, the Archives is an extremely severe building, typical of its architect's work, with four identical façades constructed of brick with stone trim.

Corner pyramids, supporting weathervanes, are the chief decorative feature.

A Baroque balustrade surmounts the roof-line.

Although Herrera was responsible for the building's design, work was executed under the direction of *Juan de Minjares* and *Alonso de Vandelvira*.

The building is entered from its west façade, facing Avenida de la Constitución.

Interior   Immediately ahead, but only glimpsed through the railings, is the arcaded two-storey patio around which the complex is built. This layout, typical of Seville but unusual in a Renaissance building, lessens its severity and has been described as looking 'as if the sun of Andalusia had melted the frigidity of the Escorial'.

Upper galleries, overlooking the patio, were constructed in the mid nineteenth century to provide much-needed additional storage space.

The staircase, of pink and black marble, was designed by *Lucas Cintora*.

Permission is freely given to visit the Archives, but visitors must give their name and their Seville address.

The same type of marble that forms the staircase steps provides the flooring.

An audio-visual display (Spanish only) traces the history of the building.

More than 38,000 files, containing 4 million items, include autograph letters from Columbus, Cortés, Magellan, Cervantes and Napoleon. One of the most important documents is the papal bull of Alexander VI dividing America between Spain and Portugal. Unfortunately, although original plans and drawings of early Spanish buildings in the American colonies are displayed, the letters on view are photostats and therefore of limited interest.

The elegant bookcases of Cuban wood were designed by *Blas Molner*.

Good views of the Gothic upper parts of the cathedral, unobtainable from the street, may be gained from the windows.

The last section of the gallery (roped off) displays a wall plaque commemorating the foundation here of the Bellas Artes de Santa Isabel de Hungria (Fine Arts of St Isabella of Hungary), a society that still exists. One of its founders was the painter Murillo.

Leave the building and turn left and left again to reach Calle Santo Tomás.

Location 4 MUSEUM OF CONTEMPORARY ARTS (MUSEO DE ARTE CONTEMPORANEO) *Pedro de Silva 1770*

5 Calle Santo Tomás.

Open Winter, Tuesday to Sunday, 10.00–14.00 and 17.00–20.00; Summer 09.00–15.00.

Admission charge to non-Spaniards.

Works by contemporary artists are changed at regular intervals. This art gallery, therefore, will be of specialist interest only.

The building, which formerly belonged to the cathedral's Chapter, serving as its tax collection house, was erected in 1770. *Pedro de Silva*, the architect, designed the work to blend with the Archives of the Indies opposite and it is, therefore, similar in style. Conversion to an art gallery took place in 1970: an attic floor was added and a basement created. During excavations, a small tower and remains of a section of the eleventh-century wall from the Alcázar to the Tower of Gold were discovered.

At the south end of Calle Santo Tomás, the **Tower of Abdelaziz**, or **Tower of Victory**, occupies the corner with Avenida de la Constitución. This was a watch tower in the Alcázar wall which, at this point, also served as the inner city wall.

Blocked lobed windows survive at upper level, but these and other embellishments are later, Mudéjar, work.

Further south, facing Avenida de la Constitución (just before the tourist office), stands the picturesque **Postern Gate of the Alcázar**, known as the **Arch of Mañara**, which pierced the same wall of which the Tower of Abdelaziz formed a part. This gateway now consists of an early fourteenth-century Gothic vault within a blocked Moorish horseshoe arch of brick, which probably dates from the eleventh century.

The ceramic plaque commemorates the reference to this 'Postigo del Alcázar' (minor gateway of the Alcázar) by Cervantes, in his novel *Rinconete y Cortadillo*. Complete restoration of the archway, now incorporated in the Crédit Lyonnais building, took place in 1990.

Laid out in the nineteenth century, **Avenida de la Constitución** is the main north/south artery bisecting the city centre. The cathedral and the General Archives of the Indies occupy much of the east side, but the remainder, dominated as it is by banks and tourist offices, contains little of interest. However, an ancient survival in the thoroughfare may be seen at **No. 28**, facing the north-west door of the cathedral. Surprisingly, considering its setting, the Gothic entrance is genuine medieval work; it is all that remains of the College of San Miguel, where the canons of the cathedral once lived.

The house in which it has been inserted is Neo-Gothic, as is the adjoining building, **No. 26**.

If the door to **No. 28** is open, proceed to the arcaded patio with its central fountain, a cool oasis in this commercial part of the city.

Return to Avenida de Constitución, left.

A plaque on the wall of the passage beside **No. 24** commemorates San Miguel College and the founding of the El Candelero brotherhood in the fourteenth century. The passage leads to **Plaza del Cabildo**, an unusual, semi-circular patio. The alleyway ahead passes one of Seville's best-known restaurants, Figon del Cabildo (page 313).

From the passage turn left and follow Calle Arfe to the castellated gate at its south end.

Location 5 'OIL' POSTERN GATE (POSTIGO DEL ACEITE)
Calle Almirantazgo.

Occupying one of the most picturesque, and therefore most

photographed corners of Seville, this minor gateway in the city wall was where the providers of cooking oil (*aceite*) gathered to sell their wares. Most Sevillanos refer to it simply as 'El Postigo'.

Major alterations were made to the structure in 1573.

From the east side, a ceramic plaque on the wall of the adjacent bar illustrates its earlier appearance (from the other side).

Calle Santo Tomás de Ibarra leads southward, from Calle Almirantazgo, passing the central Post Office.

No. 14 has one of the best pastiche 'Mudéjar' exteriors in Seville.

The former Royal Mint closes the vista at the end of the street.

Location 6 FORMER ROYAL MINT (CASA DE LA MONEDA)
5 Calle de Santander.

Scheduled for complete renovation in various stages, beginning in 1989, the former Royal Mint is a huge complex of terraces and patios that had been allowed to reach a state of almost complete decay.

An impressive Baroque entrance, *c.* 1789, leads to a great courtyard, known as Habana, around which are grouped the buildings where 200 workers minted coinage from precious metals taken from the New World. Coins sent back to America from here were the first European currency to be used on that continent. The only sign of life for many years has been from the Bodega Blanco Cerrillo, approached via the archway right. Extremely popular with youngsters at night, partly due to the courtyard outside on to which the crowds spill, the *bodega* is dark and atmospheric within.

From the archway immediately ahead, Calle Maese Rodrigo leads back to Avenida de la Constitución, where a small, brick chapel occupies the corner site.

Location 7 MAESE RODRIGO CHAPEL (CAPILLA DE MAESE RODRIGO)
Puerta de Jerez.

In spite of its prominent situation, the late Gothic/Mudéjar brick exterior of this small chapel is one of Seville's lesser-known jewels.

History   The chapel is all that remains of Seville's first university, founded here by *Maese Rodrigo de Santaella*. It was consecrated in 1506, although not completed for another three years.

Exterior   The simple portal, of two-tone brickwork, was added by *Martín Sánchez*, *c.* 1514.

Urgent structural restoration to the building was carried out in 1991.

Mudéjar work on the south façade is exhibited by the stepped castellation and belfry, although the gargoyles on the corners are Gothic.

A late Gothic window, incorporating three quatrefoils, lights the south wall. Its delicacy and perfect proportions make it one of the architectural delights of the city.

The east façade, facing Calle San Gregorio, incorporates a Mudéjar window and large gargoyles.

Interior   At the time of writing, even before restoration, the chapel had rarely been open. Its interior is austere and airless, with a Mudéjar roof to the nave and a Gothic rib vault to the sanctuary.

The reredos, with its painting by *Alejo Fernández*, *c.* 1520, is dedicated to Santa María de Jesús. In style it is reminiscent of the Virgen de la Antigua reredos in the cathedral. Maese Rodrigo, who is believed to have presented the reredos to the chapel, is depicted kneeling before the Virgin in the central panel.

The dado in the sanctuary, and the altar frontal, are of seventeenth-century ceramic tiles.

Opposite the chapel, in Calle San Gregorio, but with its main entrance facing Puerta de Jerez, is the **Banco Santander**, formerly the Yanduri Palace. Built in the nineteenth century, the palace was the birthplace of the poet *Vicente Aleixandre*, winner of the 1977 Nobel Prize for Literature.

In August 1936 General Franco occupied the building, as his first headquarters on the Spanish mainland.

The formerly open patio, now roofed, may be entered.

Puerta de Jerez, little more than a traffic roundabout,

commemorates the south gateway in the city wall, from which the road once led to the city of Jerez. Carved on the gateway was a resumé of Seville's traditional history: 'Hercules built me, Caesar surrounded me with walls and towers, the King Saint took me.' Of the major gates, only the Córdoba and the Macarena survive, but both have been much altered.

Seville's greatest hotel, the **Alfonso XIII**, stands by the south-east corner. Built in Andalusian neo-Baroque style, it was opened to coincide with the 1929 exhibition. A member of the international CIGA group, this is the highest-rated hotel in the city. Upgrading of rooms, begun in 1990, will result in even higher standards and, of course, prices. Non-residents are welcome to view the sumptuous public areas and patronize the San Fernando bar and Itálica restaurant.

Pass the north façade of the hotel by following Calle San Fernando eastward. The great complex ahead will make an opera-lover's heart beat faster.

Location 8 'CARMEN'S' TOBACCO FACTORY (UNIVERSIDAD), 1728–71
Calle San Fernando.
> *Open daily.*
> *Admission free.*

The former royal tobacco factory, now Seville University, is the second largest building in Spain – Madrid's Escorial is the largest. Scenes in Bizet's *Carmen* were set here.

History A tobacco factory was built opposite San Pablo church in 1610, but, due to the rapid gain in popularity of cigarette-smoking, it became too small and was replaced by the present complex. Commissioned in 1725, it was begun three years later by *Ignacio Sala*, continued by the Flemish engineer, *Sebastián van der Borcht*, 1750–66, and completed by *Juan Vicente Catalan i Bengoechea* in 1771. At its production peak in the nineteenth century, approximately 10,000 *cigarreras* (female cigar- and cigarette-makers) were employed. The fictitious character, Carmen, who first appeared in a novel by the Frenchman, Prosper Mérimée, but is better known for her leading role in Bizet's *Carmen*, was based on one of the girls who were described by Richard Ford as 'more impertinent than chaste'. Ford also related methods of preventing the girls from stealing tobacco: '... an ingeniously minute search on leaving their work, for they sometimes carry off the filthy weed in a manner that her Catholic majesty never dreamt of'. A prison was incorporated in the scheme for the speedy incarceration of guilty employees. In recent years, the function of the factory has been transferred to a modern building on the Triana side of the river, and the University has occupied the premises since 1956. Most technical faculties will eventually transfer to the site of Expo '92, on La Cartuja island, where some of the structures have already been designed for easy adaptation to accommodate them when the great show has ended.

The factory was built in Baroque style around a series of patios, many of them arcaded, to ensure that the workers were supplied with ample natural light.

Van der Borcht was chiefly responsible for building the façade, but he apparently followed the original designs of *Sala*.

Ornamentation, by *Cayetanes de Acosta*, included the roof-line sculptures and the portals.

The entrance arch of the main portal incorporates medallion busts of Columbus (Colón) and Cortés.

Reliefs depict aspects of tobacco and its discovery in America.

Above the keystone of the arch is a lion's head. Flanking trophies possibly commemorate the military engineers involved in the building.

All columns and pilasters follow the Ionic order.

On the second stage, somewhat oriental lions flank the royal coat of arms, which is surmounted by a figure of a trumpeting *Fame*, also by *Acosta* but originally gilded.

The vestibule leads to the **Clock Patio**.

The complex was originally divided into residential quarters, with galleried, manufacturing areas at upper level.

The central fountain of the **Fountain Patio**, which follows, is an original Baroque feature.

A stairway from the passage, right, gives access to the **galleries**; the tobacco was processed in the areas leading from them, natural illumination being increased by skylights set in truncated domes.

From the Clock Patio, follow the short passage, immediately right, to the **cafeteria**, the only approach to the main patio of the complex from this point.

The University's cafeteria is open to all. Food matches the city's commercial *tapas* bars in range and quality, but prices are very low – one of the least-known 'best buys' of Seville.

The main patio is reached from the far end of the cafeteria.

Formerly accommodating the *cuadras* (stables), the **Main Patio** was once much larger but, in the nineteenth century, coldly Classical ranges on all four sides, by *Colonel Diego Bordick*, significantly diminished its size.

Continue ahead and exit from the University.

Occupying the north-west corner of the site is the factory's former **chapel**, by *van der Borcht*.

Rarely open, its reredos, dedicated to the Virgin de los Remedios, was made by *Julián Ximénez* in 1762.

On the opposite side of Avenida del Cid, facing the University, the rather forlorn **Prado de San Sebastián**, now a vast car-park, gives no hint of its former glories (and iniquities). For long the site of Seville's renowned *feria*, which is now held in Triana's Parque de los Príncipes, it was here also that those found guilty of heresy at the Inquisition's *auto-de-fe*, held either in a church or in the Plaza San Fernando, were burned at the stake. The place of burning was known as the Quemadero; nobody was ever burned at an *auto-de-fe* itself. Huge, jeering crowds enjoyed the agonizingly slow death of the victims, a spectacle held under the jurisdiction of the civil authorities, not the clergy. A last-minute repentance earned the benevolent favour of prior strangulation. Blanco White, as a child of ten, witnessed Seville's last burning for heresy in 1783. He described bundles of wood being placed on barrels of tar and a poor, blind woman being burned to ashes.

To the south, on a traffic island, stands the bronze equestrian monument to El Cid.

Location 9 EL CID MONUMENT
Avenida del Cid.

Presented by the Hispanic Society of America, the monument is inscribed to record the return to Seville of El Cid, at that time the ambassador of Alfonso VI of Castile, following his victory over the King of Granada in 1080. Aided by García Ordóñez, the Muslim King of Granada was preparing to invade Seville, then ruled by the 'poet' king Al Mutamid and his 'golden' court. El Cid's intervention tipped the scales, and the superior Granadine army was defeated at Cabra, near Seville, Ordóñez being captured. El Cid, who came from Burgos, where his remains now lie, was a brilliant and successful warrior, his main achievement being the capture and effective rule of Valencia. However, his role as a defender of Christendom is largely mythical.

The equestrian bronze figure is the work of **Rodrigo Diaz el Vilar**, 1980.

Immediately behind the monument, on the east side of Avenida del Cid, the **Portuguese Consulate** is accommodated in a delightful neo-Baroque pavilion, built in 1929.

The domed Lope de Vega Theatre occupies the south-west corner, right, of the major road junction, rather glamorously known as the Glorieta de San Diego.

Location 10 LOPE DE VEGA THEATRE (TEATRO LOPE DE VEGA)
Glorieta de San Diego.
 Tickets for performances are sold daily, 11.00–14.00 and 17.00–20.00.

Opera, ballet and plays are performed in this neo-Baroque theatre, built in 1929 as the Ibero-American Exhibition's casino.

The vast entrance hall is one of Europe's most impressive, and more than 700 spectators can be seated in the auditorium.

A performance of *Carmen*, followed by a moonlit stroll through the Santa Cruz quarter, would appear to be the ingredients for a magical evening.

Avenida Isabel la Católica, running diagonally south-eastward from Glorieta de San Diego, is the main approach to Seville's most attractive park.

Location 11 MARÍA LUISA PARK (PARQUE DE MARÍA LUISA)

Half the grounds of San Telmo Palace were given to the city by Princess María Luisa de Orléans, Dowager Duchess of Montpensier, in 1893, and remodelled by the French engineer *Le Forestier*. He followed the informal English style of garden layout, but pools, tiled arbours and statues were added later, many of the latter honouring Andalusian romantic writers. All these changes were in conjunction with the Ibero-American Exhibition of 1929. However, the most important additions were the pavilions, each one specially designed to accommodate the exhibits of a Latin-American country: most of them are now consulates or private schools.

Horse-drawn carriages may be hired at the entrance to the park.

First right, Avenida Bécquer leads to a small bower, left, where the park's most famous monument is built around a tree. This honours the Sevillano poet *Gustavo Adolfo Bécquer* (1836–70). His marble bust is surrounded by an allegorical group of females representing love: hopeful, possessed and lost. All are the work of *Coullaut-Valera*.

Return to Avenida Isabel la Católica, where Plaza de España has been created on its east side.

Location 12 PLAZA DE ESPAÑA *Anibal González*

This semi-circular *plaza*, the most ambitious of the exhibition's projects, was laid out in 1914 but the buildings were not completed until 1929. Fortunately retained is the long stream, crossed by picturesque bridges. Rowing boats may be hired throughout the year from the Avenida side.

The buildings, not open to visitors, now accommodate the Capitanía General (Military), the Gobierno Civil (Local Civil Government) and the Gobierno Militar (Local Military Government).

Within the great colonnade, allegorical mosaics illustrate Spanish provinces and historical events.

Coats of arms and maps are depicted on the pavement.

The most enjoyable route to the two museums in Plaza de América, at the far end of María Luisa Park, is through the park, via any of the paths that lead south-eastward in their direction.

Although the first building reached is the Museum of Folk Arts and Popular Customs, the Archaeological Museum on the south side of the *plaza* will be of greater importance to most and, bearing in mind that both close at two o'clock, it may be preferable to proceed immediately to the latter.

Anibal González also laid out this *plaza*, 1911–19. Different styles were then adopted for its three large pavilions: the Royal Pavilion, in Gothic style, to the east, which now accommodates the Junta de Andalusia; to the north, what is now the Museum of Folk Arts, in Mudéjar style; and to the south, the present Archaeological Museum, in Renaissance style.

Location 13 ARCHAEOLOGICAL MUSEUM (MUSEO ARQUEOLÓGICO)
Plaza de América.
  Open Tuesday to Saturday 10.00–14.00.
  Admission charge.

Important finds in the Andalusian provinces are displayed, outstanding among them being gold artefacts from Carambolo and Roman statues from Itálica. The museum opened here in 1942, transferring from the Convento de la Merced, now the home of Seville's Fine Arts Museum. It comprises twenty-seven galleries on two floors and takes some time to explore thoroughly: enthusiasts should allocate at least two hours. At the time of writing, captions were in Spanish only, and a brief indication of each gallery's contents is therefore given here.

From the entrance, descend the steps to the Pre-History exhibits.

Hall I Paleolithic and Neolithic. Instruments made from stone and bone, bones from a mammoth.

Hall II Aeneolithic. Bronze artefacts, decorated pots, cylindrical stone idols.

Hall III Early Bronze Age (2000–1500 BC). Pots, necklaces, bronze arrowheads.

Hall IV Bronze Age, last stages (to 800 BC). Decorated

funerary stelae from Carmona and Ecija span the transition from bronze to iron ages.

Hall V   Colonies. Finds from Carambolo (8th–6th centuries BC).

Hall VI   Carambolo Treasures. Displayed in a darkened room, dramatically illuminated, are Tartessian gold jewellery, 6th century BC, comprising mainly bracelets and necklaces. This extraordinary find was made just two miles from Seville, in 1958.

Hall VII   Ebora Treasures. Ceramics from Ebora. Items of gold from Sanlúcar de Barrameda, including the Lebrija Candelabrum, are generally on view.

Hall VIII   Colonies. Items from Phoenician, Carthaginian and Greek colonial periods, including drinking vessels and votive offerings.

Hall IX   Carmona. Busts from Itálica are of greatest interest.

Hall X   Iberian. Roman coins.

Ascend the stairs to the major Roman exhibits.

A gallery by gallery description of the upper floor is unnecessary, as everything on display comes from the Roman colonization of Spain. Major exhibits are second-century work from Itálica. This includes busts, torsos, capitals and tessellated pavements; among the emperors depicted are Hadrian (Adriano) and Trajan (Trajano), both natives of Itálica.

Large architectural sections of stone from ruins in Carteja are in **Hall XVIII**.

Hall XXIV deals with finds at Malva, including a model of a temple. An important and rare head of Hispania is displayed.

The last galleries, **XXVI** and **XXVII**, exhibit post-Roman work – Paleochristian, Visigothic, Arabic, Muslim and Mudéjar.

Facing the museum, on the north side of Plaza de América, is the Folk Arts and Customs Museum. By its very nature it will appeal to those with more specialized interests.

Location 14 MUSEUM OF FOLK ARTS AND CUSTOMS (MUSEO DE ARTES Y COSTUMBRES POPULARES)
Plaza de América.
Open Tuesday to Sunday 10.00–14.00. Admission charge.

Surprisingly, a brief guide in English is provided.

Created in 1972 and spread over two floors, the museum, as may be expected, is entirely eclectic in nature – dress, musical instruments, rural implements, ceramics, etc.

Hall VII reconstructs various room settings from peasant and middle-class environments.

Just west of the museum, towards the river, runs the delightful **Paseo de las Delicias**, a continuation of the tree-lined Avenida de la Victoria, which itself continues the Avenida de la Palmera, Seville's southern approach road, with its famous palm trees.

Bus 34, from Paseo de las Delicias, returns northward, via Avenida de la Constitución, to Plaza Nueva.

ITINERARY 5

FINE ARTS MUSEUM, TOWER OF GOLD AND MAESTRANZA BULLRING

Places of interest in the western sector of the city are explored, keeping close to the river. Much of the area covered, El Arenal, was the former dockyard quarter of Seville, but only fragments survive as a reminder. The Tower of Gold is, after the Giralda, Seville's best-known symbol, while the historic bullring may be viewed as part of a visit to its museum, without having to witness a bullfight.

The Fine Arts (Bellas Artes) Museum, together with its paintings, recently restored to a pristine state, is the most important art gallery in Spain after Madrid's Prado.

Definitely not to be missed is the seventeenth-century Charity Hospital, a virtual museum of Murillo's works, all of them painted specifically for the foundation.

Concentrated in the Arenal centre are Seville's most varied *tapas* bars – unless great control is exercised, all cultural pursuits may well be terminated for the day when they have been reached!

Timing *The Tower of Gold's Nautical Museum is closed Monday.*

The Charity Hospital and the Maestranza Bullring's museum are closed Sunday.

The Provincial Museum of Fine Arts (Bellas Artes) is closed Monday, and Saturday and Sunday evening.

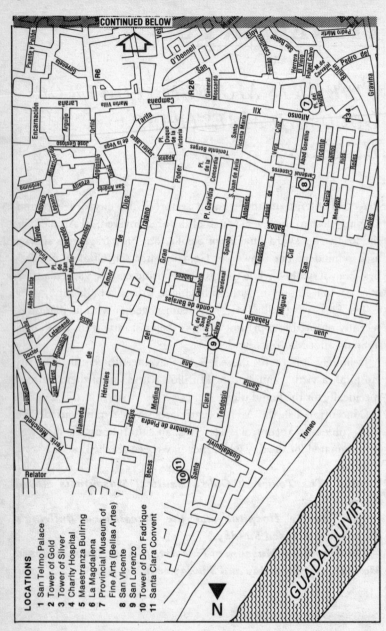

CONTINUED BELOW

LOCATIONS
1 San Telmo Palace
2 Tower of Gold
3 Tower of Silver
4 Charity Hospital
5 Maestranza Bullring
6 La Magdalena
7 Provincial Museum of
  Fine Arts (Bellas Artes)
8 San Vicente
9 San Lorenzo
10 Tower of Don Fadrique
11 Santa Clara Convent

GUADALQUIVIR

N

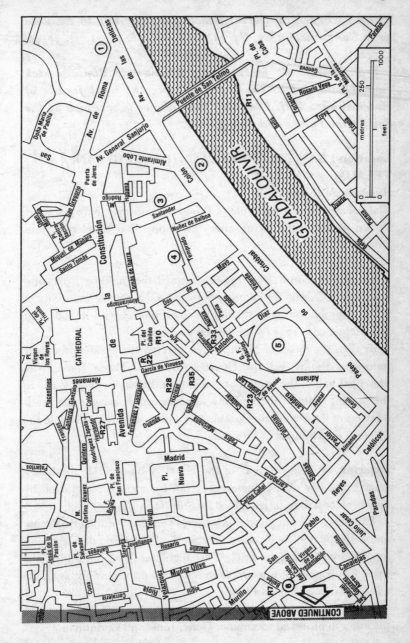

START *Puerta de Jerez. Reached by any bus to Avenida de la Constitución: C3, C4, 21, 22, 23, 25, 26, 30, 31, 33, 34, 40, 41, 42.*

From Puerta de Jerez follow Avenida de Roma, which runs southward to the river, passing the west façade of Hotel Alfonso XIII. The block that follows is occupied by the San Telmo Palace and its grounds.

Location 1 SAN TELMO PALACE (PALACIO SAN TELMO)
Avenida de Roma.

The palace is a rare example of the most exuberant Baroque style, known as Churrigueresque after the family that developed it in Salamanca.

History *Antonio Rodríguez* designed the building to accommodate the Colegio de Pilotos y Navegantes, a marine university of pilots, captains and high-ranking officers. Work began in 1682 and was completed *c.* 1734 by the *Figueroa* family.

In 1849 the dukes of Montpensier adapted the building for their residence, and it was the Dowager Duchess, María Luisa, who presented half of the enormous grounds to the city in 1893. Early in the present century, the building was adapted to become the headquarters of the Seminario Consular. It will shortly accommodate the offices of the Diputación Provincial.

Exterior Facing the rear of the Hotel Alfonso XIII, the balustraded roof line of the single-storey north façade is punctuated by figures of local dignitaries, added by *Susillo* in 1895.

The palace's main façade, however, overlooks Avenida de Roma, and is dominated by its portal, the work of Leonardo de Figueroa's son, *Antonio Matías*, 1734. This highly elaborate portal is the finest Churrigueresque example in the city, apart, possibly, from the abandoned church of San Luis.

Built in three stages, each Classical order is superimposed above the other in historical succession: Doric, Ionic and Corinthian.

Around the Ionic columns of the second stage are allegorical figures of the Sciences and the Arts.

A figure of St Telmo, patron saint of navigators – an allusion to the building's original use – stands in the window of the upper stage.

Flanking him, between Corinthian columns, are St Fernando and St Hermenegildo, both greatly revered in Seville.

Enter the complex from this side.

Interior The square, central patio may be glimpsed, but not entered from here.

Buildings combine stone, brick and a blue ceramic strip.

Rising above the patio is the Baroque belfry of the chapel, dedicated to Nuestra Señora del Buen Aire; it is the work of **Leonardo de Figueroa**.

At the time of writing, the chapel was not open; its main feature of interest is the reredos of the high altar, featuring a bas-relief *Virgin and Child* carved by **Juan de Oviedo** in 1600; followers of **Cornejo** transformed the relief into three-dimensional form in the eighteenth century.

Paintings in the cupola are the eighteenth-century work of **Cabral Bejarano**.

Between the palace and the river, overlooking the San Telmo bridge, are the **Vicente Aleixandre Gardens**, laid out in 1830. They were originally much larger and were called the Cristina Gardens, forming part of the new residential area developed by the river. That side was reduced in 1929 with the construction of hotels, thoroughfares and the San Telmo bridge, all, of course, in connection with the Iberico-American Exhibition. The present name of the gardens commemorates the Nobel literary prizewinner, who was born in a house adjacent to the Maese Rodrigo Chapel in Puerta de Jerez.

Avenida de las Delicias skirts the river end of the gardens as far as San Telmo bridge, where it changes its name to Paseo de Cristóbal Colón.

The Tower of Gold, a famous Seville landmark, overlooks the river.

On the other side of the Paseo is the outrageously undistinguished Prevision Española building, of which more anon.

Location 2 TOWER OF GOLD (TORRE DEL ORO)
Paseo de Cristóbal Colón.

Nautical Museum open Tuesday to Sunday 10.00–14.00 (closes 13.00 Saturday and Sunday).

Admission charge (nominal).

After the Giralda, the Tower of Gold is Seville's most representative individual structure and like the Giralda, it was erected during the Muslim era.

History   Abu-i-Ula, governor of Seville, commissioned this military watchtower in the Arenal quarter of Seville, together with a similar edifice on the opposite side of the river, during the middle period of the Almohad occupation. It formerly stood at the junction of a fortified wall extending from the Alcázar and the main defensive wall of the city. In addition to being lookout posts, the purpose of the towers was to defend the city against invasion from the river, a heavy chain linking their stone bases across the water and thus preventing ships from passing upstream. The Castilian squadron of Ramón de Bonifaz had to sever this link before St Fernando could take Seville in 1248. Paris was defended in a similar way, but London relied on a riverside wall, combined with the great Tower of London.

Ortiz de Zuniga records that the name of the Tower of Gold was established in the Muslim era, during the reign of Borg-al-Dsayed, and that it evolved because the tower was then clad with gilded tiles. However, there is no further evidence of this and some have suggested that the name may refer to the gold plundered from America, all of which was shipped to Seville's port, past the tower, for tax assessment during the sixteenth century.

After the Reconquest, the towers lost their defensive importance and the Tower of Gold served as a prison and, possibly, a storehouse for precious metals brought from the Americas.

According to the Duke of Rivas, it was here that Pedro the Cruel imprisoned the nun Aldonza, after having her kidnapped from the Santa Clara Convent.

The fate of the tower's twin, on the Triana side of the river, is unknown.

It is easier to appreciate the external elements that make up the tower from a short distance away.

Exterior   When built, the tower consisted only of its two polygonal stages; the circular superstructure is an eighteenth-century addition.

Twelve-sided, the first stage is of stone, with ashlar trim and horseshoe arches above the cornice.

The second stage, of brick, retains some lobed arches.

Green ribbons of ceramics around the arches are a later addition.

Surmounting the tower, the domed, circular structure was added by *van der Borcht* in 1760.

The Nautical Museum (Museo Naútico) occupies two floors and displays exhibits relating to Seville's maritime history.

An enlarged engraving of 1740 illustrates the old dockyards and the defensive wall, with its extension to the Tower of Gold.

At the entrance to the stairs, a plaque commemorates Alfonso XIII's visit to the tower in 1923.

Exhibits continue on the upper floor.

Steps flanking the tower lead to the promenade where, from this point, boats leave for cruises on the river Guadalquivir. Since 1991 these have been extended to La Cartuja island, site of Expo '92, made possible by moving the river's barrage further north. Facilities offered by the boats vary from a straightforward cruise, with bar, to *flamenco* evenings. During the period of Expo '92 a virtually non-stop ferry service from here to the site is planned.

Paseo de Cristóbal Colón continues northward, and the castellated top of a less well-known tower, the Tower of Silver, may be glimpsed from Calle Santander, first right.

Location 3 TOWER OF SILVER (TORRE DE PLATA)
13 Calle Santander.

This octagonal, castellated watchtower also dates from the Muslim period, but remnants of the wall in which it was inserted represent Christian rebuilding work. Restoration of the tower, the house built around it and the wall fragment was completed in 1991.

It is probable that the tower was named simply to correspond with the nearby Tower of Gold; there is no record of silver tiles or any reference to its adoption as a silver store.

Obscured by the house, nothing can be seen close up from Calle Santander, but most of the structure comes into view half-way along Calle Temprado, the street that leads northward from it.

It is also from Calle Temprado that one of Seville's two late seventeenth-century hospitals is approached.

Location 4 CHARITY HOSPITAL (HOSPITAL DE LA CARIDAD) *Bernardo Simón de Pineda, 1674*
3 Calle Temprado.
Open Monday to Saturday 10.00–13.00 and 15.30–18.00, Sunday 10.00–12.30.
Admission charge.

The church of this seventeenth-century hospital, contemporary with that of the Venerable Priests, is virtually an exhibition of religious paintings. Its founder, Mañara, was obsessed with death, and many of the works displayed reflect his horror of it.

History *Miguel de Mañara* (1626–79), the son of a wealthy shipping agent of Italian descent, spent his adolescent years womanizing and indulging in riotous drinking bouts. He has even been attributed with inspiring the Don Juan legend, but as Mañara was only four when the character first made his literary appearance in 1630, this seems to be unlikely. He became a changed man at the age of thirty-four after meeting Pedro Martínez, who had created a charitable society whose chief purpose was to provide funds for the Christian burial of the poor and of executed criminals. Mañara was depressed, as his wife had recently died, and this may also have played some part in his decision to devote the remainder of his life to religion and charity. Eventually Mañara became leader of the charitable (de la Caridad) society of Martínez, drawing up rules for its 'very humble brotherhood' and providing funds for the hospital that the brotherhood would operate. Plans for the hospital were prepared by Bernardo Simón de Pineda and it was completed in 1674. The complex was built on the site of medieval shipyards and the hermitage of San Jorge, where it had been customary for voyagers to the New World to attend their last Mass before departing. Mañara left his Seville mansion to spend the last years of his life in the hospital, where he died five years after its completion.

Exterior The hospital's church, left of the entrance, is painted white, with exposed stone decorative elements, typical of Seville Baroque.

Behind the arch lies the **main patio**. Its walls are decorated with large ceramic panels, attributed to *Murillo*.

A double row of columns divides the rectangular area into two squares. In the centre of each, marble fountains incorporate groups of figures representing *Charity* and *Mercy*, brought here from Italy in 1682.

Pass between the columns, to the north-east corner, and proceed to the internal patio, which is known as the **Patio de los Rosales** (Patio of the Roses) because Mañara grew roses in flower-pots suspended from its walls.

The Moorish shipyards that once stood on the hospital site were rebuilt for Alfonso X in 1252, and a plaque commemorates their construction. The one-and-a-half brick arches in this patio are all that survive.

Behind the arches lies the rear patio; its bust of Mañara, on a pedestal, was made in 1920.

Fixed to a wall is the original ceramic street sign of Calle Ataúd, a short thoroughfare that disappeared in 1924 when Plaza de Doña Elvira was enlarged. Below this, a plaque records the experience of Mañara in that street, as related by his page. According to him, Mañara was struck down by a blow from an unseen hand and heard a mysterious voice calling for his coffin (*ataúd*) to be brought. This is often held to be the reason for the conversion of Mañara but, knowing his reputation at the time, it seems more likely to have been a story concocted by the two of them to explain the results of a good evening out.

The hospital's church is entered from the north-west corner of the main patio, via a vestibule.

In the vestibule, where tickets are purchased, are displayed photographs of the complete series of canvases painted for the church by **Murillo**, 1660–74. During the Napoleonic occupation of Seville, Marshal Soult took five of them back to France and they are now distributed between several art galleries, including London's National Gallery; six remain here.

Above the aisleless nave of the church, at the west end, is the **choir's gallery** (not open).

Immediately above the entrance door hangs *End of World's Glories*, one of the cadaverous paintings by **Valdés Leal**, 1672. Portrayed is a dead bishop, rotten with worms.

The face of the corpse in the coffin to the right is a portrait of Mañara. At the top of the painting, God's hand holds scales, inscribed in Latin 'Neither more' and 'Nor less'. Murillo is reported to have complained that the work made him hold his nose when looking at it.

Projecting from the west wall, another door leads to the small vestibule that fronts the door to the street, which is generally closed. In the pavement of this vestibule is set Mañara's first burial stone.

Both biblical scenes, flanking the west door, are attributed to the seventeenth-century painter **Miguel Luna**; they replaced four of the **Murillo** works taken by Soult.

Above the north door hangs the second of **Valdés Leal**'s grisly works: *Triumph of Death*, featuring a skeleton in armour, and the words in Latin, 'In the twinkling of an eye.'

Murillo's painting of the winged *St John of God Taking a Sick Man to Hospital* forms the reredos of the altar in the next bay. The saint's face is another portrait of Mañara.

Similarities in style with Caravaggio have been noted. Another work by **Murillo**, *The Annunciation*, hangs above the altar in the following bay. The great number of works commissioned for this church from Murillo reflects the close friendship between Mañara and the painter.

The mahogany pulpit is the work of **Pineda**, its sounding board surmounted by a figure of *Charity* by **Pedro Roldán**.

On the upper part of the wall, in the most easterly north bay, hangs the large *Moses Striking Water from the Rock*, by **Murillo**.

Other works on this wall are a reredos with an early *Virgin of Charity* and a painted panel, *Jesus as a Child*, by **Murillo**.

Frescoes on the cupola are by **Valdés Leal**.

Its spandrels, painted by **Lucas Valdés**, portray the Evangelists.

From here can be seen the painting *Exaltation of the Holy Cross*, by **Valdés Leal**, in the west gallery.

The reredos, designed by the architect of the hospital, **Bernardo Simón de Pineda**, was carved by **Pedro Roldán** and is considered to be his masterpiece. Its theme, *The Holy Burial*, was expressly commissioned by Mañara, who lies in the crypt, which is approached by stairs leading from the sanctuary.

The first reredos on the south wall incorporates a figure of St Joseph, by **Cristóbal Ramos**.

This is surmounted by a painted panel, *John the Baptist as a Boy*, by **Murillo**.

Above is a large **Murillo**, *Miracle of the Loaves and Fishes*, which serves as a counterpart to the same artist's work facing it on the opposite wall.

Against the central pillar of the same wall, a small reredos, reputedly presented by Mañara, incorporates a painting of *The Crucifixion* by **Murillo**.

In the reredos, the figure of *Christ of Charity*, once thought to be the work of Roldán, is now attributed, like the accompanying angels, to **Francisco Gijón**.

Against the pilaster, right, is a seventeenth-century bas-relief, *Ecce Homo*, by the **García** sisters, who worked in Granada.

The lower painting in the next bay, by **Murillo**, 1672, depicts *St Elizabeth of Hungary Treating Lepers*.

Before leaving the hospital, visitors should request permission, if convenient, to view the former Chapter House (Sala de Cabildos).

Displayed within are souvenirs of Mañara, including his portrait by **Valdés Leal**, *c.* 1672, reputedly still hanging in the position for which it was originally painted.

Exhibited in a glass cabinet is the founder's deathmask, while on the wall hangs his sword.

Immediately opposite the hospital, in the small **Jardín de la Caridad**, the statue of Mañara supporting a poor person in his arms is by the Sevillano *Antonio Susillo*, 1902.

Adjacent to the Charity Hospital, at 5 Calle Temprado, is the **Maestranza de Artillería**. Completed in 1786, during the reign of Carlos III, this Baroque headquarters of the artillery regiment was named to reflect its proximity to the Maestranza bullring. Although the complex may not be entered, it is possible to see an immense fanlight window behind the courtyard.

Occupying the entire block between the artillery buildings and the river is the new opera house, **Teatro de la Maestranza**, completed in 1991 in conjunction with Expo '92. It is entered from the riverside façade, much of which is formed by nineteenth-century remnants from the Artillería's ammunitions works, which previously occupied the site. A dome above the auditorium is the only other architectural feature of interest.

From Calle Temprado, admittedly the rear of the building, it appears that the architect was inspired by a brief visit to Croydon. The detrimental effect of the complex on the world-famous view of Seville from across the river is observed later.

Calle Dos de Mayo, which runs down to the river, also continues eastward, and it is from this stretch that one of Seville's most picturesque views is obtained, with the Giralda rising above the Postern Gate.

Calle Arfe, second left, leads to a typical Sevillian multiple road intersection and it is here that one of the city's greatest concentrations of *tapas* bars may be found.

At **No. 18** Calle Arfe, a grocer's, displaying a multiplicity of names, retains one of Seville's few outstanding shop fronts (the city lacks the numerous attractive nineteenth-century pharmacies boasted by Barcelona). Unusually for Seville, a clock is incorporated in the wooden façade.

By regarding the road junction as a *plaza* and proceeding anti-clockwise, Calle Harinas, third right, leads north-eastward where, at No. 21, **El Rincon Gallego del Pulpo** specializes in dishes from Galicia, particularly marinated octopus (see page 316).

Returning to Calle Arfe, at No. 5, on the corner, right, with Calle

Harinas, **Mesón Sevilla Jabugo I** is a popular *tapas* bar, specializing in charcuterie from the famous Jabugo producer Sánchez Romero Carvajal (see page 317).

From Calle Arfe, right, follow Calle Antonia Díaz, first left. **El Buzo** (The Diver), at No. 5, will strike English visitors as an amusing name for a bar, but no linguistic pun is intended.

Mesón Serranito, No. 11, is a *tapas* bar with an extravagant display of ceramic tiles and bullfight photographs.

From the bar, left, Calle García Fernández Palacios, first right, leads to the tree-lined Calle Adriano, unusually wide for Seville. Turn left and follow, first right, Calle Lope de Arenas. At No. 5, on the corner, **Jamón Real** is a *bodega* that 'imports' produce from the neighbouring province of Extremadura. The quality of the food is exceptional, particularly the cheeses, most of which are a revelation as they can be found nowhere else in Seville. Definitely not to be missed (see page 315).

Return to Calle Adriano and continue to the riverside, where Paseo de Cristóbal Colón leads to the bullring's entrance.

Location 5 MAESTRANZA BULLRING (PLAZA DE TORO) *Vicente San Martín 1761–87*
Paseo de Cristóbal Colón.
Museum open, apart from bullfight days, Monday to Saturday, 10.00–14.00.
Admission charge.
Bullfights are held daily during the **feria** *and the preceding week when the season commences. Thereafter, Sunday evenings until October. Advance tickets are sold at the bullring.*
The Maestranza, the world's most famous and beautiful bullring, is a must for the bullfight *aficionado*; those who are not attracted by its spectacle of ritual slaughter are still able to view the historic arena as part of a visit to the museum.

History The Maestranza bullring was completed in the second half of the eighteenth century on the site of an earlier arena, to accommodate the Real Maestranza de Caballería (Royal Masters of Horsemanship), founded in 1725. It is certainly one of the oldest bullrings to survive in Spain – possibly, as many claim, *the* oldest to be designed, although Ronda's was opened two years earlier. Architecturally, little has changed.

All the great bullfighters have performed in the Maestranza and it is the aim of would-be heroes to be carried from the arena shoulder-high, through the Prince's Gate, the ultimate accolade.

It was not until the eighteenth century that the modern style of bullfight, including the colourful costumes, evolved. This was originally an aristocratic pursuit, the bulls being killed by riders on horseback or, as frequently happened, by dogs that were set on the hapless beasts. These 'bull feasts' often lasted three days. Until fairly recently, the bulls were much bigger, and, lacking adequate protection, more horses were killed and maimed than now.

Completed in 1787, the gleaming white, Baroque façade overlooks the river. Its stone portal is inscribed Plaza de Toros.

Many of the spectators at bullfights are women, who wear traditional Andalusian dress for the occasion, often including a *mantilla*. On hot evenings, their splendid fans will be waved vigorously. The colourful dress of those appearing in the *corrida* – *matadores*, *toreros*, *picadores* – is equally well known, and the spectacle evokes what many tourists mistakenly think is the 'real' Spain.

A bullfight at the Maestranza undoubtedly combines bravery, artistry and beauty. Whether this will compensate for having to witness the grievous suffering which is always inflicted on the bull, sometimes on the horses and occasionally on the bullfighters themselves, is up to the individual to decide. Lord Nelson witnessed a bullfight at Cádiz in 1786 and recorded that he was sickened by the spectacle.

The museum includes the expected posters, costumes, prints and photographs, but for most people the most impressive 'exhibit' will be the great arena itself.

From the bullring, exit right. First right Calle Adriano. Second left, Calle Arenal flanks the great market building, entered from Calle Pastor y Landero, first left. Seville's most important food market, the **Arenal Market** (Mercado del Arenal), is believed to have been built on the site of the prison, where the Italian Renaissance sculptor, Torrigiano, died in 1522. All types of food are sold but, as usual, it closes in the afternoon.

On leaving the market, turn left and second right, following Calle Reyes Católicos to, fourth left, Calle Cristo del Calvario.

Immediately left, the **Montserrat Church**, completed in 1696, with its brick façade, is open only for Mass, when its Baroque reredos and several paintings may be seen.

Immediately facing this church, but entered from Calle San Pablo, the extension of Calle Reyes Católicos, is La Magdalena.

Location 6 LA MAGDALENA *Leonardo de Figueroa 1709 Calle San Pablo.*
Open daily but closes 14.00–18.00.

One of Seville's most important churches, Baroque in style, La Magdalena incorporates a fourteenth-century Mudéjar chapel with three delightful cupolas. *Murillo* was baptized in the previous building and the font used may be seen. Surprisingly, considering the ubiquity of his works in Seville, there are no Murillo paintings within; however, works by *Zurbarán*, *Valdés* and *Roldán* compensate.

History The church of the convent of San Pablo el Real (St Paul the Royal), an earlier building on the site, collapsed in 1691, due to faulty rebuilding, only one of its chapels surviving. A new church was commissioned from *Leonardo de Figueroa* on the site of the former building and this was completed in 1709; the Mudéjar chapel that had survived was incorporated.

In 1810, a church dedicated to La Magdalena (St Mary Magdalene), but sited elsewhere in Seville, was demolished and its parish transferred to St Pablo, which shortly adopted the name.

Restoration of the buiding took place in 1991.

Exterior The three tiled Mudéjar cupolas in the south-west corner of the church were constructed in the late fourteenth century. They are best viewed from the west end in summer, as trees then obscure the view from Calle San Pablo.

The remainder of the church is entirely Baroque.

The east doorway, leading to the south transept, incorporates in its pediment a carving of *St Domingo de Guzmán* by **Roldán**.

La Magdalena is generally entered from its main doorway.

Interior The aisled interior, with side chapels, is believed to follow the plan of the earlier building. A Tuscan influence is indicated by the width of the nave.

Immediately left of the entrance is the **Mudéjar Chapel** (not always open), retained from the previous church. This was vaulted in the late fourteenth century and its central cupola decorated *c.* 1400.

Incorporated in the *Descent from the Cross* reredos is the figure of Christ, attributed to **Roldán**, 1660.

Other figures of saints, etc. are by **Pedro Nieto**, 1633.

Immediately north-west of the chapel, in the **baptistery**, is the font in which **Bartolomé Esteban Murillo**, the painter, was baptized on 1 January 1618. Then, of course, it stood in the earlier church.

The organ, in two sections, is situated at the west end.

In the north-west corner, the **Sacrament Chapel**'s reredos features *The Virgin of the Rosary*, completed by **Cristóbal Ramós** in the eighteenth century.

Paintings of *St Dominic* and *The Miraculous Cure of Reginald of Orléans* were painted by **Zurbarán** for the earlier church, 1622–6.

In the **second north chapel**, *Christ Resurrected* was painted by *Jerónimo Hernández II*, to form its reredos.

Three important reredoses are sited in the **north transept**. On the west wall, the *Virgin of Sorrows* is attributed to **Roldán**; it is certainly by a member of the Seville School and dates from the second half of the seventeenth century.

Immediately left of the transept's door, the *Virgin of the Fevers* reredos is from the school of *Juan Bautista Vázquez*, *c.* 1566.

Against the same wall, right of the door, the reredos depicts *St Joachim, St Anne and the Virgin*. This is late seventeenth-century work attributed to **Gijón**.

On the north wall, above the gilded, screened pew, a fresco depicts a medieval *auto-da-fé*.

The cupola above the **crossing** is painted with Dominican saints, by *Valdés*. Wooden emblems of St John and St Mark, together with Old Testament themes, are by *Roldán*.

The pulpit is of polychrome marble.

Faith Triumphant was the theme adopted by *Valdés* for the fresco on the vault of the **sanctuary**.

Large paintings on the side walls of the sanctuary, by either *Valdés* or *Matiás de Arega y Alfonso*, are seventeenth-century work. They illustrate *David Playing a Harp* and *The Offering of the People of Israel in the Temple*.

Dedicated to St Paul, the reredos of the high altar incorporates a figure of *Mary Magdalene* by *Felipe Malo de Molina*, 1704.

The clothed figure of *The Virgin of Amparo*, in the **chapel** immediately north of the sanctuary, is mid-sixteenth-century work, from the studio of *Balduque*.

Francisco de Ocampo sculpted the figure of *Christ Crucified*, in the **south transept's east chapel**, in 1612. This is flanked by *The Virgin and St John the Evangelist*, the nineteenth-century work of *Astorga*.

Matching the north transept, the **south transept** has a similar private pew.

The fresco above depicts *St Fernando Entering Seville at the Reconquest*.

Against the second south pier from the east is a relief of *The Ascension* by *Juan de Mesa*, 1619.

Exit from the church, left. First left, Calle Bailén, third right, Calle Manuel de Carvajal, first left, Plaza del Museo.

Location 7 PROVINCIAL MUSEUM OF FINE ARTS (MUSEO PROVINCIAL DE BELLAS ARTES)

9 Plaza del Museo.

Open Tuesday to Friday 10.00–14.00, 16.00–19.00, Saturday and Sunday 10.00–14.00.

Admission charge.

A long period of restoration to the building and its works of art ended in 1991. Seville's Fine Arts Museum is, after the Prado in Madrid, the most important art gallery in the country, the majority of the works exhibited being painted by Spanish artists or foreigners, mostly Flemish, working in Spain. Only here, in Seville, can major works by the city's greatest painter, Velázquez, be seen. Nevertheless, it should be remembered that religious paintings of equal quality to many of those in the museum are to be found in abundance in Seville's cathedral and churches.

History   Opened in 1838, the nucleus of the museum is the collection of Dean Manuel López Cepero, comprising works that he rescued from convents at their suppression. Since 1942 they have been displayed here in the former Convent de la Merced Calzada, which was completed in Mannerist style by *Juan de Oviedo y de la Bandera* in 1612. The Mercedarians (Merciful) had been founded in the thirteenth century by St Peter Nolasco, to secure ransoms for Christians captured by the Moors.

Above the door of the great stone portal, added in the eighteenth century, are the figures of the Virgin Mary, St Peter Nolasco and Jaime I, carved by *Francisco Tirado*. Prior to the formation of this doorway, the convent was entered from Calle Bailén.

Immediately ahead through the entrance is the **Patio del Aljibe**, one of the three cloistered patios, each in a different style, around which the buildings are grouped. Ceramic tiles came from other secularized convents.

A double staircase links this patio, to the left, with the **Patio de los Bojes**, on one side of which is the former refectory.

To its right lies the **Claustro Grande** (Great Cloister), fronting the former church. *Leonardo de Figueroa* remodelled the cloister in Baroque style in 1724, but the paired columns are *Oviedo*'s work.

Paintings within the museum were restored and rehung, together with some carvings, in 1991. As a group, they provide a complete history of the Seville School. At the time of writing, the final location of each work had not been fully established. The convent lost most of the original paintings commissioned for it when the buildings were secularized. Remaining, however, are portraits of the founders by *Pacheco* and *Vázquez*, *The Mercedarians* by *Zurbarán*, *The Virgin and St Anne* by *Roelas*, and the mural in the church by *Domingo Martínez*.

Other selected highlights of the museum are *Velázquez*'s *Portrait of Cristóbal Suarez de Ribera* and *The Virgin with St Ildefonso*; **Zurbarán**'s *Apotheosis of St Thomas Aquinas, The Pope with St Bruno, The Virgin of the Cave* and *St Ambrose*; **Murillo**'s *Adoration of the Shepherds, St Thomas of Villanueva, Apparition of the Virgin to St Felix of Cantalicio, St Justa and St Rufina* (from the reredos of the Capuchin church) and *The Vision of St Francis*; **Valdés Leal**'s *Ascension of the Virgin* and *The Temptation of St Jerome*; **Herrera the Elder**'s *Apotheosis of St Hermenegildo*; **El Greco**'s *Portrait of His Son*; **Montañés**'s *St Bruno*; and **Torrigiano**'s *Virgin and Child* and *St Jerome*.

From the museum, turn left and continue to Calle Alfonso XII, first right.

Nos. 27–29, rare examples of Catalan Modernism in Seville, incorporate floral plaster decoration reminiscent of work in Barcelona by **Doménech i Montaner**.

Return westward and follow Calle San Vicente, second right.

Location 8 SAN VICENTE
Calle San Vicente.
Open 09.30–10.30 and 18.00–20.30.
An ancient church, somewhat spoiled by remodelling, San Vicente nevertheless retains some features of interest, including a Gothic portal and arcades and a Mudéjar roof. There are also some carvings by **Roldán** and **Balduque**, but the interior is not exceptional.

History Built on the site of a mosque, according to tradition, San Vicente is a Gothic/Mudéjar structure that has been restored: poorly in the eighteenth century, and very poorly in the nineteenth.

Exterior Although most work is post eighteenth century, some features from the original church have been preserved.

A blocked Gothic portal on the west, Calle San Vicente, façade, denotes the original main entrance.

Interior Arches of the **aisles** maintain their pointed, Gothic form. The Mudéjar timber roof has been little altered.

Choir stalls at the west end are the work of **Luis de Vilches**,

1736. *Jesus, Bearing His Cross*, in the **chapel north of the west door**, was carved by the Cordóban, **Felipe de Ribas**, in 1641.

Within the **Rosario Chapel**, the first on the north side, *The Virgin of the Rosary* is by **Cristóbal Ramos**.

The **sacristy**, approached from the north aisle, displays paintings from the high altar's former reredos: a *Virgin of the Assumption* and three works depicting *St Vincent's Martyrdom*, by **Juan de Uceda Castroverde** and **Francisco Varela**. Three more paintings, which made up the set, have been lost.

The ceiling is sixteenth-century Mudéjar work.

In the **sanctuary**, replacing an earlier piece, the present Baroque reredos of the high altar was designed by **Cristóbal de Guadix**, 1690–1706.

The figure of St Vincent is by **Roldán**.

Four relief panels depict scenes from the saint's life.

The *Crucifixion* surmounting the piece is by **Roque Balduque** and **Juan Giralte**.

Flanking this, the mitred saints are Leonardo and Isidoro.

In the **south-east corner chapel** are the two most important figures in the church: *The Virgin of the Sorrows*, attributed to **Molner**, and *Christ of the Suffering*, carved in the second half of the seventeenth century, possibly by **Roldán**.

Ceramic tiles are by **Hernando de Valladares**, 1602.

Two reliefs at the east end were originally part of the reredos. *Exaltation of the Serpent in the Desert* formed the top section, and the large *Descent from the Cross*, by **Andrés de Ocampo**, was positioned below.

Immediately right of the south door, a figure of *The Archangel St Michael*, mid eighteenth-century work, provides the altarpiece.

The Virgin de los Remedios, by **Pedro Villegas de Marmoléjo**, stands in the **most westerly of the north chapels**.

On leaving the church, right, follow Calle San Vicente northward. Second right, Calle Baños leads to **Plaza de la Gavidia**.

In the centre of the *plaza*, a bronze statue on a marble plinth, erected in 1889, commemorates Daoiz, a Sevillano who became a national hero fighting Napoleon's forces on 2 May 1808. Bronze reliefs at the sides depict the epic battle.

From the north-west corner of the *plaza*, follow Calle Cardinal Spinola northward.

Passed, right, is the **Santa Rosario Convent**. Its Baroque church, although not outstandingly interesting, is open daily 16.00–18.15.

Immediately ahead, the church of San Lorenzo occupies the entire north side of Plaza de San Lorenzo.

Location 9 SAN LORENZO
Plaza de San Lorenzo.
Open daily but closes 13.00–18.30.

History The original Gothic/Mudéjar church, probably begun in the late fourteenth century, was widened and mostly rebuilt early in the seventeenth; further remodelling has since taken place.

Exterior Both entrances from the *plaza* were seventeenth-century additions, by *Diego Lopez Bueno*. The doors show a Mudéjar influence within their Baroque frames.

The west tower was built in the fifteenth century above the Gothic main portal, now blocked.

Three Mudéjar windows in the tower survive.

Interior Entering from Plaza de San Lorenzo, turn left and proceed to the west end of the nave.

On the inner wall of the **outer south aisle** (left of the choir) a Baroque reredos incorporates *The Virgin of Rocamador*. This was painted in the first half of the fourteenth century, and a Sienese influence is apparent.

Two great stone corbels, in the form of re-used capitals and demi-columns, support the most westerly arches of the arcades; these, and the blocked west portal, partly concealed by the choir, are all that survive from the original building.

Both **outer aisles** were added in the seventeenth century, forming the major part of San Lorenzo's extension.

Originally rib-vaulted, the **sanctuary** was rebuilt in the seventeenth century and a cupola was erected.

The ceramic dado is also seventeenth-century work.

Although *Montañés* was commissioned for the reredos of the high altar, failing health and the pressure of other work led to the sculptures being executed by *Felipe* and *Dionisio de Rivas*.

Exit from the church and turn left.

Occupying the site of the house of Hernán Cortés, the discoverer of Mexico, is the church of Jesús del Gran Poder, at a right angle with San Lorenzo.

Consecrated in 1965, **Jesús del Gran Poder** was designed in the manner of Seville's Baroque churches, to provide more impressive accommodation for the revered figure in the reredos of the high altar, *Christ Bearing his Cross*, carved by *Juan de Mesa* in 1620. The figure itself is known as Jesús del Gran Poder (Jesus of Great Power) and plays an important part in Holy Week, when it leaves the church on a float at two o'clock on Good Friday morning. Before the present church was completed, the carving stood in a chapel within San Lorenzo.

Flanking the figure are an eighteenth-century Virgin, attributed to *Astorga*, and a seventeenth-century St John the Evangelist.

Unusually for Seville, the church is circular.

From the west side of the *plaza*, Calle Eslava leads to Calle Santa Clara, from where, occupying the first corner right, stretches the great Santa Ana Convent. Its late thirteenth-century church of brick faces Calle Santa Ana. Not generally open to the public, the most important work within is *St Anne and the Virgin* by *Montañés*, 1627.

Further northward, **No. 12 Calle Santa Clara**, formerly an eighteenth-century palace, retains a severely Classical stone entrance.

No. 23 is a Baroque mansion of brick, but with a stone portal that incorporates a particularly decorative window.

On the opposite side of the road, at **No. 40**, enter another of Seville's delightful patios; this one is planted with orange trees and belongs to the Santa Clara Convent.

The Tower of Don Fadrique cannot be seen from here in spite of its height, and must be approached through the archway, left, which leads to another courtyard fronting it.

Location 10 TOWER OF DON FADRIQUE (TORRE DE DON FADRIQUE) *1252*

40 Calle Santa Clara.
  Open daily 11.30–14.00 and 15.30–17.30.
  Admission free.

Not only is this medieval tower a unique survivor in Andalusia, but the Romanesque detailing is rare in the city and its figure corbels are the earliest examples of Sevillano carving to survive.

The brick-built tower, rising ahead, was built as a medieval defensive bastion. Lying well within the area encompassed by the city wall, its purpose was to defend the palace of the Infante Don Fadrique, which stood beside it. After the palace was demolished, the tower remained in isolation in the orchard of the Santa Clara Convent, the monks caring for the venerable structure.

Exterior Transitional in style, the tower's Romanesque windows at the third stage are a rare sight in Seville; upper stage windows are Gothic.

In spite of a battlement and slits for firing arrows, the tower is not particularly military in appearance, and has gargoyles decorating the corners.

The Gothic portal on the far side is fifteenth-century and was transferred here from the demolished college, Seville's first university, founded by Maese Rodrigo.

A Latin plaque records the erection of the tower in 1252.

Interior The **vestibule** is rib-vaulted.

Stone steps, with a wooden balustrade, lead to the first level, where the walls are pierced with niches from which arrows could be fired.

The rib vault retains its boss.

A much higher rib vault crowns the upper stage, but of far greater interest are the figure corbels, the earliest examples of Seville School sculpture to survive.

Distant views of the Giralda are seen, while immediately ahead is the apse of the Santa Clara Convent's church and, to its left, the arcaded patio that forms part of the monastic domestic quarters.

Returning from the tower to the entrance patio, it may be that because of its adoption by the city of Seville for Expo purposes in 1992, the church of the Santa Clara Convent will be open. It previously opened, rather frustratingly, one hour after the entrance to the Don Fadrique Tower closed.

Location 11 SANTA CLARA CONVENT (CONVENTO DE SANTA CLARA)
40 Calle Santa Clara.
Church open (prior to 1992) Tuesday to Thursday 18.30.
Works by *Montañés* and his school, particularly the Santa Clara reredos of the high altar, are the outstanding treasures of the convent's church. Some alterations to general layout are possible, following restoration of the building in 1991.

History St Fernando founded the monastery of Santa Clara in 1260, one of the earliest in Seville. Its present church was built in the fifteenth century, in Gothic/Mudéjar style. Restoration and some remodelling took place in the sixteenth century and, more drastically, in the seventeenth.

Facing the patio, the tiled entrance porch is the work of *Diego de Quesada*, 1622.

Interior The church is aisleless, its nave retaining the original coffered Mudéjar ceiling.

A ceramic dado decorates the entire church; apart from the section within the chancel it is seventeenth-century work by *Hernando de Valladares*.

Behind a grille, at the west end, the **nuns' choir** may be glimpsed.

Plaster decoration to the **nave**'s wall is by *Juan de Oviedo* and *Miguel de Zumarraga*, 1620.

It is recorded that the high altar's reredos is by *Montañés* and his followers, and from their style, the other four reredoses in the church also appear to be, at least partly, the work of the master.

Those passed on the north wall are dedicated to, respectively, St John the Baptist and the Immaculate Conception.

The **sanctuary** occupies the polygonal apse of the church, which is rib-vaulted.

Some amendments were made in the eighteenth century to the high altar's reredos, dedicated to St Clare, but little harm was done.

Designed by *Montañés*, 1621–3, much of the work is by his own hand, although members of his workshop certainly assisted.

The figure right, representing *The Miracle of St Clare*, is exceptional.

On the south wall, reredoses are dedicated respectively to St Francis and St John the Evangelist.

Facing the entrance is a mid sixteenth-century Mannerist painting of St Roque.

Leave the convent's patio and turn left into Calle Santa Clara. Calle Guadalquivir, first right, leads to the river at Calle Torneo. From the same side of the street, bus C1 follows the ring road clockwise, passing La Macarena and Calle Santa María la Blanca.

Alternatively, from the opposite side of the road, bus C2 follows the Triana side of the river to Plaza de Cuba, on the west side of the San Telmo bridge.

ITINERARY 6

HOUSE OF PILATE, CITY HALL AND ROMAN COLUMNS

After the Alcázar, the House of Pilate, with its sensitive mix of architectural styles, is Seville's most important domestic building. The City Hall and the House of the Pinelo Family exhibit outstanding Renaissance decoration. San Esteban is the quintessential Gothic/Mudéjar church, and the convents of Buen Suceso and Santa Inés are rare examples of monasteries that permit the public to enter their churches.

Timing   *The House of the Pinelo Family is closed at weekends.*
   San Isidoro is open 19.00–21.00 (Sunday 10.30–12.00).
   San Ildefonso is open 18.30–20.00.
   San Pedro is open 08.00–10.00 and 19.00–20.30.
   The Buen Suceso Convent is open 07.30–10.00 and 19.30–21.00 (Sunday 11.00–14.00).
   The Santa Inés Convent is open daily 19.15–20.00.

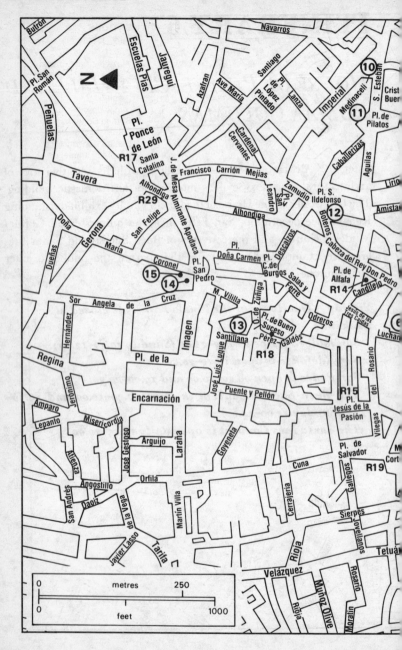

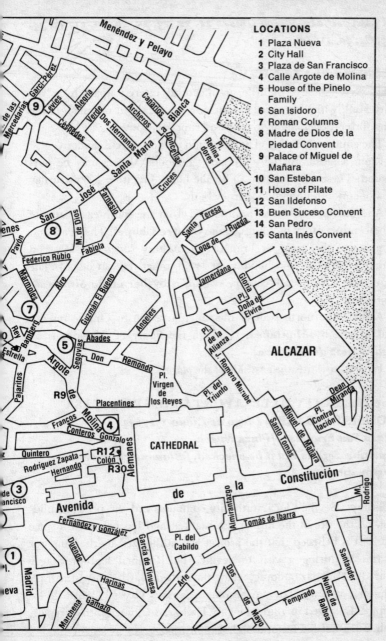

START *Plaza Nueva (Buses 21, 22, 23, 25, 26, 30, 31, 33, 34, C3, C4, 40, 41, 42).*

Location 1 PLAZA NUEVA

The 'New' square, of little architectural interest apart from the City Hall, which occupies its east side, was laid out on much of the land formerly belonging to the San Francisco Convent.

The equestrian statue of St Fernando in the centre is modern.

From a kiosk, on the south side, 'Bonobus' tickets may be purchased. These are valid for all Seville buses, on either a ten-journey or a one-month unlimited journey basis.

Also on the south side, approached from the south-east range of nineteenth-century buildings, is the **Onofre Chapel**. This is all that remains of the great St Francisco monastery (open for Mass on Sunday, Monday and holidays at 12.30, other days at 08.00). The high altar's eighteenth-century reredos is by *Bernardo Simón de Pineda*.

Against the north wall of the sanctuary, the St Onofre reredos was carved by *Montañés*, although the figure of the saint is by *Pedro Diaz de la Cueva*.

Proceed towards the east side of the *plaza*.

Location 2 CITY HALL (AYUNTAMIENTO or CASA CONSISTORIALES) *Diego de Riaño 1527–34*
Plaza San Francisco/Plaza Nueva.
Opening details must be checked, following comprehensive restoration.

History Seville's local authority commissioned the present building, on the site of the former fish market, and has occupied it since 1568. It is believed that the project was authorized by the Emperor Carlos V during a visit to Seville. The Council had previously shared a Mudéjar building, facing the cathedral, with the cathedral's Chapter; this was later to become a famous tavern, Corral de los Olmos. Enlarged in 1891, the City Hall gradually fell into disrepair, and much-needed restoration began in 1990.

Exterior The Plaza Nueva façade is entirely the nineteenth-century work of *Demetrio Ríos*, who began the extension of the City Hall in 1891. This matches the dimensions of the main façade, which faces Plaza San Francisco, but forgoes the exuberant decoration, the only noteworthy features being pedimented windows, balustrades and Ionic pilasters.

Calle Madrid passes the south façade of the building, and the first section of Renaissance work is seen at this point.

Before continuing to Plaza San Francisco, it is worth noting the nineteenth-century neo-Mudéjar building that occupies the corner of Avenida de la Constitución, at **No. 2.** Its ground floor accommodates Confitería Filella, the confectioners.

The Plaza San Francisco façade of the City Hall is best observed from its east side. *Diego de Riaño*, who worked on the building during 1527–34, was a master of the Plateresque style, and his sculpted façade is one of the finest examples in the country.

Historical and allegorical figures are the work of numerous craftsmen, including *Diego de Guillén*, *Pedro de Pamanes*, *Toribio de Liebana* and *Juan Vizcaíno*. All fit into the rhythmic framework established by *Riaño*, but no motifs are exactly repeated.

It will be noted that stonework to the north appears to have been prepared for carving which, presumably due to financial problems, never took place.

At the time of writing, it is not clear where the public entrance will be, but the historic interiors of the building are approached directly from Plaza San Francisco.

The **vestibule** is star-vaulted, a demonstration of Riaño's affection for the Gothic style, even within this Renaissance building. However, it also incorporates very un-Gothic circles, twisted columns and Plateresque flowers.

From the vestibule, a narrow corridor leads to the **Sala de Consistorio**, the lower meeting room of the council. This was where the renowned twenty-four knights of Seville convened. Walls are decorated with arabesques and medallions and a large city arms, carved by *Roque Balduque*.

A gilded Latin frieze extols the integrity and independence of the councillors.

The ceiling incorporates *casonetes*, carved with the heads of Spanish kings. An archway by **Juan Sánchez**, 1535, gives access to the Plaza Nueva from the hall.

Built in 1571, under the direction of **Benvenuto Tortello**, the former **chapel** retains a frieze.

Leading from the vestibule is the **stairway** to the archives, on the first floor.

At landing level, the vault, designed by **Juan Sánchez**, is decorated with small animals, flowers and cherubim.

The cupola above the stairwell is entirely Renaissance, the work of **Hernán Ruiz the Younger**, the architect who was also responsible for the upper stage of the Giralda.

A door leads, right, from the head of the stairs to the library, where historic and beautiful books are kept. The **Municipal Archives** (Archivo Municipal) comprises one of the most important collections of ancient documents to be found in Spain. Of particular interest are the six books known as the *Tome of the Catholic Monarchs*, created in 1498 from many separate documents relating to royal privileges that had been granted.

The most important section of the Archives is accommodated within the upper **Sala de Consistorio**, lying directly above the lower Sala de Consistorio.

Document cases now occupy what was formerly seating for the council members.

The coffered ceiling was decorated and gilded during the reign of Philip II. Exhibits of particular interest include the painting of *St Justa and St Rufina* by **Juan de Espinal**, 1760, and, in a display case, the silver mace of Juan de Córdoba, and the banner of Seville. The latter is a modern copy of the fifteenth-century original, now displayed in the Alcázar.

Location 3 PLAZA DE SAN FRANCISCO

Named to commemorate the great monastery that occupied much of the *plaza*, delightful houses, mostly post eighteenth-century, complement the City Hall. During the Franco period, the eastern section was renamed Plaza Falange Española.

Tournaments were held in the square from the early fifteenth century, but in 1478, Pope Sixtus IV authorized the Spanish Inquisition, which first operated in Seville, and the sinister *autos-de-fe* (acts of faith) became an even greater attraction. An *auto-de-fe* was the trial of those accused of heresy by the Roman Catholic Church, no one actually being burned during its proceedings. All trials were under the jurisdiction of the clergy, and most took place within a church – an *auto particular*. Occasionally an *auto publico*, a grand trial in a public place, Plaza San Francisco in the case of Seville, was arranged, and this took on the aspect of a pageant. Stands were erected and those to be tried, initially Jews whose conversion to Christianity was suspect, were led in procession to the square. Beginning at six o'clock in the morning, the trials usually lasted until the early afternoon. Those found innocent were reconciled to the church, those guilty were 'relaxed' to the civil authorities, with a hypocritical request that they should be dealt with leniently – it was known that death by burning was the invariable sentence. The crowds then moved to the Quemadero (burning place) at Prado de San Sebastián, where the stakes had been set up.

Today, the processions that pass through annually during Holy Week and Corpus Christi, watched by spectators from the specially erected stands, are the main events in the *plaza*. For some, the pointed black hoods of the penitent *cofradías*, identical to those worn by the Inquisitors and by members of the Klu Klux Klan, disturbingly evoke reflections on the enormity of the crimes committed by mankind in the name of God.

Calle Hernando Colón leads from the south-east corner of the *plaza*; passed at No. 8 is **Bodega Pez de Espada**, one of Seville's most popular fried fish bars (page 316).

An excursion is now made into Seville's most baffling quarter. Every few yards, narrow alleyways meet, wriggling away at varying angles. Intersections are not named and some streets appear to have no identification at any point. Even the largest-scale maps available, i.e. those in this book, will be difficult to follow here – a compass and a ball of string are probably the best bet!

Follow Calle Rodríguez Zapata, first left, to Calle Alvárez Quintero, first right. Towards the end, another *tapas* bar centre is reached, some of the *bodegas* providing extremely good value for money.

The short Calle Gonzalo, first left, connects with Calle Argote de Molina.

Location 4 CALLE ARGOTE DE MOLINA

Lying within the Santa Cruz quarter, like many of its streets, Calle Argote de Molina commemorates one of Seville's sixteenth-century men of letters.

Most buildings are eighteenth-century houses, but the famous Las Escobas Tavern, founded in the fourteenth century and patronized by Cervantes, Byron and Dumas, disappeared long ago. At No. 26, approached by a short passage, second left, is **Mesón Don Raimundo**, one of Seville's finest restaurants, specializing in Andalusian dishes, particularly game in winter (see page 313). The restaurant occupies an ancient house which has been well restored and sympathetically furnished. It was once known as the Horno de las Brujas (Bruges bakery), as its owners, who baked biscuits, came from Bruges in Belgium: the building later accommodated the city's first pawnbroking establishment.

A ceramic plaque, fixed to the wall of **No. 13** in 1924, denotes that this was the house of Gloria Bermúdez, heroine of the novel *La Hermana San Sulpicio*, by **Armando Valdéz**.

Calle Segovias, the right fork, preserves two ancient mansions with roof-level viewing galleries. The first, on the corner, left, at **No. 7**, retains a Baroque doorway but has been abandoned. However, the second, fronting Calle Abades, first left, is in immaculate condition. Great millstones have been built into its base for strength.

Location 5 HOUSE OF THE PINELO FAMILY *sixteenth century*
12–14 Calle Abades.
   Open Monday to Friday 10.00–13.00 and 16.00–20.00.

Now the seat of Seville's Literary Academy, this beautiful sixteenth-century mansion displays some of the finest Plateresque plasterwork in the city. The name of the house commemorates its first occupants, the wealthy Genoese Pinelo family of merchants. Francisco Pinelo knew Columbus and was appointed first commissioning agent for the Casa de Contratación.

Plasterwork of the arcades' spandrels in the main (second) patio is exceptionally decorative and incorporates Renaissance medallion busts.

The hybrid, composite capitals to the columns, ubiquitous in Seville, follow the contemporary prototypes first designed in Genoa for the House of Pilate.

The ceiling above the staircase is Mudéjar.

Stairs may be ascended to first-floor level, but no rooms are open to the public, nor may the roof gallery be approached.

On leaving the building, the roof gallery, with its rare, Gothic balustrade, is best seen from Calle Guzmán el Bueno, which stretches ahead eastward.

Return, following Calle Segovias westward. First right, Calle Argote de Molina. Immediately ahead, in Calle Estrella, first left, rises the tower of San Alberto church.

No. 3, **Bar Estrella**, is one of the city's most attractive bars. No television. No juke box. No fruit machine. Just an ancient radio that doesn't work. What a relief!

Renaissance columns, one of them leaning alarmingly, support the timber beams; once more, the House of Pilate's capitals are to be seen. Blue ceramic strips and a gleaming zinc bar are further attractions (see page 314).

San Alberto, ahead left, built in the eighteenth century, has been much remodelled. In a niche above the portal is the figure of *St Alonso* by **Alvarez de Albarrán**, 1626. The church is rarely open, but little within is of great interest. The figure of Christ in the high altar's reredos is a copy (1791) of a work by Montañés.

Continue northward, following Calle Luchana, to the church of San Isidoro.

Location 6 SAN ISIDORO
Calle San Isidoro.
  Open Monday to Saturday 08.00–9.30 and 19.00–21.00, Sunday 10.30–12.00.
Now, after many years of virtual dereliction, San Isidoro is in tip-top condition, its brilliant internal lighting being an example that others might well follow. By tradition the oldest established of Seville's churches, Mudéjar and Gothic features survive.

History It has been suggested that this Gothic/Mudéjar church, built *c.* 1360, may be the oldest in Seville. Nevertheless, remodelling in the sixteenth century, and the addition of north chapels in the eighteenth, has greatly altered its original appearance.

Exterior The mid fourteenth-century tower's superstructure is seventeenth-century.

  Its portal, facing Calle San Isidoro, is Gothic, apart from the Mudéjar stars, and almost certainly a later addition.

  A simple Gothic portal, with a double arch, provides the west entrance from Calle Luchana.

  Perhaps the most picturesque aspect of the church, however, is gained from the north side, fronting Calle Augusto Plasencia. Here, 1990 repainting provides a Knickerbocker Glory of colour – orange, pink, white and yellow, above a black plinth – even the mindless graffiti hooligans can't spoil it, though they are having a good try.

Interior Entered from Calle San Isidoro, at the base of the tower, the **vestibule** is rib-vaulted.

  High Gothic arches of brick form the arcades of the **aisles**.

  A painted Mudéjar ceiling stretches across the **nave**.

  At the west end, against the south wall, left of the entrance, the figure of Christ by *Francisco Villegas*, 1614, originally provided the main feature of the former reredos of the high altar. The **baptistery** is accommodated, as usual, in the most westerly of the north chapels. Its brick vault is Mudéjar.

  Immediately east of the north door, the **Señor of the Three Falls Chapel** displays, on the wall, left, an early sixteenth-century figure of the Virgin, mostly concealed by clothing. She is known as *The Virgin of the Salud*, or *The Virgin Canaria*.

A famous carving, *Christ Falling with His Cross*, by **Francisco Antonio Gijón**, 1687, gives this chapel its name. It is one of Gijón's major works: the same sculptor was also responsible for carving the figure coming to Christ's assistance.

Against the chapel's east wall stands the Renaissance tomb, made in 1579, of **Gonzalo Herrera de Olivares**, Bishop of Laodicea.

The **Sacrament Chapel**, which follows, is decorated with plaster-work in high relief.

Its incredibly ornate reredos is in the style of **Duque Cornejo**.

Large paintings, based on New Testament themes, are by **Lucas Valdés**.

Facing down the north aisle, the **Chapel of the Maestres** (an aristocratic Seville family) is embellished with a ceramic seventeenth-century dado.

The figure of *Christ on the Cross* is fourteenth-century.

A simple cupola surmounts the **crossing**.

Above the **sanctuary**, the frescos on the vault are from the school of **Juan Espinal**.

The high altar's reredos, by **Felipe Castillo** and **Pedro Tortolero**, is eighteenth-century work.

Its *St Isidoro* was painted by **Juan de Roelas** in 1613.

Facing down the south aisle is the **Chapel of the Villapando Family**.

Tiled dados were made in 1609.

The Baroque reredos is dedicated to St Alberto.

Against the south wall stands the St Joseph reredos by **Pérez Caballero**, 1742.

The figure was carved for it by **José Montes de Oca**.

Mudéjar brickwork decorates the **Milagrosa Chapel**, which follows.

On the south wall, before the exit, the painting of *Purgatory* is by **Esteban Márquez**.

Follow Calle San Isidoro, left, on leaving the church. An intricate maze of alleyways is now entered, in which it is quite hard not to get lost. First right, Calle Corral del Rey. Second left, Calle Abades. First left, Calle Aire. First left, Calle Mármoles.

Location 7 ROMAN COLUMNS (MONOLITOS ROMANOS)
Calle Mármoles.

Three columns, apparently in situ at the ground level of Roman times, are the remains of a great Roman temple, probably created during the reign of Hadrian. There were formerly six columns, but one was taken to the Alcázar by Pedro I; this broke before it could be erected, and the pieces were dumped in what is now Calle Mateos Gago. The other two were removed in the sixteenth century, to stand at the south end of the newly formed boulevard, the Alameda de Hércules, where they may still be seen, side by side.

Cardus, the main north/south thoroughfare of Roman Seville, passed here, and the temple stood on its east side. The columns supported the temple's portico, which must have rivalled that of Rome's Pantheon in grandeur.

Alfonso X believed that the columns were physically erected by Hercules, and later it was alleged, without evidence, that the temple had been dedicated to Hercules.

Seville historians referred to the columns as marbles (*mármoles*), and this is recorded by the name of the street in which they stand.

Buttressed by crude blocks of wood, and standing in a pool of green algae with 'islands' of half-submerged bottles, the columns can no longer be said to hint at the splendour of Roman Seville.

At the far end of Calle Mármoles, in Calle Muñoz y Pavón, is the church of San Nicolás de Bari.

A gate formerly stood in the ghetto wall, at this point, one of the most important to lead from the ghetto to the rest of the city.

Built in 1781, and completely restored in 1991, **San Nicolás de Bari** possesses a double-aisled interior, with red marble columns, in the style of a mosque. Its fittings, however, are Baroque and include a figure of Christ carved by *Pedro Roldán* in 1650.

Exit from the church immediately ahead, following Calle San José.

Calle San José, together with its southern continuation, Calle Santa María la Blanca, once formed the most important thorough-fare in the Jewish quarter. Immediately right stretches the long, plastered wall of the Madre de Dios Convent.

Location 8 MADRE DE DIOS DE LA PIEDAD CONVENT
1572
Calle San José.
Opening times to be established following restoration.
This is a historic Seville convent church, where the wife and daughter of the explorer Cortés are buried. Mudéjar features combine inter-nally with great Baroque altarpieces.

History Isabella I founded the convent in 1496. It has been sug-gested that *Hernán Ruiz the Younger* was responsible for the design of the church; but in any event, *Juan de Simanca* and *Pedro Díaz de Palacios* completed the building in 1572. Simi-larities with synagogues at Toledo and Lorca indicate that the church may occupy the site of an ancient synagogue.

Exterior The convent's exterior incorporates Mudéjar features: horseshoe arches to the portals, star windows and stepped castel-lation.

Painted brickwork indicates the location of the convent's church.

Above the lintel of its stone portal, a bas-relief medallion depicts *The Virgin of the Rosary*, with God above, and St Dominic at her feet, carved by *Juan de Oviedo* in 1590.

Immediately right of the portal, a plaque, erected in 1971, com-memorates the founding of the convent by the Catholic Queen (Isabella) on 6 June 1496, and gives details of its construction.

Interior Immediately right, behind rails, is the **nuns' choir**.

The aisleless church has been extended westward since it was originally built.

Its Mudéjar ceiling to the **nave** and **sanctuary** was erected by *Francisco Ramírez*, *Alonso Ruiz* and *Alonso Castillo*.

The murals are believed to have been painted by *Lucas Valdés*.

Against the north wall, the early seventeenth-century reredos depicts *The Entombment*.

Visitors are not permitted to approach the **sanctuary** closely, and this, combined with the usually inadequate lighting, prohibits a clear view of important objects at the east end of the church.

Just before the **sanctuary** stands the St John the Evangelist reredos; the figure of the saint, in the central niche, and reliefs depicting scenes from his life, are by *J. Hernández*.

Against the north wall of the **sanctuary** lies the recumbent figure of *Juana Zúñiga*, widow of *Hernán Cortés*, the discoverer of Mexico. The explorer's real love, however, was a Mexican 'Indian' princess, Malinche, and he spent little time with Juana.

Opposite, a similar figure commemorates *Catalina Cortés*, the explorer's daughter. Both figures were carved by *Juan de Oviedo* and *Miguel Adán* in 1590.

The two ladies are buried beneath the floor of the sanctuary.

A huge gilded Baroque reredos covering the entire east wall of the sanctuary is the work of *Francisco de Barahona*, 1684–90.

Also by *Barahona* are the flanking 'angels' and the *Last Supper* medallion, in the lower section.

The Virgin of the Rosary with the Infant Jesus, in the central niche, is by *Jerónimo Hernández*, 1573.

Above, added from an earlier reredos, is a Calvary group, also by *Hernández*.

A delightful altar rail by *Pedro Valera*, on the south wall, protects the *Correo* reredos, so called because it was assigned to the Correo Mayor of Seville. The work was completed in 1571 and its ceramic dado, together with the altar frontal, was made two years later by *Alonso García*.

Another *Virgin of the Rosary* reredos follows, a late sixteenth-century work attributed to *Jerónimo de Guzmán*.

The *Virgin and Child* painting, also late sixteenth-century, which forms the upper feature, depicts the *Virgen de Populo*, to whom the altar was formerly dedicated.

At the west end, the *Sagrada Lanzada* (Holy Lance) reredos, incorporating a Crucifixion scene, is by a member of the Seville School, c. 1570.

From the church, turn right to the Fernando III Hotel, and then, immediately left, follow Calle Céspedes.

The visitor has now entered the historic **Barrio San Bartolomé**. It is believed that the Flemish ghetto at some period extended into this *barrio* from Santa Cruz. Although a prestigious area in the seventeenth century, it was allowed to become run down and, unlike Santa Cruz, no great restoration scheme was put in hand. At last an effort is being made, and many of the major buildings have already been rehabilitated: further work is planned.

Facing the north end of Calle Céspedes is the former palace of Miguel de Mañara.

Location 9 PALACE OF MIGUEL DE MAÑARA
27 Calle Levies.

Under complete restoration in 1991, for adaptation to local government offices, the palace was originally the home of the wealthy Mañara family. Tomás, the father of Miguel, was the consul to Seville's traders. A plaque records the birth here, on 3 March 1627, of Miguel Mañara, founder of the Charity Hospital (page 146). Towards the end of his life, Mañara vacated the palace for his hospital, where he died on 9 May 1679.

Two fluted Doric columns flank the main portal, which is decorated with busts and sheep's skulls.

The remainder of the façade of this rather severely Classical, early seventeenth-century palace is of stuccoed brick, decoration being restricted to simple pilasters and cornices. Little of importance within appears to have survived the decay of the building, and it seems unlikely that the public will be admitted.

Facing the palace, on the west side of Plaza de las Mercedarías, stands the Mercedarías college of San José. Its church is not open to the public.

Ahead, the Saleses Convent's great brick-built church is modern work. Blind horseshoe arches are Mudéjar-inspired. Internally, there is little of artistic value.

Follow Calle Vidrio, skirting the south end of the church. Second left, a narrow passage, unnamed at this end, does a dog-leg turn, finally revealing that it is called Calle Cristo del Buen Viaje. At its end, immediately ahead, in Calle Esteban, appears the east apse of San Esteban church.

Location 10 SAN ESTEBAN
Calle San Esteban.
Opening times should be established following comprehensive restoration in 1991.

The building of San Esteban was begun in the second half of the fourteenth century. The west portal of the church is the finest Gothic/Mudéjar example in Seville.

Inside are outstanding paintings by *Zurbarán*.

Exterior   The polygonal apse retains a Mudéjar battlement.

Short and castellated, the Mudéjar tower was given a typical Sevillian belfry in the seventeenth century.

Although less impressive than the west portal, as is usually the case, the early fifteenth-century south doorway retains some original work, with deep corbels supporting the cornice.

Within a niche, dated 1618, stands a figure of St Stephen.

The west portal, facing Calle Medinaceli, is the jewel of the church: also early fifteenth-century, it is a complete example of Gothic form with Mudéjar decoration, all remaining in exceptional condition.

Each of the lion's-head corbels, supporting the upper cornice, varies slightly in design.

Around the door, lobed arches form a *sebka* frieze, in the style of the Giralda.

Niches have Gothic canopies, but Mudéjar lion's-head pedestals; the figures are quite obviously replacements of the originals.

Outer archivolts are carved with the usual diamonds, but clover leaves are also incorporated in the pattern.

Capitals to the colonettes are floral Mudéjar work.

Interior   A coffered Mudéjar ceiling roofs the **nave** and its **aisles**, while the **sanctuary** is rib-vaulted; an oft-repeated combination in churches of this period.

The baptism, in San Esteban, of the painter *Juan de Valdés Leal* on 4 May 1622 is recorded on a stone in the **baptistery**, looking up the north aisle.

Heavy Baroque decoration to the **Capilla Sacramento**, in 1679, included the polychromatic tiles, with medallions.

The high altar's reredos, by *Luis de Figueroa*, 1629, incorporates a *Martyrdom of St Stephen* scene and an *Adoration of the Shepherds* by *Polanco*.

Other paintings, featuring saints, are excellent examples of the skill of *Zurbarán*. It is not yet clear whether all these outstanding works will form part of the reredos, as originally, or whether they will be dispersed around the walls of the church.

Ceramic tiles, made in the sixteenth century, decorate the altar.

Looking down the south aisle, the **south-west chapel** retains Mudéjar work; before restoration, an early seventeenth-century figure of Christ was displayed within.

On leaving the church, follow Calle Esteban westward to **Plaza de Pilatos**, which is rather spoilt by the unsympathetic apartment block that closes its south side.

In the centre, a statue commemorates *Zurbarán*, now generally regarded, after Velázquez, as the greatest painter of the Seville School.

The **plaza** was originally incorporated within the House of Pilate, on the north side, and locked up at night. Bullfights and equestrian events were frequently staged.

Location 11 HOUSE OF PILATE (CASA DE PILATOS)
Plaza de Pilatos.
Open daily 10.00–20.00 (closes 18.00 in winter).
Admission charge, with additional charge for optional visit to the upper floor (guided tours of the latter only).
Apart from the Alcázar, this is the most sumptuous private residence in the city that the public may enter. Combining Mudéjar, Gothic and Renaissance work, the house, virtually a palace, had great

influence on Seville architecture, following its sixteenth-century extension and Classical embellishments by the first Marquess of Tarifa. The strange name of the complex, the House of Pilate, was acquired from an unfounded tradition that it was a replica of the praetorium in Jerusalem, where Christ was arraigned before Pontius Pilate. Restored in recent years to its former glory, Casa de Pilatos remains the family home of the Dukes of Medinaceli, who occupy private quarters on the upper floor. In addition to being classed as a public monument, it also sometimes serves as the venue for concerts, seminars and other events of a cultural nature.

History Pedro Enríquez and his wife Catalina de Ribera purchased the property in 1483, after it had been confiscated from its former owner, Pedro Ejecutor, the city magistrate, following his conviction for heresy by the Inquisition. Its relatively high price reflected the value of the fresh water supply to the estate. At the time, all water in Seville belonged to the King, and most citizens had to obtain their requirements from public fountains. Although it is unclear which existing sections of the house were built by Pedro, it is generally believed that the chapel was constructed for him.

Pedro's son Fadríquez, who became first Marquess of Tarifa in 1514, is chiefly responsible for the present appearance of Casa de Pilatos. Around 1530 he began its great expansion, which continued for almost fifty years until the estate covered a huge area bounded, from north to west, by Calle Imperial, Calle Medinaceli, Calle San Esteban, Plaza de Pilatos, Calle Caballerizas and Calle Zamudio.

In 1518 Fadríquez began his Grand Tour of Europe, which incorporated Italy, then experiencing the peak of the High Renaissance. He continued to the Holy Land and on his return journey commissioned, in Genoa, two monumental sepulchres for his parents, destined for the family mausoleum within the monastic church of La Cartuja. In 1528 he ordered further sepulchres for some of his more important ancestors, and the following year he commissioned architectural embellishments for the House of Pilate. The modified

Classical style of the latter had great influence on the appearance of houses in Seville, which can still be noted to this day.

On returning to Seville, Fadríquez noted that the distance from his house to the Cruz de Campo (Cross in the Field), a small temple built on the outskirts of the city by **Diego de Merlo** in 1482, was exactly the same as that between what was believed to be the ruins of the praetorium in Jerusalem and Golgotha. Roman Catholics depict the route from the praetorium, where Pontius Pilate 'washed his hands' of Christ, to Golgotha Hill, scene of the Crucifixion, by illustrating the main events of the Passion, usually fourteen in number, known as the Stations of the Cross. Fadríquez, therefore, decided to mark these stations between his house and the Cruz de Campo, beginning with the first, representing Christ before Pilate at the praetorium.

Seeing this, the people of Seville created the myth that the design of the residence was a replica of 'Pilate's House'. Pilate, in fact, only lodged at the praetorium while performing his official duties in Jerusalem, preferring to live at Caesarea, on the Mediterranean. Rooms gradually acquired names that supported the legend, e.g. Salón del Pretorio, and these have survived. Although popularly known as Casa de Pilatos since the sixteenth century, it was not until the nineteenth century that the name was established officially.

Per Afán, who inherited the estate following the death of Fadríquez in 1539, became the first Duke of Alcalá in 1558 and was later entrusted with diplomatic missions to Italy. While there, he collected antiquities, acquiring existing collections of importance, and Pope Pius V presented him with additional valuable pieces. All these were sent to Seville, beginning in 1568, accompanied by an Italian architect, **Benvenuto Tortello**, who was responsible for some remodelling work on the house and the display of the collection.

After the death of Per Afán, little of consequence happened to the house until its ownership by Fernando, third Duke of Alcalá, who completed unfinished work, added new lodgings for servants, and remodelled the south façade, *c.* 1630. Much of the work, which was designed by **Juan de Oviedo**, was badly affected by the 1755 earthquake and was rebuilt in the nineteenth century.

Fernando had acquired an outstanding collection of paintings, but most of them went to Genoa after his death in 1637.

When the family moved to Madrid in the mid seventeenth century, the house was stripped of most of its treasures, functioning only as administrative quarters and servants' accommodation. As might be expected, dilapidation set in, frescos were overpainted and rooms subdivided. Fortunately the prevailing 'Romantic' taste of the nineteenth century was the saviour of the House of Pilate, the fifteenth Duchess of Medinaceli initiating its complete restoration, though it was not until after the Civil War had ended that the complex became, for the first time, the main residence of the Dukes of Medinaceli. A modern apartment was constructed where the great library, lost in the earthquake, had stood, and by 1950 most of the restoration work had been completed and the family treasures were installed.

Exterior The House of Pilate is constructed around a series of internal patios and gardens, with little of note visible from the surrounding streets; an exception is the arcaded loggia, right, that stands at an angle to the entrance wall, once referred to by Sevillanos as the place of the 'Ecce Homo', as they believed that it was a reproduction of the room in which Christ appeared before Pilate, crowned with thorns.

Definitely of note, however, is the archway of white Carrara marble, made in the Genoese studio of *Alfonso María de Aprile* in 1529 for the first Marquess of Tarifa. Its Corinthian pilasters are Roman in style.

The monumental and open character of the entrance marked a significant change in Seville fashion, which had, until then, reflected the Muslim preference for insignificant portals that concealed rather than revealed the quality of an interior.

In the spandrels are bas-relief busts of Roman emperors.

Standing within the polychrome marble niche, left of the arch, is the cross that initiated the Way of the Cross from the House of Pilate to the Cruz de Campo. The piece, including its Latin inscription, was made for Fernando, third Duke of Alcalá, by *Andrés Correa* and *Nicolás de Ferrero y Lorrea* in 1630, as a replacement for the former cross that had stood within the complex.

Tickets are purchased immediately left of the entrance, one ticket being necessary for the ground floor and another, optional, for the upper floor (admirably, each ticket is printed with an area and room plan). The following description keeps to the sequential order as now visited, the plan number being given in bold type.

Apeadero (1) The Apeadero – meaning, in Spanish, an area where transport is awaited – is arcaded on two sides, thus giving protection from the elements (chiefly, in Seville, the hot sun).

To the left is the **Caballerizas** (stable block) with its **Picadero** (riding school) **(8)**, approached from a monumental vestibule, its vault supported by columns. The hall originally served as the wardrobe or 'cabinet of curiosity' of the first Marquess of Tarifa. Remodelling took place, 1568–70, by *Tortello*, for the first Duke of Alcalá, to house Classical sculptures; although later adapted to stables, its appearance is basically unchanged.

Directly above, the Library and Armaments Room were badly damaged by the 1755 earthquake and were rebuilt in the nineteenth century, both disappearing as entities; the area now forms private accommodation.

One of Seville's most extravagant displays of bougainvillaea cascades over the wall ahead throughout most of the year. The iron gate leading to the main patio is a nineteenth-century addition, in Romantic style. The entrance was originally from the corner, right, giving the patio a greater sense of enclosure.

The much-faded medieval bust of Pedro the Cruel, on the wall left of the entrance, was acquired by the third Duke of Alcalá in the seventeenth century, when he learned that it was to be replaced by a new version in its original position in Calle Cabeza del Rey Don Pedro. A legend connected with the bust is related on page 193, when the street is reached.

The plaque, right of the gate, commemorates the creation of the library and archives by the third Duke of Alcalá.

Patio Principal (Main Patio) **(2)** Although the design of the arcaded patio adheres strictly to Mudéjar taste, other elements are delicately incorporated. Plasterwork, the use of ceramics, and the unequal dimensions of the arches are Muslim; gallery balustrades are Gothic; the fountain, columns, statues and dimensions are Renaissance.

The pavement, originally tiled, wore out and was replaced by marble in the nineteenth century. At the same time, the windows were restyled in Muslim form, imitating work at Granada.

The central fountain, supported by dolphins, was made in Genoa by *Aprile* in 1529. It is crowned by the two-headed god Janus.

A colossal statue occupies each corner of the patio. Athene (with spear) is a copy of the Greek Médicis Athene, attributed to a follower of *Phidias*, fifth century BC. The other statues are all Roman; clockwise from Athene they are Minerva, Ceres and a Muse. Busts of Roman emperors, occupying niches within the arcades, were brought from Italy by the first Duke of Alcalá: most needed restoration. The high ceramic dado is the work of *Diego* and *Juan Polido* from Triana, 1536–8.

Enter the first room right of the patio's entrance.

Salón del Pretorio (Praetorium) **(3)** *Juan Rodríguez* and *Diego Hernández* designed this hall, the name of which commemorates residences provided for Roman provincial governors, such as Pontius Pilate.

The coffered ceiling incorporates the arms of the Ribera family.

Windows are provided with seventeenth-century Plateresque grilles and Mudéjar shutters.

A ceramic frieze decorates the walls.

Leading from the long side of the Salón del Pretorio is an arcaded passage, **Corredor del Zaquizamí (5)**. Displayed in the passage are Roman and Renaissance busts, stones and inscriptions.

Continue ahead.

Anteroom (not identified on plan) Columns with Caliphate capitals flank the entrance. Exhibited are Roman busts, a sleeping nymph, a Renaissance bas-relief arms, copied from Trajan's Column in Rome, and a bas-relief, *Leda and the Swan*, from the first century BC.

Off the far end of the arcade, right, lies a small pavilion.

Salón Dorado (Gilded Hall) (not identified on plan) This pavilion gained its name from the gilded, interlaced ceiling, one of the best examples of its type in Seville. Roman busts, reliefs and sections of friezes are displayed.

The Grotesque Roman heads served as models for the monumental fountain in Plaza de la Virgen de los Reyes.

Immediately right of the door is a Greek bust.

Jardín Chico (Small Garden)   The garden was originally much smaller, consisting only of the section facing the Corredor del Zaquizamí, but when a yard was demolished early in the present century this provided the opportunity for its extension.

Various figures decorate the ponds and fountains, notably a bronze of a young Bacchus by *Mariano Benlliure*.

Return to the main patio, via the Salón del Pretorio, and enter the range, right.

Salón de Descanso de los Jueces (Resting Room of the Judges) (unnumbered on the plan but fronting the chapel (**5**), to which it serves as an anteroom). Its ceramic dado incorporates panels with the coats of arms of the Enríquez and Ribera families.

A Mudéjar plaster frieze and a plaster portal, combining Mudéjar and Plateresque work, have both been over-restored.

Capilla (Chapel) (**5**)   It is believed that the chapel, although once larger, is the oldest part of the House of Pilate. According to tradition, it was built for Pedro Enríquez and Catalina de Ribera. However, entrances to other rooms from the chapel were certainly opened up later for Fadrique Enríquez de Ribera.

The impressive rib vault and archivolts to the windows are Gothic in style, but some have doubted their authenticity.

A copy of a Visigothic figure of *Christ the Good Shepherd* stands on the altar; the original is in the Vatican.

The central column has given the chapel the unofficial name of Capilla de la Flagelación (Flagellation Chapel), in the erroneous belief that it represented the column to which Christ was tied for his beating.

Approached from the far end of the Descanso de los Jueces is a small study, **Gabinete de Pilatos** (Pilate's Study) (**6**). The central fountain has given this room the alternative name of Salón de la Fuente.

A frieze of pine surrounds the Mudéjar lacework ceiling.

The ceramic dado incorporates square panels depicting the arms of the Enríquez and Ribera families.

From this room is approached the Large Garden.

Jardín Grande (Large Garden) When the garden, originally the orchard, was made it was significantly more extensive than the Small Garden but, as already explained, the latter has since been extended.

Ahead, the arcade had a great influence on architecture in Seville. Marble for the columns was imported from Genoa and their shafts designed without entasis, i.e. they were completely regular in dimensions, without the usual swelling. Even more innovative, the capitals were of a stylized Composite design, now referred to as *monas*, which soon became a popular decorative feature in the city.

Tortello built two identical ranges, 1568–70, incorporating loggias, the arches of which were supported by ancient columns. One range survives, little altered, but the other was disastrously remodelled by filling in its ground floor arcade to provide additional domestic accommodation.

The single-storey pavilion, facing the entrance arcade, was also built by *Tortello*. An interesting tradition is that the first Duke of Alcalá obtained from Pius V the ashes of the Emperor Trajan, a native of nearby Itálica. These were kept in a vase displayed in the library, until a servant unwittingly scattered them in the garden. As might be expected, it is said that citrus fruit grew in profusion where the ashes fell.

Return to the Main Patio, via the Gabinete de Pilatos, and proceed to the stairway in the corner of the arcade's passage, right. Ensure that tickets for the upper floor have already been purchased at the entrance. Numbers corresponding with the rooms indicated on the ticket's first-floor plan are again shown in bold type.

Escalera (Stairway) **(1)** Immediately left, against the wall, is the decorative door that originally gave access to the stairway.

Ceramic tiles are noted for their rainbow-hue effect.

At the second landing hangs a copy of **Murillo**'s *Virgin of the Serviette*.

The outstanding 'half-orange' ceiling of the cupola above the stairwell was made by **Cristóbal Sánchez** in 1537. **Andrés Pérez** was responsible for its decoration, including the gilding.

At the top of the stairs, wait for the guide. Visitors are led along the gallery to its far end and return in the same direction, but through the rooms. The guides do not generally speak English, and a detailed description of the rooms is therefore given here.

Galería Alta (Upper Gallery) Remains of frescos, depicting Classical personalities – Cicero, Croesus, etc. – were discovered quite recently and have been preserved. They were painted, 1538–9, by **Andrés Martín**, **Alonso Hernández Jusado** and **Diego Rodríguez**.

Salón de los Frescos (Fresco Room) **(2)** It is recorded that this was formerly known as the Glass Windows Room, as it was fitted with stained glass by Flemish masters. The present name reflects the recently discovered *Triumph of the Four Seasons* fresco, painted by **Diego Rodríguez** in 1539 and based on contemporary engravings by **Pieter Coecke van Aalst**, published in Antwerp.

The trussed ceiling is Mudéjar work.

Two Roman busts are displayed.

Salita de Fumar (Smoking Room) **(3)** Family portraits include an equestrian portrait of the Count of Ribadavia, a copy of the original, which remains in Galicia.

St Andrew, patron of the House of Pilate, and St Juan de Ribera, natural son of the first Duke of Alcalá, are both painted by an anonymous artist.

Comedor (Dining Room) **(4)** The trussed ceiling is sixteenth-century Mudéjar work.

Two cloths by **Teniers**, 1680, depict the Medinaceli arms, among others.

Paintings include two Evangelists and a Mary Magdalene, by **Sebastián de Llanos Valdés**, 1668, and, above the fireplace, a still-life by the Neapolitan **Giuseppe Recco**, 1629.

The fireplace, of black stone, came from the former library.

An early eighteenth-century folding screen of Córdoba leather, and a pair of eighteenth-century Japanese vases, are noteworthy pieces.

From here it is now more usual for the visitor to be conducted directly ahead to the library, via the Salón del Torreón, a change from the route indicated on the ticket's plan necessitated by curtailment of the original itinerary. However, the Salón del Torreón may be examined at this stage.

Librería (Library) **(9)**   The bookcases were made in Ireland in the nineteenth century. Paintings are: on the entrance wall, *St Paula*, an anonymous mid seventeenth-century work, probably from the Madrid School, an *Immaculate Conception*, the Virgin unusually accompanied by two youths, a copy by **Arpino** of the **Murillo** original, and, ahead, a *Penitent Mary Magdalene*, by an anonymous Spanish painter, early sixteenth century.

Salón de Retratos Este (East Retiring Room) **(10)**   Family portraits dominate: a large seventeenth-century portrait of the Dowager Duchess of Medinaceli, mother of the present Duke, by **Sotomayor**; and *Bárbara de Braganza*, from the studio of **Van Loo**.

Rooms 11–13 on the ticket plan are no longer visited, as they now form part of the private quarters. A return is made to the Tower Room.

Salón del Torréon (Tower Room) **(5)**   This room is situated in the tower of the house, which was built as a defensive measure and fortified.

The large sixteenth-century Brussels tapestry, right, is the work of **Panenemacker**.

Above the fireplace hangs an equestrian portrait of the Marquess of Aytona, by **Gaspar de Crayer**.

It is flanked by heraldic cloths.

Below, the elongated *Adoration of the Magi* is from the school of **Jordán**.

Opposite, works by **Jordán** include, below, *Erminia and the Shepherds*.

Christ and the Samaritan and *Prometheus*, both on the remaining wall, are seventeenth-century Neapolitan works.

Salón de Oviedo (Oviedo Room) **(6)**   The name of the room commemorates the seventeenth-century architect who was responsible for its plaster ceiling. Other décor by him was superseded in the eighteenth century.

Immediately left of the entrance is a small bullfighting scene by **Goya**.

Family portraits are by followers of **Agustín Esteve**.

Salón de Pacheco (Pacheco Room) **(7)**   **Fernando Francesco Pacheco**, the painter, was a leading member of the group of artists and intellectuals that met at the House of Pilate in the early seventeenth century. Many of his paintings were among the outstanding collection of the third Duke of Alcalá, most of which left Spain for Genoa, following his death in 1637. However, the Pacheco ceiling of this room, completed in 1603, survives, featuring *The Apotheosis of Hercules* and other mythical themes.

A sycophantic inscription in Latin, on the ceiling, praises the young Duke of Alcalá as 'a model of virtues'.

Not to be missed is the outstanding, early sixteenth-century Plateresque bench, incorporating the Medinaceli arms.

Gabinete (Cabinet or small room)   A mythological Olympian banquet is painted on the ceiling. By an unknown artist, it is believed to precede Pacheco's work at the house.

The fireplace is decorated with exquisite Second Empire panels of Sèvres porcelain.

Views of the Bay of Naples, flanking the fireplace, are by **Gaspar Vanvitelli**.

The Spanish landscape is by **Battagioli**.

On the wall, right of the fireplace, stands a Flemish panel by **Pieter Coecke**.

A return to the patio is now made by the same staircase.

On leaving the House of Pilate, turn right and immediately right again, following Calle Caballerizas, which passes the stables (hence its name) and leads to Plaza de San Ildefonso.

Location 12 SAN ILDEFONSO, *José Echamaros 1794–1841*
Plaza de San Ildefonso.
   Open daily 18.30–20.00.
A fourteenth-century fresco from the earlier building, and carvings by **Montañés** and **Roldán**, are the chief items of interest in this Baroque church.

History   San Ildefonso, formerly a fourteenth-century church, was rebuilt in Classical style by the city's chief architect, *José Echamaros*, under the auspices of the Fine Arts Academy.

Exterior   The brightly-painted west façade is entered via its portal, flanked by twin towers.

Interior   In the second north bay of the **nave**, a sixteenth-century *Virgin of the Kings* is flanked by carved wooden figures of St Fernando and St Hermenegildo, both by *Roldán*. *Christ Captive*, the subject of the reredos that follows, was made in the second half of the seventeenth century.

A cupola, with lantern, roofs the **crossing**.

Decorating the wall behind the altar that looks down the north aisle is the *Virgin of the Coral* fresco, painted *c*. 1375 and exhibiting Italian influence.

This wall is all that survives structurally from the fourteenth-century church.

Above the **sanctuary**'s inner arch, the effigies of St Peter, St Paul and St Ildefonso came from the high altar's reredos of the earlier church; they were carved by *Felipe de Rivas* in 1637, but heavily restored in the nineteenth century.

Behind the present high altar's reredos stands a *baldacchino* of jasper.

Immediately left of the doorway, at the west end of the church, the base of the tower accommodates the **baptistery**.

Against the wall, left, stands a bas-relief of *The Trinity* by *Montañés*, 1609.

On leaving the church, proceed directly ahead to the courtyard of **San Leandro Convent**. San Leandro was one of the first convents to be founded in the thirteenth century, following the Reconquest. However, its site changed several times, until Pedro the Cruel donated the present land in the fourteenth century.

Sold from an enclosed, revolving cupboard, facing the courtyard, are products made by the nuns from exclusive recipes. *Yemas de San Leandro*, based on egg-yolks, is the most popular of all the confectionery that can be purchased from Seville's convents. Prices are listed for varying weights, and change is given, so transactions are simple, even though the nuns serving cannot be seen. Goods are appropriately packaged, making welcome gifts.

Return to Plaza de San Ildefonso from the courtyard and follow, immediately right, Calle Zamudio, which leads to Plaza de San Leandro, where the Baroque doorway to San Leandro convent's church is passed, right.

Rarely open to the public, the building was remodelled by *Juan de Oviedo*, *c.* 1600.

Reredoses dedicated to St John the Baptist and St John the Evangelist incorporate work attributed to *Montañés*.

From the *plaza*, Calle Imperial, first right, runs eastward. Third left (including the short dead-end passage), Calle Lanza leads to, first left, Plaza de López Pintado.

Immediately right stands **Santiago church** (open at 18.30).

An earlier structure was completely rebuilt, in Classical style, in 1789.

Its high altar's reredos, designed by *Vermondo Resta* in 1599, was carved by *Andrés de Ocampo*.

On the west wall hangs a sixteenth-century painting of St James (Santiago) slaying the Moors at the battle of Albelda, by the Italian, *Mateo Perez de Alesio*.

Return to Plaza de San Ildefonso and continue ahead to Calle Boteros. First left, **Calle Cabeza del Rey Don Pedro** leads to a small *plaza*.

In a first-floor Baroque niche, on the corner of **No. 30**, the seventeenth-century bust of a king depicts Pedro I, illustrating the legend, almost certainly apocryphal, that gave the street its name (Head of the King Don Pedro). The story was told by the Duke of Rivas in his book *El Candilejo*. According to this, a man was murdered in the street by a cloaked assassin. Pedro vowed to discover the murderer and display his head in the street. An old woman, who had witnessed the event, then revealed that she was certain that Pedro himself had been the assailant, as she had heard the 'crackling' of his bones – a well-known characteristic of the

King, who presumably suffered from chronic rheumatism. Admitting his guilt, Pedro 'kept' his promise but craftily displayed a carved bust rather than his actual head. The medieval version of the bust that stood here until replaced in the seventeenth century has been described on page 185.

Returning eastward, Plaza de Alfafa, rectangular in shape, forms the second turning, left.

With its plane trees, rectangular dimensions and café terraces spilling on to the pavements, **Plaza de Alfafa** evokes squares in Provence. On Sunday, there is a bird market that lasts most of the day. For those who find it abhorrent to see caged birds, often crammed together in restricted areas, Sundays are probably best avoided. Most of the poor creatures on offer are rather dreary pigeons, presumably intended for the table, as pigeon-fanciers of the north of England variety are rather thin on the ground in Andalusia.

Nevertheless, at most times Plaza de Alfafa is an extremely pleasant location, providing yet another *tapas* bar centre in the city.

Ahead, from the north side of the square, Calle Odreros leads, via Calle Salas y Ferre, to an even longer but much more tranquil square, **Plaza del Cristo de Burgos**. Many of its shady trees are very old and have grown to a great size.

On the corner, immediately right and adjacent to Tito's Bar, **No. 21**, formerly a palace, is now a greengrocers' warehouse; its watch-tower is retained.

After entering the square, take the second turning left, Calle Ortiz de Zuñiga. A tiny *plaza*, right, **Plaza del Buen Suceso**, was named from the convent that occupies its east side.

Location 13 BUEN SUCESO CONVENT
Plaza del Buen Suceso.
Open Monday to Saturday 07.30–10.00 and 19.30–21.00,
Sunday 11.00 and 14.00.

The pretty, Baroque interior, with exuberant pink marble, is a delight, cupolas heightening the Baroque effect.

Immediately right of the entrance, against the south wall, is the convent's greatest treasure, the figure of *St Anne with the Virgin as a Child*, a masterpiece by **Montañés**.

Two streets branch from the north side of the *plaza*. Calle M. Vililla, right, leads directly to Plaza de San Pedro.

Location 14 SAN PEDRO
Plaza de San Pedro.
Open daily 08.00–10.00 and 19.00–20.30.

San Pedro (St Peter) boasts an outstanding collection of paintings, and retains, in the lace-like Mudéjar ceiling to its San Antonio chapel, one of the finest examples of its type in Seville.

History Although possessing mid fourteenth-century Gothic/ Mudéjar origins, San Pedro has been greatly remodelled, particularly in the seventeenth century. Velázquez, Seville's greatest painter, was baptized here in 1599. Regrettably, little of his work may be seen in the city and there is no example whatsoever in this church.

Exterior San Pedro is built of brick, with stone portals.

Facing the *plaza*, the Baroque main portal was begun by **Diego de Quesada** in 1613.

Martín Cardino added the figure of St Peter in 1624.

The brick Mudéjar tower, with lobed windows, was given a Baroque belfry in the seventeenth century; everything was restored in the eighteenth.

The west portal, also of stone, was built in 1612.

NB On entering the church, be careful not to trip on the projecting threshold.

Interior The timber roof of the nave is coffered Mudéjar work.

Also Mudéjar are the ornate west door and the organ gallery above.

Proceed to the north aisle's third chapel from the west, the **Christ of Burgos Chapel**.

Its reredos's late sixteenth-century figure of *Christ Crucified*, by **Juan Bautista Vázquez**, is flanked by *The Virgin of La Palma*, attributed to **Astorga**, and *John the Evangelist*.

On the north wall, immediately to the east, a plaque, inserted in

1899, commemorates the tricentenary of the baptism within San Pedro of Diego Velázquez de Silva on 6 June 1599. The great artist, known internationally simply as **Velázquez**, became court painter in Madrid when only twenty-four, and few of his works, therefore, are to be seen in the city of his birth. It would be a pleasant gesture if, in 1999, at least a small work by the master could be presented to this church to mark the quatercentenary of his baptism.

As usual, while the **nave** has a timber ceiling, the more important **sanctuary** is rib-vaulted in stone.

Many paintings decorate the sanctuary, but because of generally inadequate lighting, they are all difficult to see.

The high altar's reredos was begun by **Felipe de Ribas** in 1641 but completed by his brother **Francisco** twenty-five years later.

Six reliefs depict scenes from the life of St Peter.

The saint's effigy, by **Andrés de Ocampo**, 1691, stands in the central niche, at lower level.

Facing down the south aisle, the **San Antonio Chapel** retains an outstanding Mudéjar vault, built in 1379.

Of narrow, interwoven strips of brick, the lace-like (*lacería*) result is one of Seville's finest examples.

The most easterly of the south chapels displays an outstanding Eucharist painting by **Lucas Valdés**, depicting *The Entry of Souls into Heaven*.

At upper level, on the south wall, hangs the famous *St Peter Liberated by an Angel*, painted by **Juan de Roelas** in 1612.

Leave the church and turn left. First left, Calle Doña María Coronel passes the east end of San Pablo, although its octagonal apse is partly concealed by adjacent houses. Nevertheless, Mudéjar detailing, particularly castellation, may be observed.

Adjacent to San Pablo is the Santa Inés convent.

Location 15 SANTA INÉS CONVENT
5 Calle Doña María Coronel.
   Church open daily 19.15–20.00.

History   The convent of Santa Inés was founded in the fourteenth century by Doña María Coronel, a member of a wealthy Seville family. A legend records that María was pursued by Pedro the Cruel, who murdered her husband in order to clear his path. To escape the King's unwanted attentions, María disfigured her face with boiling oil and retired to this small convent, where her body is preserved.

Construction of the church was begun in the fourteenth century, and it was built in the Gothic style, although seventeenth-century remodelling has since given it Baroque features. The nuns who now live here belong to a closed order.

Exterior   Arcaded on two sides, the patio is one of the most attractive to front a Seville church.

Opposite the entrance to the building, a ceramic wall-plaque records that Bécquer was inspired by the organ of Santa Inés to write his ghost story, *Maese Pérez el Organista* (Master Pérez the Organist).

Produce made by the nuns is sold from the revolving wooden dispenser at the end of the patio. Cakes, confectionery, dried fruit and nuts are available at most times; consult the price list.

Above the Baroque stone portal, a seventeenth-century addition, the carved *Agnus Dei* is a Latin pun, referring to St Agnes, an alternative and more common version of St Inés.

Interior   Plasterwork throughout the church, and the murals on the west wall, are by **Francisco de Herrera**, the murals being completely restored in 1991. Behind the screen, at the west end, is the **nuns' choir**; the famous Baroque organ of the church, *c.* 1700, is hidden from view.

Paintings on the vault of the **sanctuary** are also the work of **Herrera**.

Made in the eighteenth century, the reredos of the high altar incorporates a figure of St Inés in the central niche, a survivor from its predecessor.

On the east wall, right of the sanctuary, the paintings are by sixteenth-century Flemish artists.

Return to Plaza de San Pedro, right, and follow the main

thoroughfare, Calle Imagen, westward to Plaza de la Encarnación. Buses 10, 11, 12, 20, 23, 32, 41 and 42. Alternatively, to extend the route to include El Rinconcillo tavern and Santa Catalina church, exit from Santa Inés left. Second right, Calle Gerona. (See pages 216 and 202.)

ITINERARY 7

LA MACARENA, ANDALUSIAN PARLIAMENT AND CITY WALL

Four important churches and Santa Paula Convent, the most welcoming to visitors of all Seville's monasteries, are seen. The finest stretch of the City Wall and the new seat of the Andalusian Parliament (the former seventeenth-century Hospital de la Sangre) are also included.

Timing *An early start is necessary to see the interior of Santa Catalina, as it closes at 09.30 (it opens again for an hour in the evening but is closed without fail by 19.30).*

The Terceros Convent is open at 20.30.

Santa Paula Convent, and the Macarena basilica, although open for much of the day, shut 13.00–16.30 (17.50 for the Macarena).

San Gil and San Marcos both open for Mass at 19.30.

The former church of La Paz Convent is open Sunday 08.30–11.30.

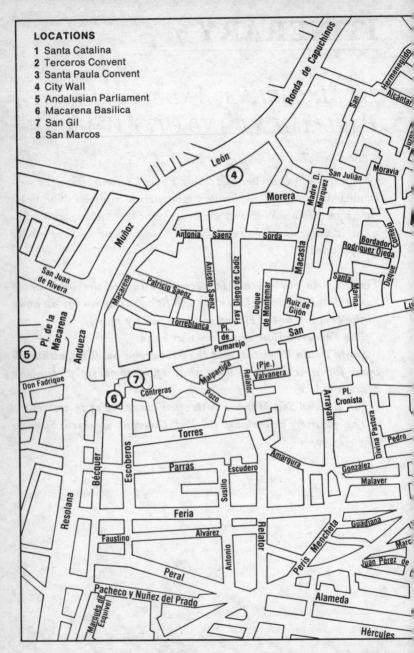

LOCATIONS
1 Santa Catalina
2 Terceros Convent
3 Santa Paula Convent
4 City Wall
5 Andalusian Parliament
6 Macarena Basilica
7 San Gil
8 San Marcos

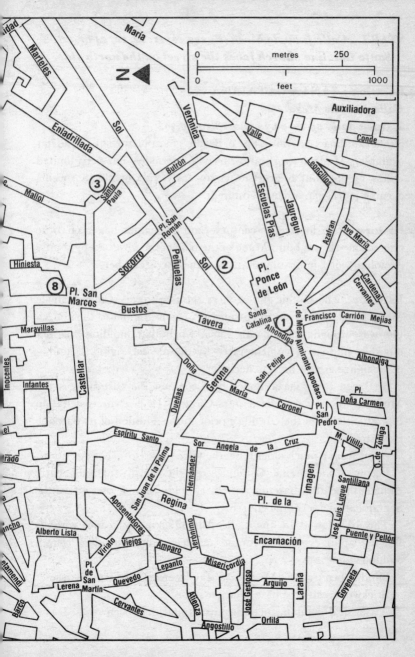

START *Calle Juan de Mesa (Buses 10, 11, 12, 20, 24 or 32).*
Santa Catalina church faces the street on the north side.

Location 1 SANTA CATALINA
Calle Juan de Mesa.
Open daily 09.00–09.30 and 18.30–19.30.

Santa Catalina's exterior is one of Seville's most picturesque Mudéjar examples. Mudéjar work also survives internally, but very limited access to the church necessitates an early visit or else a specific evening journey in order to admire it.

History The fourteenth-century Santa Catalina has been little altered since it was built. Much of the base of the tower is apparently Almohad work, indicating that a mosque once stood here.

Exterior The Gothic portal faces the main road, Calle Juan de Mesa, providing the south entrance. It is not original to the church but was brought from Santa Lucía when that building was demolished in 1930 (commemorated by the plaque, right). Detailing of the figures is now hard to decipher.

Best seen from Plaza Ponce de León, on the east side, is the Mudéjar tower, very like a mini-Giralda. In fact, its castellation reproduces that of the Giralda's prior to the addition of its Baroque superstructure.

Apart from a much older base, the tower dates from *c.* 1350.

Facing Calle Santa Catalina, on the north side, an early eighteenth-century Baroque structure, richly carved, rises above the Sacrament Chapel of the church.

This is followed by the Calle Alhóndiga west façade, with its bulging apses evoking a rotund maiden aunt remembered from childhood.

Blind, lobed tracery, Mudéjar work, decorates the first two apses.

Brickwork rests on a base of ashlar stone.

A Classical column, including its capital, has been re-used as a buttress.

Interior　Immediately within the portal is an extraordinary horse-shoe arch, the only entrance of its type to a church in Seville.

Brick arches of the aisle's Gothic arcades are exposed.

The ceiling is Mudéjar work.

Above the arch of the first north bay hangs *The Baptism of Christ* by *Francisco García de la Vega*.

Facing down the north aisle is the extravagantly Baroque **Sacrament Chapel**, created in the first half of the eighteenth century by *Matías* and *Ambrosio de Figueroa*. Mass is generally held in this chapel on weekdays.

Sculptural embellishments are by *Benito de Hita y Castillo*, who was also responsible for work on the chapel's reredos.

As usual, the **sanctuary** is rib-vaulted.

The high altar's reredos was the work of *Diego López Bueno*, 1629, but the central figure of St Catherine, *c.* 1800, has been attributed to *Gijón*.

In the **Cristo de la Exaltación Chapel**, the most easterly on the south side, the reredos incorporates a figure of Christ by *Roldán*.

Its painted panel, *The Repentance of St Peter*, is by *Pedro de Campaña*.

Of particular interest is the bows and ribbons design of the panelled Mudéjar ceiling, *c.* 1400.

From the north side of the church follow Calle Sol, which forks north-eastward from Plaza de los Terceros.

Location 2 TERCEROS CONVENT
10 Calle Sol.
Church open Monday to Saturday 20.30, Sunday 11.30.

History　The convent was founded by a Franciscan order in the early seventeenth century. Building work progressed slowly, extending into the eighteenth century. The Brotherhood of the Last Supper now occupy the complex.

Exterior　Situated on the east side of the road, the convent's church precedes its extensive domestic buildings.

Some of the features of the early eighteenth-century portal are unique in Seville; it is possible that **Manuel Ramos**, a Portuguese friar, was responsible for its design, as the convent's staircase (not open) is known to be his work.

The overall Spanish Colonial appearance of the portal is emphasized by brickwork and terracotta decoration.

Interior   *Francisco Ribas* designed the high altar's reredos.

The **Holy Sacrament Chapel** is the work of the *Figueroa* family. Choir-stalls were made in 1630.

Calle Sol leads to Plaza San Román, a short distance away, with **San Román Church**, a Gothic/Mudéjar building, probably fourteenth century.

The eighteenth-century tower is of the common Seville type: a steeply-pitched, tiled roof surmounts an open belfry with twisted columns.

Both portals are Gothic, the main one flanked by brick Mudéjar windows; the other portal, facing Calle Sol, is blocked.

The aisled **nave** (*church open 18.30*) has a coffered Mudéjar ceiling.

From the *plaza*, Calle Enladrillada follows the north façade of the church. Second left, Calle Santa Paula.

Location 3 SANTA PAULA CONVENT
11 Calle Santa Paula.

Church, museum and shop open daily 09.30–13.00 and 16.30–19.00.

Admission free but donations welcome. Coins (25 pesetas) are needed to illuminate the interior.

A Seville rarity, this monastery still welcomes visitors to part of its domestic quarters, which have been converted to a public museum.

History   Ana de Santillán founded Santa Paula Convent in 1475, her sister Isabel Enríquez, wife of the Constable of Portugal, providing much of the finance. The church was completed *c.* 1485 in Gothic/Mudéjar style, but with some Renaissance decoration.

Exterior   A sixteenth-century brick entrance leads to the patio of the convent.

Ceramics depicting St Paula are nineteenth-century replacements of the originals.

The delicate spire of the church, rising above the white houses, has been dubbed the finest of its type in Andalusia.

From the patio, the magnificent portal to the church ahead is basically Gothic in form, while the brickwork is Mudéjar and the crestings and medallions are Renaissance.

The medallions were carved by *Lucas della Robbia* and *Pedro Millán*, whose identification appears in Gothic lettering in the second medallion from the right, which depicts St Cosme and St Damian.

Ceramics are sixteenth-century work by *Niculoso Pisano*.

Marble arms of the Catholic Monarchs on the tympanum commemorate the foundation of the convent in 1475.

The church may be entered only with the attendant, who, at the time of writing, spoke in a unique language, combining German, French, English and Spanish – often in one sentence.

Interior   The aisleless **nave's** early seventeenth-century roof is the work of *Diego López de Arenas*.

Occupying the west end is the **nuns' choir**, embellished with blue ceramic tiles.

Towards the east end of the north wall is a fifteenth-century crucifix.

This is followed by the *St John the Evangelist* reredos by *Alonso Cano*, 1638, decorated by Cano's friend *Juan del Castillo*.

The paintings are substitutes for the originals, which were taken back to France by the acquisitive Marshal Soult in the nineteenth century.

Montañés was responsible for the outstanding figure of John the Baptist (1637) in the central niche.

The arch to the **sanctuary**, and its rib vault, are Gothic.

Inset in the north wall is the ceramic-decorated tomb of Don Juan, Constable of Portugal.

The tombs of his wife Isabel and her sister Ana, founder of the church, lie on either side of the high altar.

All are late nineteenth-century copies of the originals by *Gestoso*.

Inset in the south wall, and serving as the model for the other tombs, is that of León Enríquez, brother of Isabel and Ana. Original sixteenth-century work, its ceramic decoration combines the arms of the Enríquez family and of Portugal.

The high altar's reredos, carved by *Fernando de Medinilla* in 1730, replaced an earlier work of 1592 by *Ocampo*; this has been lost, apart, perhaps, from its figure of St Paula, believed to be the one that is incorporated in the present reredos.

At upper level, the Virgin, angels and *Crowning of St Jerome* scene are mid-eighteenth-century additions.

Ceramics in the **sanctuary**, including the altar frontal, are by *Pisano*.

Facing the *St John the Evangelist* reredos is the *St John the Baptist* reredos, against the south wall, the work of *Felipe de Ribas*, 1637.

Montañés carved the figure of St John the Baptist in 1638; others are attributed to *José de Arce*.

The reredos that follows, dedicated to *Santo Cristo* (Holy Christ), was made by *Felipe de Ribas* in 1638, although its Crucifixion scene is a later addition. Finally, the *Virgin of the Rosary* reredos is by *Gaspar de Ribas*, 1642; its figure of the Virgin is mid-eighteenth-century.

Paintings are by *Francisco Cubrián*, a follower of *Zurbarán*.

The **sacristy**, not generally open, has a Mudéjar vault.

The convent's museum is approached from a small patio left of the exit from the church. Visitors will be accompanied by a nun.

Museum   The museum is divided into two halls.

Hall 1   Books, paintings and ornaments are displayed.

On the wall left is *St Jerome*, by *Ribera*, followed by *The Immaculate Conception* by *Matéo Cerezo*.

Hall 3 contains the treasures of greatest interest. Immediately left is a painted half-figure of the Virgin by *Pedro de Mena*.

The Adoration of the Shepherds is attributed to *Ribera*.

Also by *Pedro de Mena* is the *Ecce Homo* in the corner.

Windows provide views of the nuns' seventeenth-century arcaded cloister: all other examples in Seville's convents are hidden from public view.

At the far end of the entrance wall is a painting of St Michael, by *Caxés*. The Crucifixion scene immediately before the exit was painted by *Zurbarán*.

Confectionery and preserves made by the nuns are sold from a small shop facing the patio. Favourites include marmalade (from Seville oranges of course), bitter orange sweets and 'angel hair'.

Facing the patio's entrance, and commemorated by the usual plaque, is the house occupied by Isabella and her parents in *La Española Inglesa* by *Cervantes*.

On leaving the convent, right, Pasaje Mallol, first right, leads to Calle Moravia (the left fork) and Calle San Julián.

San Julián is a mid-fourteenth-century church with a simple, Gothic Mudéjar entrance. Lions' heads and canopied figures are now much faded.

The aisled nave has a coffered ceiling.

Ahead, Calle Madre Dolores Márquez leads to the unique Seville example of an important Moorish gate in the city wall.

The **Córdoba Gate** (Puerta de Córdoba), although much restored, some of it badly, with concrete, retains the original horseshoe arch.

The gateway earned its present name after the Moors had been defeated, from the road to Córdoba that led directly from it.

Proceed to **San Hermenegildo Church**, attached to the gate.

Built of brick, with a Baroque portal, the church occupies the site where, according to tradition, St Hermenegildo, a Visigothic king, was martyred.

On the other side of the Ronda de Capuchinos (unnecessary to cross the road) stands the **Capuchinos Chapel**, which gave the busy thoroughfare its name. According to tradition, the Virgin, dressed as a shepherdess, appeared here to Friar Isidoro in 1703.

The finest remnants of the wall are now passed by following the main road, Calle Muñoz León, in an anti-clockwise direction.

Location 4 CITY WALL

Roman Seville, covering a much smaller area than the present city, would certainly have been walled, but no structural remnants of that fortification have been identified with certainty. The Almoravids walled the city again *c.* 1112, and their enclosure was restored by the Almohads and later by the Christians.

At its zenith, the wall stretched 6,000 metres and was punctuated by 166 watchtowers. It was entered from twelve main gates and three minor or postern gates, the latter being grouped around the Alcázar. Towards the city centre, the wall lay well back from the river to allow for flooding. Most of the wall was demolished in the mid nineteenth century.

Part of the garden wall of the Alcázar, which was incorporated in its length, survives, and there is also a short stretch east of Calle Sol, but by far the most impressive section links Puerta de Córdoba with Puerta de la Macarena, following the line of Calle Muñoz León and its extension, Calle Andueza.

A path runs between the main wall and the outer wall, which originally served as a barbican; however, the fortification appears more impressive when viewed from the road.

The wall is approximately two metres thick and consists primarily of sun-dried bricks, lime and rubble. Seven square turrets are passed until, facing Calle San Juan de Rivera, the polygonal Torre Blanca (White Tower) is reached. This tower was first known as the Torre Blanca in the fifteenth century, presumably because its walls were then whitewashed. In the nineteenth century it was called Tía Tomasa.

Only the outer face is polygonal (to provide all-round external visibility); the rear is flat.

When open, the tower is entered from Calle Macarena, at the rear.

A circular passage encompasses the first floor.

Steps lead to the second floor and the roof turret. Ceilings follow the polygonal shape of the structure.

After this tower has been left, one more is passed before the wall ends at the **Puerta de la Macarena.**

The Macarena Gate is the only surviving example in Seville to retain its pre-Christian name, which commemorates a Moorish princess. The gateway's arch was originally the entrance to a fort, but then it was horseshoe-shaped. The present Baroque form was established during rebuilding in 1795, although much remodelling from the sixteenth century had already taken place by then.

On the north side of Calle Andueza, in Plaza de la Macarena, stands the Andalusian Parliament. It is the only location in Seville outside the ring road to be featured in this book, indicative of the compressed nature of the historic core of the city, all of which was built within the ancient wall that the ring road and the river now follow.

Location 5 ANDALUSIAN PARLIAMENT (PARLAMENTO DE ANDALUCÍA)
Former Hospital de la Sangre.
Plaza de la Macarena.
Public gallery open when Parliament is in session. Times for visits to be ascertained after comprehensive restoration has been completed.

Completely restored to provide a permanent seat for the Andalusian Parliament, this great Renaissance building, originally a hospital, provides one of Seville's most powerful façades. Of greatest interest internally is the church, now converted to Parliament House.

History Catalina de Ribera founded the Hospital de la Sangre (Hospital of the Blood), also known as the Hospital de las Cinco Llagas (Hospital of the Five Wounds), in 1500, obtaining a papal bull for the purpose. Her son Enríquez de Ribera, first Marquess of Tarifa, extended the hospital, originally sited in Calle de Santiago, and left sufficient money in his will for a much larger complex to be built elsewhere. The site chosen was the present one, and an architectural competition was held, administered by the monasteries of La Cartuja, San Jerónimo and San Isidoro. *Martín de Gaínza*'s scheme was chosen and work began in 1546. After the death of *de Gaínza*, work continued, led by *Hernán Ruiz the Younger*, who was aided, from 1570, by the Neapolitan *Benvenuto Tortello*. *Asensio Maeda* took over in 1572, completing the hospital in 1613, sixty-seven years after work had begun. The Infirmary, private until 1837, eventually became the Hospital Provincial. Gradually its buildings fell into disrepair, and they were closed in the 1960s.

Complete restoration, to provide the seat of the Andalusian Parliament, has taken place, most of the area now being earmarked for administrative offices.

Exterior The hospital was designed around courtyards divided by ranges that formed a central cross, a layout favoured in Spain by contemporary infirmaries, e.g. at Toledo.

The rusticated stone façade, forming the entire north side of Plaza de la Macarena, is regarded as one of the finest in the city; it is entirely the work of *Hernán Ruiz*, and typical of Seville Mannerism.

All windows are pedimented.

Doric pilasters at ground-floor level are surmounted by Ionic pilasters to the first floor.

The Baroque central portal, of white marble, is crested with the arms of the foundation.

Flanking the balustrade are the arms of Catalina de Ribera and her son Enríquez.

Follow Calle Don Fadrique, which skirts the west façade of the hospital.

Towers, evoking belfries, occupy each of the four corners.

The long side and rear walls match each other, with gargoyles, at roof level, providing a Gothic feature.

It is expected that the public will be admitted to the **debating chamber** from the *plaza* façade. This is accommodated in the former church, which stands in the centre of the main patio. It was designed by *Hernán Ruiz* in 1560 and provides a typical example of his work.

The Classical portal is of Portuguese rose jasper.

Juan Bautista Vázquez the Elder carved the tympanum's *Charity* medallion, together with *Faith* and *Hope*, from Genoese marble, in 1563.

It is not clear at the time of writing how much of the interior of the former church will be retained after its conversion. However, the high altar's severely Classical reredos is expected to be kept in situ, albeit covered during parliamentary sessions.

The aisleless building is Classical in style, but less austere than most contemporary examples in Seville.

Asensio Maeda designed the high altar's reredos in 1601, but it was made by **Diego López Bueno**. Sculptures from the sixteenth and seventeenth centuries are incorporated.

Paintings by **Alonso Vázquez** are considered to be some of his most important.

The Virgin of the Rosary, in the central niche, is Sevillian work from the second half of the sixteenth century.

Christ, the Virgin and the Apostles, a famous work by **Esteban Márquez**, a follower of **Murillo**, will probably also still be displayed within the building.

Returning to the Macarena Gate, a visit is now made to the adjoining basilica, of the same name.

Location 6 MACARENA BASILICA *Gomez Millán 1941–9 Calle Macarena.*
Open daily 08.00–13.00 and 17.00–21.00.
Museum open daily 09.30–12.30 and 17.30–19.30.
Admission charge.

The modern church itself is of no great interest, but is popular with visitors due to its outstanding reredos figures, primarily that of the Macarena Virgin, the most revered in Seville.

History Given minor basilica status by Pius XII, the church was built to provide a more imposing setting for the Macarena Virgin, which formerly stood in the adjoining church of San Gil.

The Seville Baroque style of the seventeenth century was adopted.

Interior A profusion of pink marble and murals give the basilica a sumptuous appearance.

North and south walls are each punctuated by two chapels.

In the second north chapel, the figure of *Christ under Sentence of Death* (*Jesús de la Sentencia*), now clad in an embroidered cloak, is by **Morales**, 1654.

Duque Cornejo is attributed with the **south-east chapel**'s *Virgin of the Rosary*.

The Macarena Virgin presides over the reredos of the high altar. Its full title is María Santísima de la Esperanza Macarena (Sanctified Mary of Hope); the sculptor is unknown, but the style is not dissimilar from that of *Roldán* or his daughter *La Roldana*.

Seville's most renowned bullfighter, Joselito, spent half his earnings on emeralds for the figure, but received scant gratitude from above as he was killed in the bullring in 1920, aged twenty-five; the statue was draped in black for a month. In spite of this tragedy it is still a tradition that bullfighters pray to the Macarena Virgin before entering the Maestranza bullring.

In 1937, General Queipo de Llano appointed the figure Captain-General of the Nationalist Forces. The Macarena Virgin has also been given the Medal of Honour.

Proceed to the museum, approached from the east end of the north aisle.

The **Museo Devocional y Artístico** (entry charge) displays the basilica's treasures, primarily costumes and jewels that decorate the Macarena Virgin.

The church of San Gil is linked with the Macarena basilica; however, it is more interesting to approach the building from Calle San Luis, which runs southward.

Location 7 SAN GIL
Calle San Luis.
Open for Mass 19.30.
Of greatest interest within the church are the timber Mudéjar roof of the nave and the rail and the early fourteenth-century tiles of the sanctuary.

History   The parish church of San Gil (Giles) was founded shortly after the Reconquest. Bishop Remondo dedicated the building towards the end of the thirteenth century, to record the name of the church in Segovia where he had been baptized. It is possible that San Gil, as has been suggested, occupies the site of a mosque, due to its proximity to the Macarena Gate; however, no evidence for this has been discovered. Most of the nave dates from the second half of the fourteenth century, but there are some thirteenth-century remains. Remodelling in the eighteenth and nineteenth centuries took away much of the Gothic/Mudéjar character of San Gil, and during the Civil War the building was damaged, some of its treasures being looted.

Exterior   Facing Calle San Luis, the octagonal apse and the tower represent the oldest parts of the structure to survive.

Only the lower sections of the tower, however, are Mudéjar.

The Baroque belfry was added in the eighteenth century.

The south doorway is simple Gothic work from the first half of the fourteenth century, but entirely reworked.

Interior   Gothic arcades of brick form the aisles, possibly additions to what was originally an aisleless church.

The timber Mudéjar roof of the **nave** is trussed, while that above the **transept** and **sanctuary** is a simple timber structure.

The sanctuary's rail was made in 1630.

Forming the sanctuary's dado, the glazed tiles are believed to be c. 1300, the oldest decorative feature of San Gil.

The former reredos of the high altar, which incorporated the Macarena Virgin, has been replaced by a *baldacchino* and a *Christ the Good Shepherd* figure, clothed in black.

In the **south-east chapel**, the *Virgin of the Rosary* reredos is attributed to *Cornejo*.

After leaving the church, follow Calle San Luis southward to Plaza Pumarejo. Occupying the entire north side of the square is **Edificio Pumarejo**, now a furniture store; it was formerly a Classical palace and its Doric doorway of stone is original.

Further south, lying back in a small *plaza*, is the church of **Santa Marina**. Since being virtually gutted by arsonists at the outbreak of the Civil War in 1936, the building has been closed, and even Seville's loot, acquired for the Expo '92 bonanza, seems unlikely to alter the situation here.

Santa Marina, founded shortly after the Reconquest, in the thirteenth century, was designed in Gothic/Mudéjar style.

According to tradition, a fugitive from justice who had hidden in the tower made a hole in its wall and discovered a *Pietà* (a figure of the Virgin supporting the dead Christ in her arms). The fugitive immediately requested the Virgin's protection, which, presumably, he received. Known as the Virgin of Mercy, she has been adopted as patron by the Brotherhood of the Sacred Shroud, now established in the former Convent de la Paz (page 216).

The fourteenth-century Mudéjar tower has a typically castellated roof.

Created *c.* 1300, the portal is probably the oldest feature of Santa Marina to survive.

The central figure, representing God, is flanked by those of the Virgin and saints.

The archivolts are entirely Gothic, apart from the Mudéjar star decoration on the outer band.

The north and south walls of the church both retain circular Mudéjar windows, some of the best examples in Seville.

Apparently the south-east chapel's Mudéjar lacework frieze survived the fire.

An equally sad case is the parish church of **San Luis de los Franceses**, a little further south, on the opposite side of Calle San Luis. It was built for worship by Jesuit novitiates, and *Lionel de Figueroa*, aided by others, was responsible for its construction, 1699–1723. San Luis is Seville's outstanding example of Chirrugueresque, a highly decorative Spanish elaboration of Baroque, and is the only circular church in the city. Its profusion of verdant growth is indicative of neglect, and in 1991 it was announced that San Luis would be abandoned. This brought forth a howl of protest from conservationists and it remains to be seen, at the time of writing, if a reprieve can be gained.

The stone and brickwork of the façade combine to give a polychromatic effect, particularly impressive at night (it is still floodlit).

Most important of all is the exuberant portal, matched in Seville only by that of the San Telmo Palace, also Chirrugueresque work.

Best observed from Calle Duque Cornejo is the Italian-style cupola.

Continuing southward, Calle San Luis is interrupted by Plaza San Marcos where, thankfully, the church is still in good order.

Location 8 SAN MARCOS
Plaza San Marcos.
Open daily 19.30.

This mid-fourteenth-century Gothic/Mudéjar church escaped Baroque embellishments and is, therefore, one of the least altered examples in Seville. The horseshoe arches of the aisles are very Islamic in appearance, a unique feature in the city.

Exterior   The Mudéjar tower, *c.* 1350, is built on the base of the minaret of a former mosque. Its design appears to have been influenced by the Giralda. Another untouched survival of San Marcos is its portal, the usual combination of pointed Gothic archivolts and Mudéjar decoration.

Lobed arches intertwine to form a frieze of rhomboids.

Lion corbels are in quite good order but the surrounding figures are very worn.

Interior   A Mudéjar feature, unique in Seville to San Marcos, is the rows of horseshoe arches that divide the **aisles** from the nave.

The timber ceiling was rebuilt in 1987.

Facing down the north aisle, the wooden figure of St Mark is attributed to *Juan de Mesa*.

South of Plaza San Marcos, the long Calle San Luis becomes Calle Bustos Tavera. Second right, Calle Doña María Coronel. First right, Calle Dueñas, leads to a small *plaza* where, at No. 5, stands the **Palacio de las Dueñas.** Almost equal in status to the House of Pilate, this fifteenth-century palace similarly combines Gothic, Mudéjar and Plateresque styles. However, a detailed description of its contents in a guidebook of this nature would be like sending a penniless child to a sweet shop: the public are never admitted. The Palacio de las Dueñas is the private residence of the Duke and

Duchess of Alba. One gleam of hope for those visiting Seville in 1992 is that the Duke has been appointed Seville's Expo supremo and might be persuaded to permit limited entry to sections of the palace – but this is conjecture.

An open gateway permits a glimpse of the fine gardens.

Returning, somewhat wistfully, to Calle Bustos Tavera, turn right.

The name of Calle Bustos Tavera commemorates the brother of the heroine of *La Estrella de Sevilla*, a legendary tale by the dramatist **Lope de Vega**, who sited the family house in this street; it had formerly accommodated the Inquisition's tribunal.

Adjoining No. 17, approached from its patio, is the former **La Paz Convent**, known as La Mortaja. This now accommodates the Hermanidad de la Sagrado Mortaja (Brotherhood of the Holy Shroud), and is open Sunday morning 08.30–11.30, when photography is permitted.

A plaque in the delightful patio recounts the tale of the fugitive in the tower of Santa Marina (see page 214).

Within, the *Pietà* forms the high altar's reredos. It is eighteenth-century work and was brought here from Santa Marina church.

At the far end of Calle Bustos Tavera, occupying the Calle Gerona/Calle Alhóndiga corner, is **El Rinconcillo**, Seville's oldest tavern. Founded in 1670, it will remind Londoners somewhat of Fleet Street's *Ye Olde Cheshire Cheese*, which predates it by just three years. Wood predominates, in spite of the ceramic tiles, and some of the beams appear to be original. There are two bars and a small area reserved for diners.

A slight drawback, at least for gentlemen, are the primitive toilets, only a small urinal being provided.

From the Calle Alhóndiga exit, turn right and proceed to Calle Juan de Mesa (buses 10, 11, 12, 20, 24, 32).

ITINERARY 8

SHOPPING STREETS, EL SALVADOR AND PALACE OF THE COUNTESS OF LEBRIJA

The great church of El Salvador, virtually a second cathedral, is one of many passed on this route. In contrast, the 'Capillita' San José, a Baroque jewel, is one of the tiniest religious buildings in the city. Both are close to Calle Sierpes, the most famous shopping street in Seville. This is situated between Calle Cuna and Calle Tetuán, the three parallel thoroughfares providing an unusually concentrated shopping centre for a major city. The Palace of the Countess of Lebrija is a fifteenth-century Mudéjar mansion, containing outstanding Roman work brought from Itálica.

Timing *If El Salvador is to be entered in the morning, an early start is necessary, as the great church closes 10.00–18.30.*

Calle Sierpes and Calle Cuna should be visited either in the morning or the evening: most of their shops close 13.30–16.30.

The Palace of the Countess of Lebrija is open Monday and Friday 17.00–19.00.

The Anunciación church opens at 12.00 and San Antonio Abad at 13.00.

The three last churches visited, San Martín, Omnium Sanctorum and San Juan de la Palma, open, respectively, at 20.00, 19.00 and 20.30. An evening return will therefore be necessary in order to go inside.

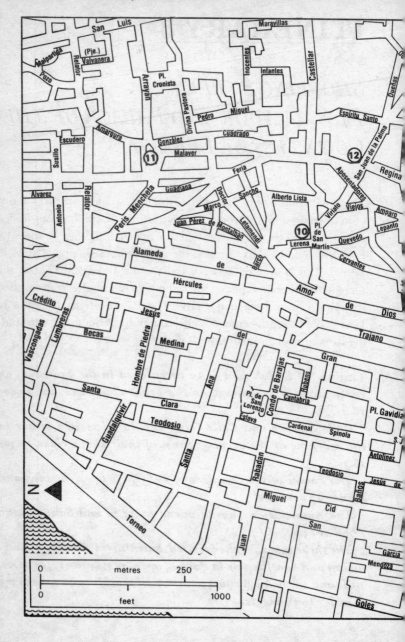

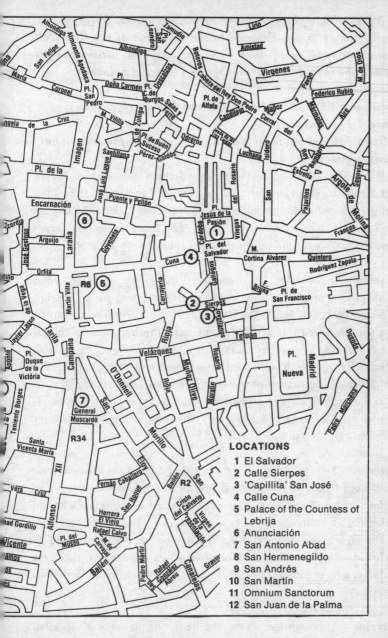

LOCATIONS

1 El Salvador
2 Calle Sierpes
3 'Capillita' San José
4 Calle Cuna
5 Palace of the Countess of Lebrija
6 Anunciación
7 San Antonio Abad
8 San Hermenegildo
9 San Andrés
10 San Martín
11 Omnium Sanctorum
12 San Juan de la Palma

START *Plaza Nueva (Buses 21, 22, 23, 25, 26, 30, 31, 33, 34, C3, C4, 40, 41 or 42). Proceed to the east side of the City Hall (Ayuntamiento) and follow Calle Bruna, from the north-east corner of Plaza de San Francisco to Plaza del Salvador.*

Location 1 EL SALVADOR *Esteban García 1674–1712*
Plaza del Salvador.

Open daily 08.00–10.00 and 18.30–21.00. Also for occasional evening concerts.

This vast Baroque church matches, in its dimensions, many important cathedrals. Incorporated around its patio are remnants of Seville's first great mosque. Outstanding reredos carvings include the famous *Jesus of the Passion* by **Montañés**, and *The Transfiguration* by **Cayetano de Acosta**, one of the most exuberant Baroque works in Seville.

History El Salvador (the Saviour) occupies the site of the first great mosque of Seville, built in the ninth century, during the reign of Abdul Rahman II. At the Reconquest the mosque was adapted to a church, but by 1671 the Islamic structure had become dilapidated and was demolished. **Esteban García** designed its replacement in Baroque style and construction began three years later. On the death of the master of works, **Francisco Gómez Septier**, in 1696, **Leonardo de Figueroa** took over and completed the building, which was consecrated in 1712. The mosque's patio and tower were incorporated in the church and have survived in part.

Exterior Due to the restricted opening hours of the church, only the Plaza del Salvador façade is described at this stage.

Built of brick and stone, the massive scale suggests a cathedral rather than a church.

This façade, of brick and stone, in dire need of weeding in 1991, is embellished with carving by **Juan Martínez Montañés**, the great sculptor, who is commemorated by the bronze monument facing the church.

Interior Although less severe, the design of the nave is modelled on that of Granada Cathedral, created by Siloé. *José Granados*, then master of works at Granada, suggested the scheme, and it was executed by *Francisco Gómez Septier*.

Fluted Corinthian pilasters cluster around the piers.

The **nave** is barrel-vaulted.

Pass, for the moment, the door to the patio.

The reredos featuring *St Anne Teaching the Virgin* is by *Montes de Oca*.

Set in the north transept's **Sagrario (Sacrament) Chapel** is the famous *Jesus of the Passion* figure, bearing a black cross, by *Montañés*, 1619. On occasions the figure is moved to the high altar.

Fire in 1902 destroyed the remainder of the reredos, and its silver frame is modern.

At the east end of the **north aisle**, immediately north of the sanctuary, the reredos incorporates a *Jesus of Nazareth* figure by *Gaspar de Ginés*, 1635.

A cupola roofs the **crossing**; like the vault of the nave, it is by *Figueroa*.

Generally difficult to appreciate, due to poor illumination, the vault of the **sanctuary** was painted by *Juan de Espinal*.

The high altar was made by *Reciente* in 1753.

A *Transfiguration*, by *Cayetano de Acosta*, 1779, dominates the high altar's reredos, its dramatically gesticulating figures creating one of Seville's most exuberant Baroque works.

Immediately right of the sanctuary, the reredos incorporates *Christ of Love (Cristo del Amor)*, carved by *Juan de Mesa* in 1620.

In the second south bay from the sanctuary, the *Virgin of the Waters* reredos, by *José Maestre*, 1724, incorporates thirteenth-century figures, though the child's head was replaced in the seventeenth century.

St Christopher Carrying Christ across the Water was carved by *Montañés* in 1619.

The last bay is occupied by the *St Justa and St Rufina* reredos, with figures by *Cornejo*, 1730.

Immediately left of the exit, the *Resurrection* relief, like its partner on the other side of the doorway, comes from the seventeenth-century reredos.

Within the north door's vestibule, immediately right, a stone tablet commemorates, in Cufic lettering, the foundation of the mosque. Within the patio, immediately ahead, is the **Chapel of the Homeless**, designed by *Antonio de Figueroa*.

Its vaults are elliptical and decorated with frescos.

The **patio** was formerly the ablutions courtyard of the mosque, and its brick arcades survive, their stunted columns surmounted by Roman and Visigothic capitals, re-used by the Moors.

The arches were remodelled in the seventeenth century.

Rising ahead is the tower of the church, described later.

A covered passage leads from the patio to Calle Córdoba, right.

The **tower**, more clearly observed from this street, was built as a minaret in the ninth century, when the mosque was founded. The upper part collapsed during an earthquake in 1079, the central section was destroyed later by another earthquake and was rebuilt in the fourteenth century. Only the lower stage, therefore, dates from the Muslim period.

Figueroa added the belfry early in the eighteenth century.

Shops nestle against the apse of El Salvador, facing Plaza Jesús de la Pasión, in a medieval manner.

No. 13C bears a plaque recording episodes in Cervantes's *Rinconete y Cortadillo* that were set in this *plaza*, then a butchers' quarter. Side streets, since renamed, once included Calle de la Caza (game) and Calle de la Gallinería (poultry).

Calle Villegas del Rosario passes the south façade of the church, and from the shop **Lirola**, on the south-east corner of the *plaza*, may be obtained one of the most picturesque viewpoints, particularly at night, when the great building is floodlit.

Continue clockwise to Calle Alvárez Quintero (this forms part of Plaza del Salvador).

No. 2, **Farmacia del Salvador**, boasts a fine collection of jars, displayed on nineteenth-century dressers.

Nuestra Señora de la Paz, facing El Salvador's main façade, was built in the seventeenth century. Its polychrome façade incorporates a Baroque centrepiece of stone above the portal.

Rare in Seville, twin towers flank the church.

Calle Gallegos runs westward from the *plaza* to Calle Sierpes, second right, Seville's most famous shopping street. Turn right.

Location 2 CALLE SIERPES

Calle Sierpes is now pedestrianized and devoted almost exclusively to shops, cafés and bars, with little surviving to reveal its historic past. However, it is not, like its sister streets Cuna, Tetuán and Velázquez, dominated by clothes boutiques.

(Many visitors will wish, at some time, to traverse the entire length of Calle Sierpes for window-shopping and purchasing souvenirs. Shops of particular interest, as passed from Plaza San Fernando are: No. 89, **Segundo Antiguedades**, antiques; No. 56, **Casa Rubio** and No. 69, **Diaz** – the two shops face each other and specialize in fans; No. 61, **Casa Damas**, guitars and records of Spanish music; No. 45, **Ochoa**, cakes and tearoom; No. 1, **La Campana**, Seville's most famous *patisserie* – with stand-up bar.)

Continue northward. **Ignacio Pérez**, No. 58, an antique shop, retains its wooden shop front from the nineteenth century.

Circulo Mercantil e Industria, No. 65, displays a wall plaque commemorating the Cárcel Real (Royal Prison) that formerly stood here. Cervantes was incarcerated in the prison for tax debts, and it is alleged that he began to write *Don Quixote* during his sojourn.

On the Calle Rioja corner, first left, **No. 1** is decorated with a large ceramic panel depicting the Greek god Hermes.

No. 3, adjoining, possesses noteworthy Gothic Revival balustrades at upper level – a whiff of Modernism from Barcelona.

Follow Calle Rioja westward, crossing Calle Tetuán, and continue to **Santo Angel**, an early seventeenth-century church. Its completion date, 1640, is proclaimed above the Baroque portal.

Within, the walls of the nave are tiled to dado level. Geometric plasterwork to the **aisles** and **chancel** has been crisply executed.

Return northward to **Calle Tetuán**, right.

No. 9 retains an extensive ceramic mural of 1924, promoting the latest Studebaker motor-car. One wonders if those commissioning this long-lived poster expected the model to remain in production for almost seventy years!

Calle Jovellanos, second left, leads to the exquisite 'Capillita'. Continue past its Baroque side door to the main entrance.

Location 3 'CAPILLITA' SAN JOSÉ c. 1690
Calle Jovellanos.
Open daily, morning and evening.

For concentrated Baroque exuberance, this 'Little Chapel of St Joseph' is hard to beat. A lack of natural light, combined with its renown, ensures that the building is always illuminated from within, and the gilding shimmers with almost blinding intensity. Not to be missed.

History   This was originally the chapel of a small hospital, founded by the Carpenters' Guild in the Middle Ages. Following dilapidation, it was all rebuilt in the late seventeenth century, but now only the chapel remains. *Pedro Romero* is attributed with its design, *Sancho Corbacho* continuing the work. The building was extended eastward by *Estebán Paredes*, 1747–66.

Enter the chapel either from the south door, facing Calle Jovellanos, or the main east door. The Baroque portal of the latter was made in 1766, completing the extension.

Interior   Unusually for Seville, the high altar is at the west end. Restricted natural light is provided by tiny clerestory windows, many now blocked.

Fittings date from 1766 and were made in conjunction with the extension.

At the east end, the Baroque organ stands in its **gallery**.

Late-seventeenth-century medallions in bas-relief decorate the south and north walls, depicting, respectively, *The Virgin as a Child with her Parents* and, opposite, *The Crowned Virgin with Christ*.

Gilded Baroque private pews survive at upper level.

A late seventeenth-century cupola with its lantern roofs the **crossing**.

Cayetano de Acosta is believed to have designed the high altar's eighteenth-century reredos, which covers the entire west wall.

Roldán and *Cornejo* are credited, without evidence, with the figures.

From the chapel proceed ahead, crossing Calle Sierpes, and follow Calle Gallegos to Plaza del Salvador, left. Calle Cuna leads from the north-west corner.

Location 4 CALLE CUNA

One of Seville's major shopping streets, Calle Cuna is rather more down-market than either Calle Sierpes or Calle Tetuán, which run parallel with it immediately to the west; the usual clothing stores predominate.

Azahares, No. 31, is outstanding for *flamenco* outfits.

No. 30, on the corner with Calle Cerrajería, first left, now the premises of **Ciudad de Lonores**, a linen store, was formerly a private palace, built in the nineteenth century. Its gleaming white Mudéjar-style, wedding-cake façade contrasts outrageously with its more sober neighbours.

Facing Calle Goyeneta, second right, is the undistinguished façade of No. 8, behind which lies one of Seville's loveliest palaces.

Location 5 PALACE OF THE COUNTESS OF LEBRIJA (PALACIO DE LA CONDESA DE LEBRIJA)
8 Calle Cuna.
Open Monday and Friday 17.00–19.00.
Admission free.
Built in the mid fifteenth century, this Mudéjar palace, with its second-century Roman features from Itálica, is missed by many visitors.

An austere street façade contrasts strongly with the sumptuous interior.

Vestibule The marble Roman flooring was discovered nearby at Itálica in 1914. It is the first of a series of outstanding Roman pavements, all of which came from the palace of the ancient city.

Above the staircase, the Mudéjar ceiling was brought from the palace of the dukes of Osuna at Marchena, prior to its demolition.

The tiled dado is eighteenth-century ceramic work, but the friezes date from the sixteenth century and were brought from the demolished convent of San Augustín.

The small patio ahead is the first of three patios seen, in addition to an internal garden.

Rooms are built around the central patio and may be viewed in varying order, depending on the guide. Iberian and Roman antiquities are displayed. Of particular interest are the following:

Sala de Medusa, named from the head of Medusa, portrayed in the mosaic floor.

Salón Octagonal. In its centre is a rare example of a Roman fountain (the spout, of course, is modern).

Sala de Ganimedes displays a winged figure in the centre of its mosaic floor.

Towards the end of Calle Cuna, at No. 6, a former palace, is the **San Marco** restaurant, one of Seville's finest (see page 312), its menu being international, rather than Italian as might be expected from the name.

Almost opposite, at **No. 3**, the delicate pink brickwork of the neo-Gothic building contrasts with its stone trim.

Calle Laraña, right, a busy thoroughfare, leads to **Plaza de la Encarnación**. Napoleon's occupying forces demolished the ancient complex that formed the Encarnación Convent in 1819, in order to create this *plaza*, the largest in central Seville. Like the equally bleak Plaza Nueva, the prime reason for Plaza de la Encarnación's existence appears to be its dual function of bus station (south side) and enclosed car-park (north side).

On the south corner with Calle Laraña stands the church of the Anunciación.

Location 6 ANUNCIACIÓN *Bartolomé Bustamante and Juan de Carvajal 1565–79*
Calle Laraña.
Open daily for Mass 12.00 and 20.00.

Of prime interest are the Italian Renaissance tombs of Pedro Enríquez and his wife Catalina de Ribera.

History The church was built 1565–79 for the Jesuit Compañía de Jesús. Designed by ***Bartolomé Bustamante***, assisted by ***Juan de***

Carvajal, both Jesuits, the building was consecrated in 1579. In 1771, Seville University moved into the convent's Community House, to the west, from their premises beside Puerta de Jerez, and the church eventually became attached to the University. The University transferred to the former Tobacco Factory in 1956 and the original convent's buildings were demolished, apart from the church, during the 1970s.

Exterior Built of brick, in Renaissance style, the main façade is attributed to *Bustamante*.

Its stone portal features a *Virgin and Child* medallion by *Juan Bautista Vázquez the Elder*, *c.* 1576.

Baroque eighteenth-century figures of St Joseph and St Raphael occupy flanking niches.

Interior Like other Jesuit churches, a Latin-cross plan is followed. Many paintings decorate the walls; all are early eighteenth-century works but of little artistic importance.

Set in the north wall of the **nave** is the marble tomb of Pedro Enríquez, Governor of Andalusia and first Marquess of Tarifa. It was for Enríquez that the earliest surviving parts of the House of Pilate were built. The Renaissance tomb was carved in 1520 by *Antonio María Aprile de Carona* in his Genoa studio; the sculptor's name is inscribed on the urn that surmounts the entablature, left. It is believed that Pedro himself commissioned the work, which stood in the family pantheon at La Cartuja until the nineteenth century.

A coffered dome roofs the **crossing**.

Although monumental, the early seventeenth-century reredos of the high altar, by *Alonso Matías*, has a clinical coldness, the whole being little more than a great frame for paintings.

Its central scene of *The Holy Family* is by *Juan de Roelas*.

Above this, the painting of *The Annunciation*, by *Antonio Mohedano*, is flanked by the two St Johns, early examples of the more naturalistic style adopted by the Seville School.

The *Immaculate Conception* reredos in the south transept is by *Juan Bautista Vázquez the Younger*, 1585.

Inset in the south wall of the nave is the tomb of Catalina de Ribera, matching in style that of her husband Enríquez, opposite. It was commissioned by their son Fadríquez from another Genoese, *Pace Gazzini*, and was also formerly sited at La Cartuja.

The figure of St John the Baptist in the seventeenth-century reredos, west of the tomb, was carved by *Montañés*.

Adjoining the church, immediately to its west, the **Facultad de Bellas Artes** of the University is entered, also from Calle Laraña. Request permission at the *conserjería*, immediately left, to visit the **Panteón de Sevillanos Illustres** (Pantheon of Illustrious Sevillanos). If convenient, a guide will escort visitors to this long crypt, which runs beneath the church of the Anunciación.

At the head of the steps the visitor will pass a door of the church which is dated 1568.

The crypt has been clad entirely in marble.

Renaissance tombs of the Enríquez-Ribera family, transferred from La Cartuja, lie together at the far end.

Against the wall of a side aisle are the resting places of the two Bécquer brothers, artist and poet.

Calle Laraña continues westward, where its name changes, in quick succession, to Calle Martín Villa and Calle Campaña. Lying directly to the north is Plaza Duque de la Victoria, once surrounded by palaces; its main feature now, however, is El Corte Inglés. This is the usual featureless monster that the great chain-store group has been permitted to inflict on so many important sites in Spanish cities.

An open market for clothes and leather goods is held in the *plaza* on weekdays, but there is little else of interest.

Calle Alfonso XII leads westward from the south side of Plaza del Duque de la Victoria, right. Just before Calle General Moscardó, first left, stands the church of San Antonio Abad.

Location 7 SAN ANTONIO ABAD
5 Calle Alfonso XII.
Open for Mass 13.00 and 20.00.

The exterior of the church is particularly impressive in the evenings, when the building is illuminated internally. Then, from outside the store opposite, no less than five arches standing in line are open, providing a Baroque effect of looking through a 'tunnel' to the wall of the south chapel.

History   Originally a hospital church, San Antonio Abad was built in the sixteenth century, but much remodelling took place in the eighteenth, including the addition of a south chapel.

Interior   The church is entered from its north door, via a small patio. At the east end of the **nave**, against the north and south walls, respectively, brackets support figures of the Virgin and St Joseph, by *Montañés*.

The **south chapel** was built by *Diego Antonio Díaz*, 1724–30, for the Nazarene Brotherhood, founded in 1582.

The tondo on the west wall, depicting *The Virgin with Christ and John the Baptist*, was made in Italy *c.* 1530.

Turn left when leaving the church.

Mesón Serranito, No. 9, is a popular *tapas* bar with a small street terrace entirely clad with ceramic tiles.

Calle Santa Vicenta María, first right, leads to Calle San Juan de Avila.

First right, Calle Teniente Borjes forms the south side of Plaza de la Concordia.

Location 8 SAN HERMENEGILDO
Plaza de la Concordia.

On the east side of the *plaza*, fronted by gardens, this former church serves, at the time of writing, as the seat of the Parlamento de Andalucía (Andalusian Parliament), pending completion of new accommodation in the former Hospital de la Sangre.

A white-painted Baroque building, San Hermenegildo was constructed in 1620 as the church of the Jesuit school, which had been founded in 1580.

Unusually elliptical in form, the crossing is roofed with a cupola which is visible only from within.

Exceptional stucco work by *Herrera the Elder* survives inside the church.

Facing the church, from the east side of the *plaza*, Calle Aponte, at the Calle Trajano junction, becomes Calle Javier Lasso de la Vega. Calle Angostillo, second left, leads to Calle Daoiz. The last two thoroughfares appear to have lost buildings that once separated them and now, therefore, form a *plaza*, as yet unnamed.

Location 9 SAN ANDRÉS
Calle Daoiz.
Closed for restoration in 1991.
Built in the mid fourteenth century, this is a typical Gothic/ Mudéjar example. Some remodelling took place in the fifteenth century and again in the eighteenth.

Exterior The archivolts of the portal have almost all been replaced, but the original Mudéjar stars and lions' heads survive.

Gothic figures are in excellent condition.

A plaque has been fixed, left of the portal, to commemorate the tricentenary of the burial, at San Andrés, of the painter **Juan de Valdés Leal** on 15 October 1690. It was given by the Bellas Artes Society.

From the *plaza* can be seen the Baroque belfry.

Interior Within the **sanctuary**, the eighteenth-century reredos of the high altar incorporates a figure of *The Immaculate Conception* by **Jerónimo Hernández**, 1520.

Another reredos in the church, with the same theme, was carved by **Delgado**. The late sixteenth-century paintings are by **Alonso Vázquez**.

Other paintings in the church by **Vázquez** include *St Sebastian* and *St Roque*.

The Virgin Appearing before St Bernard was painted by **Juan de Roelas**.

Valdés Leal, who lies in the church, is represented by a group of paintings on the theme of *The Mystery of the Rosary*.

The figure of *The Virgin of the Rosary* is attributed to **Roldán**.

The **south aisle** escaped the later remodelling.

From the *plaza*, Calle San Andrés, first right, skirts the north façade of the church. Calle Cervantes, first left, leads to Plaza de San Martín.

Location 10 SAN MARTÍN
Plaza de San Martín.
Open 20.00.

Another early church to have escaped Baroque embellishment; unusually, the bell of the campanile hangs from a horseshoe arch.

Exterior Built of brick early in the fifteenth century, San Martín retains its Mudéjar tower and belfry, with horseshoe arch.

A simple stone portal, in Gothic style, appears to be the oldest part of the building; it has been suggested that this was re-used from an earlier church.

Interior The north, **Sacrament Chapel** displays a Crucifixion scene; the figure of St John the Evangelist, right, is by *Roldán*.

On the north wall of the **sanctuary**, above the door, *Christ Bearing his Cross* was painted by *Lucas Valdés*.

Designed by *Vermondo Resta*, the high altar's reredos was made by *López Bueno* in 1606; unfortunate remodelling took place, however, in the eighteenth century.

Paintings of scenes from the life of St Martin, left, are the work of the Italian *Gerolamo Lucente de Correggio*, 1613. Sculptures are by *Andrés de Ocampo*, 1608.

On the south wall of the sanctuary, the late sixteenth-century reredos is by *Bautista Vázquez* and *Jerónimo Hernández*.

The Virgin of Hope, known as Divina Enfermera (Divine Nurse), a late sixteenth-century figure, looks down the south aisle.

From the church, exit right and follow, immediately right, Calle Lerena (ignoring, presumably, the blandishments of the ladies who patrol this quarter twenty-four hours a day). Second left, Calle Barco leads to the south end of the long Alameda de Hércules.

Laid out as a fashionable promenade by *Asensio de Maeda* in 1574, the **Alameda** (shaded public walk) **de Hércules** incorporated the Laguna de los Patos (duck pond).

Following its completion, two of the columns from the Temple of Hercules (page 176) were erected, side by side, at the south end, thus giving the promenade its name.

The statues of Hercules and Julius Caesar were carved by **Diego Pesquez** in 1574, specifically to surmount the columns. Now far from fashionable, the Alameda de Hércules is at present the centre of Seville's most run-down central area, much favoured by prostitutes. It is best avoided at night.

Continue to the north end of the promenade and follow Calle Peris Mencheta, right, which runs at an angle south-eastward to Calle Feria. Immediately ahead is the Omnium Sanctorum church.

Location 11 OMNIUM SANCTORUM
Calle Feria.
Open for Mass 19.00.

Some Mudéjar detailing remains, including a thirteenth-century portal, but the sixteenth-century Virgin sculpted by **Balduque** is the only figure within to have survived the 1936 arson.

History   Allegedly built on the site of a mosque, this church was founded in the thirteenth century, during the reign of Alfonso X, but was almost entirely rebuilt, in extended form, in 1356. Fire in 1936, at the outbreak of the Civil War, severely damaged the interior.

Exterior   The body of the church dates from the 1356 rebuilding, apart from the Gothic/Mudéjar south portal, facing Calle Malaver, which is all that survives of the thirteenth-century structure.

The west portal, facing Calle Feria, is Gothic, but the lobed window above is Mudéjar and is surrounded by ceramic tiles.

The bell tower, added in the fifteenth century, impersonates the decorative *sebka* brickwork of the Giralda.

Interior   Gothic arcades of painted brickwork form the aisles of the **nave**, which has a trussed timber roof with some Mudéjar detailing.

In the north-west corner, the base of the tower, with its plain Mudéjar vault, forms the baptistery.

Inset in the north wall, at its east end, are the medieval tombs of a man and a woman; both incorporate a reclining figure and a dog.

The **sanctuary** is rib-vaulted.

On the arch of the niche, left of the high altar, is delicate plaster 'knot' work, executed *c.* 1400.

The *baldacchino* is supported by twisted columns.

Incorporated in the high altar's reredos is *The Virgin of All the Saints*, by **Balduque**, 1554, the only figure to survive the 1936 arson.

Against the east wall, facing down the south aisle, the reredos features an emaciated *Cristo de la Buena Muerte* (Christ Dead on the Cross), by **Andrés de Ocampo**, 1592.

From the church, left, the long **Calle Feria** stretches southward.

Facing a small square, at No. 29 Calle Feria, is the **Capilla de Nuestra Señora del Rosario**. The original chapel was demolished in 1936 and rebuilt in 1952. Some re-used Baroque features survive within, but the chapel is rarely open.

Adjacent, at No. 25, the **Archivo de Protocolos** retains a Baroque portal.

Calle Feria is almost exactly the same length as Calle San Luis, which runs parallel with it, slightly to the east. Together, the thoroughfares provide twin 'high streets' for the western part of Seville, which lies within the area of the ancient wall. The area is basically working-class and this is reflected in Calle Feria's shops and *bodegas*, which retain a 'typical' authenticity.

A flea market is held at the south end every Thursday morning. It is of ancient standing – Cervantes refers to it in his *Rinconete y Cortadillo*.

Alimentación Santa Ana, No. 13, is an outstanding grocers' shop, specializing in *charcuterie* and very large and good value tins of seafood – including the delicious mussels in *escabeche* sauce.

Continue southward to the end of the street.

Location 12 SAN JUAN DE LA PALMA
Calle Feria.
   Open daily 20.30.

History   A Cufic inscription, now in the Archaeological Museum, confirms that San Juan was built on the site of a mosque. Nothing remains, however, of that building. Probably begun in the late fourteenth century, the detailing is typical of an early Sevillian Mudéjar church, although some remodelling has taken place since the sixteenth century.

Exterior   The body of the tower and the portal are Gothic/Mudéjar work from the early fifteenth century.

Although the figures that would have stood in the canopied niches have all been lost, the portal, with its crisp lions' heads, is in generally good condition and an outstanding example of its type.

The Baroque tiled belfry, added to the tower in 1788, was renovated in 1918.

Interior   Usually standing in the **Sacrament Chapel**, but sometimes moved to the high altar, the late seventeenth-century figure of *Christ before Herod* is from the workshop of **Roldán**.

Benito Hito del Castillo carved the reredos of the high altar in 1760.

Its figure of *The Virgin of Bitterness* (*de la Amargura*) is attributed to **La Roldana**.

Closing the south end of Calle Feria, at **No. 3**, is a dilapidated palace that retains a monumental carriage portal, surmounted by a crest. Approached through its arch are picturesque artisans' premises.

From the south side of the church, follow Calle San Juan de Palma eastward. The cream façade of the immense **Espíritu Santo Convent** stretches northward along Calle Espíritu Santo, first left.

A Baroque portal provides the entrance to the convent's seventeenth-century church which, although remodelled in the eighteenth century, retains its original fittings.

The long brick façade stretching along Calle San Juan de la Palma and its continuation, Calle de las Dueñas, marks the domestic quarters of the convent. From the junction of these streets, Calle Sor Angela de la Cruz leads southward to Calle Imagen (buses 10, 11, 12, 20, 24 or 30).

ITINERARY 9

TRIANA QUARTER

Home of the *flamenco*, the ancient centre of Triana, established on the west bank of the Guadalquivir in Roman times, is packed with interest, in spite of its relatively small size. *Tapas* bars, *flamenco* shows and historic churches proliferate. Triana's greatest appeal for most visitors, however, remains its picture-postcard views of the city from the riverside, currently the Seville 'teeny-bopper's' night spot centre.

Timing *Santa Ana and San Jacinto open in the evening at 19.00.*
  Nuestra Señora de la 'O' opens at 19.30.
  The Capilla de los Marineros is open 09.00–13.00 and 17.00–21.00.

LOCATIONS

1 River Guadalquivir
2 Los Remedios Quarter
3 Hispanic Cultural Institute
4 Triana Quarter
5 Calle Betis
6 Santa Ana
7 Capilla de los Marineros
8 San Jacinto
9 Nuestra Señora de la 'O'

START *Avenida de la Constitución: (Buses C3, C4, 21, 22, 23, 25, 26, 30, 31, 33, 34, 40, 41, 42). From the bus stop outside the Post Office building, proceed southward. Second right, Avenida General Sanjurjo leads to the San Telmo bridge and the river Guadalquivir*.

Location 1 RIVER GUADALQUIVIR

Iberia's most ancient (but possibly mythical) settlers, the Tartessians, are alleged to have lived on the banks of the Guadalquivir river, where it flowed through what is now Seville. During the Roman period, when nearby Itálica was a much more important city, the river was called Baetis. Seville eclipsed Itálica during the Visigothic occupation, but it was the Moors who gave the river its present name, *Wadi Kabir*, meaning big river in Arabic.

Seville's easy access to the Atlantic, via the Guadalquivir, led to its selection as the unique tax collection point for imports from the Americas, thus giving it a trading monopoly that proved to be a licence to print money. Unfortunately for the city, the river gradually silted up and navigation to its port became impossible for merchant shipping: the Admiralty moved to Cádiz in 1680 and Seville's monopoly ended when, in 1717, the Casa de Contratación was also transferred to Cádiz.

Until its demise, Seville's port operated from the city centre, but when it was reformed in 1928 the site chosen was much further downstream. The main course of the river was unchanged until 1948, but flooding in the wet season inspired the construction of a barrage and a diversion of its flow to the south of La Cartuja island. In 1991 the site of the barrage was moved, enabling boats to transport visitors from the Tower of Gold to the Expo '92 site, once more following the original course of the river.

Christopher Columbus, on his first voyage of discovery in 1492, did not set sail from the port of Seville. His ships, the *Santa María*, *Niña* and *Pinta*, were built forty miles away, at the small Atlantic port of Palos (now silted up) on a tributary below La Rábida monastery, where Columbus had stayed, and it was from here that his epic journey began.

The present **San Telmo bridge**, the first structure to cross the river at this point, was only the second of Seville's bridges and it was not built until 1928. Its construction and the intersecting thoroughfares were, of course, part of the infrastructure created for the exhibition of the following year.

Location 2 LOS REMEDIOS QUARTER
The San Telmo bridge leads immediately to the Los Remedios quarter, now the commercial centre of Seville. Its Avenida Republica Argentina, lined with office blocks, is the city's nearest approach to a modern, urban thoroughfare. At the west end of the Avenida lies Parque de los Príncipes, site of the annual *feria*. Apart from this, however, there is little to interest the visitor unless he is dining at one of the luxury-grade restaurants, established to service the business lunch trade. Facing the bridge is Plaza de Cuba.

Location 3 HISPANIC CULTURAL INSTITUTE (INSTITUTO ESTUDIOS HISPANICOS)
Plaza de Cuba.
Designed in Colonial style, with painted brickwork and stone trim, the Institute was built to coincide with the opening of the San Telmo bridge. Remodelling has taken place within to provide an information centre for Expo '92.

The building occupies part of the site of the dock from which **Fernando de Magallanes** (*Magellan*) set sail, with *Juan Sebastián Elcano*, on the first round-the-world voyage, 1519–22.

From the north-west corner of Plaza de Cuba, Calle Betis, in the Triana quarter, follows the riverside.

Location 4 TRIANA QUARTER
Triana adjoins Los Remedios to the north and retains a much more historic character. It was already established in Roman times as a separate town, called Trajana, to commemorate the Emperor Trajan, who was born at nearby Itálica. Even then it was renowned for ceramic work, and Seville's patron saints, Justa and Rufina, were, by tradition, female tile-makers from Triana, martyred for their Christian faith.

During the Muslim period, Triana was the Christian area and for most of its history it was also a quarter for seamen. One of them, Juan Rodríguez Bermejo, known as Rodrigo de Triana, was the first of Columbus's crew to sight the New World. A statue of a pointing sailor clinging to a mast commemorates the event. It bears the one word '*Tierra*' (land) but, strangely, does not name Rodrigo, possibly because he was born at Lepe in the adjoining province of Huelva, rather than in Triana. Designed by *J. Lemus* in 1973, the figure stands in Plaza de la Virgen Milagrosa (the *plaza* is situated nearby, towards the Avenida Republica Argentina end of Calle Pages del Corro).

Location 5 CALLE BETIS

Much of this street follows the original Triana dockland and was not built up until early in the nineteenth century. Baetis was the Roman name for the river Guadalquivir. Pretty houses, dressed in Seville's familiar white and ochre colour scheme, line much of the west side, and orange trees provide welcome shade in summer. Once Triana's 'high street', few shops now remain, their place being taken by *flamenco* shows, night-clubs and discos geared for the very young. The best general views of 'Old Seville' are still to be gained from Calle Betis, but while the Tower of Gold, the Giralda and the Maestranza bullring remain dominant, the recent additions to the river front of the uninspired **Previsión Española** and the domed **Teatro de la Maestranza** have had a detrimental effect.

Both structures, although harmless enough, are woefully inadequate as important elements in one of the world's finest urban vistas. Granted, they replaced little of great merit but here, surely, was a need for some recognition of Seville's architectural heritage to be made, possibly in a post-Modernist manner rather than 1929 pastiche. It is virtually certain that the Prince of Wales will visit Expo '92, and perhaps he will have a pioneering word in the ear of his close relative King Juan Carlos.

The splendid riverside terrace of the **Rio Grande** restaurant is hard to resist – for drinking in the view as much as a glass of sherry.

A plaque on the corner of Calle Troya, first left, records the proximity of the Monipodio Patio, featured by Cervantes as a rogues' meeting place in *Rinconete y Cortadillo*.

Santa Ana, an outstanding Seville church, is reached by following Calle Duarte, third left: ahead rises the east end of the church.

Location 6 SANTA ANA *1280*
Plaza de la Sacra Familia.
Open 19.00.

Santa Ana is virtually the 'cathedral' of Triana. Uniquely for Seville, it combines Romanesque and Gothic styles in a Transitional manner. Outstanding Plateresque work gives variety to the interior.

History Santa Ana, the oldest parish church in Seville, was built for Alfonso X, 1276–80. Internal similarities with Burgos Cathedral, completed in 1250, suggest that the same unknown architect may have been involved. Some remodelling occurred in the fourteenth and fifteenth centuries and, following damage by an earthquake, restoration took place in the eighteenth.

Exterior Ahead, at the east end, the formerly shallow, rounded apse of the sanctuary was extended in polygonal form in the fifteenth century.

Calle Vázquez de Leca skirts the north façade, where the Transitional portal combines a typical Romanesque dogtooth pattern with Mudéjar stars.

The usual lions' heads form the corbels at upper level.

At the west end of this façade, the tower was originally incorporated in the body of the church. Large stone slabs at its base are the oldest part of the structure.

Blocked Mudéjar lobed windows survive.

Forming the belfry, the two upper sections are Renaissance additions, *c.* 1625.

From Plaza de la Sacra Familia, the south face of the tower can be seen to retain a blocked, horseshoe-arched window.

Extensive damage following the Lisbon earthquake of 1755

necessitated the rebuilding of the west façade, facing the *plaza*. The Baroque portal, dated 1609, was re-used.

Facing Calle Bernardo Guerra, the south portal is simple Gothic work.

The church is usually entered from the north portal.

Interior Santa Ana's **nave** is significantly higher than its aisles, generally a northern European feature.

Romanesque clerestory windows provide the **aisles** with some natural light, which is filtered through to the nave by rather fussy apertures, also Romanesque, above the arcades.

Both aisles and the nave are rib-vaulted, the unusual long ridge ribs being a common feature in English Gothic churches.

The St Francis of Assisi reredos, against the west wall, looking up the north aisle, is Plateresque sixteenth-century work with some eighteenth-century additions.

In the manner of cathedrals, the **choir** is sited in the centre of the nave.

At its west end *trascoro*, the Virgin of the Rosary reredos is an early sixteenth-century work by *Alejo Fernández*. Combining Italian exuberance with northern severity, this is an important example of early work by the Seville School.

The east end of the **choir** is screened by splendid ironwork, incorporating an outstanding gate.

The choir stalls are plain, eighteenth-century examples.

Two Baroque organs face each other on the north and south sides.

The north door is Mudéjar.

A beautiful Plateresque arch leads to the **Sacrament Chapel**, which occupies the north wall's penultimate bay. The chapel was added in the mid sixteenth century and, like those of the south chapel that faces it, the pillars are of stone, rather than brick as elsewhere in the church.

Within, the Immaculate Conception reredos is believed to have come from the studio of *Luisa Roldán*; it is certainly late seventeenth- or early eighteenth-century work.

The two great bosses of the **sanctuary**'s vault are similar to examples in Burgos Cathedral and are the chief reason why the architect of Santa Ana is also believed to have worked there, albeit many years earlier.

The Plateresque reredos of the high altar, carved in 1542 by **Nufre de Ortega** and **Nicolás Jurati**, although virtually a great frame for paintings, is the most important in the church.

Within a niche, the outstanding figures of *St Anne and the Virgin* (heavily clothed) date from the second half of the thirteenth century, although restored in the seventeenth by **Ocampo**; the figure of the Child is modern.

Paintings, illustrating scenes from the lives of the Virgin, St Anne and St Joachim, are the work of several artists, including **Pedro de Campaña**.

Immediately right of the sanctuary, the seventeenth-century **baptistery**, facing down the south aisle, has a pentagonal vault.

The bowl of the font, made in 1499, is inscribed outside its rim with Gothic lettering.

From the church, return towards the river but turn left at Calle Pureza, an attractive street, with typical balconies, ceramic tiles and flower-pots.

Location 7 CAPILLA DE LOS MARINEROS, *1759–1815*
53 Calle Pureza.
Open 09.00–13.00 and 17.00–21.00.

This, the 'Sailors' Chapel', is now the headquarters of the Cofradía de Jesús de las Tres Caidas y Nuestra Señora de la Esperanza (Brotherhood of Jesus of the Three Falls and Our Lady of Hope), founded in the sixteenth century.

A simple Baroque façade fronts the street.

Within, a Mudéjar influence is still apparent in the timber roof.

The layout of the chapel is basic, with neither aisles nor a chancel.

An impressive Baroque reredos to the high altar, brought here from the convent at Osuna, incorporates a figure of the Virgin, known as the *Esperanza de Triana* (Hope of Triana). On Holy Thursday this is paraded through the streets of Seville.

From the chapel, continue northward to the main road, Calle San Jacinto, continuing to Plaza San Jacinto.

Location 8 SAN JACINTO *Matías de Figueroa 1740*
Calle San Jacinto.
Open 19.00.
Facing a small garden, the brick exterior is entered from a great Baroque portal of stone.

Interior The wide, aisled nave is well-proportioned and a serene ambience prevails; there are no side chapels.

Shallow **transepts** lead from the domed **crossing**, the spandrels of which are decorated with the most ornate plasterwork in the church.

The high altar's reredos is a typically Baroque gilded example, with twisted columns; the figure of St Jacinto is by *Raphael Agnes*.

A valued possession of the church is the *Simpecado* banner of the Virgin, which leads the annual pilgrimage to El Rocío, in the province of Huelva. Returning towards the river, Calle San Jorge, third left, is faced, ahead, with the remarkable glazed-tile shop-front of **Cerámica Santa Ana**, dating from 1870. As might be imagined, ceramics are sold, some of them still made in Triana.

Calle Castilla, a long street, leads westward following the river at first. The *castilla* referred to in the name is Triana Castle, which formerly occupied the open space.

At the commencement of the street, a narrow passage, **Callejón de la Inquisición**, runs down to the river. This name commemorates the fact that Triana Castle was once the headquarters of the Inquisition.

Location 9 NUESTRA SEÑORA DE LA 'O' *Felix and Pedro Romero Late seventeenth-century*
30 Calle Castilla.
Open 19.30.
A most attractive chapel-like church, with outstanding sculptures by *Cornejo* and *Roldán*.

Exterior Triana being a long-established centre for glazed-tile manufacture, it is appropriate that the tower of this church should be clad with ceramics.

Its belfry is exuberant Baroque work.

Interior The church resembles a short, wide chapel, although unlike most chapels it is aisled.

Pink marble forms the arcades, and delicate plaster flowers decorate the ceiling, providing an overall effect of great charm.

A small Baroque organ stands beside the entrance.

Mudéjar influence is apparent in the door.

Facing down the **north aisle**, adjacent to the sanctuary, the reredos of the chapel's altar incorporates a Virgin, carved by *Cornejo*.

The high altar's reredos is dominated by *The Virgin of the 'O'*, by *Castillo Lastrucci*, *c.* 1635.

In the chapel that looks down the south aisle, the sculptured group of *The Virgin with St Anne and St Joachim* was carved by **Roldán** in 1670.

Also by **Roldán**, in the south aisle's chapel, is the figure of Christ bearing his Cross; the figure is heavily clothed.

The chapel itself is decorated with local ceramics.

For Baroque enthusiasts who don't mind a dreary walk, at the far end of the long Calle Castilla is the virtually derelict **Patrocino Chapel**, built in the eighteenth century. In pastiche style, an adjacent modern chapel now houses its treasure, the *Cristo de la Expiración* (Dying Christ), a famous Baroque work of the Seville School carved by **Gijón** in 1682. The figure is also referred to as the '*Cachorro*', Spanish for puppy, in this case commemorating the nickname of a gypsy who served as Gijón's model.

The visitor should now return to Calle Betis, approaching its northern extremity from the Triana side of the Isabel II bridge. The great attraction, nestling against the bridge, is **El Kiosko de las Flores**, the ultimate fried fish establishment in Seville. Only the finest olive oil is used and (but only at the bar) half portions are sold, which are perfectly adequate for one person and amazingly cheap. At the tables (in summer on the riverside terrace), only full portions may be ordered. This Seville favourite, closed Monday, should not be missed.

The **Isabel II bridge (Puente de Isabel II)**, designed by *Gustave Eiffel* (of the Eiffel Tower), was inaugurated in 1852. It replaced one of many structures, formerly known simply as the Triana bridge, that had linked Seville and Triana at this point for centuries. The city's second central bridge, San Telmo, as has been noted, was not built until 1928. A multitude of new structures now span the water between Seville and La Cartuja island – some of them most innovative and very beautiful, all built for Expo '92.

Buses C1 and 43 cross the Isabel II bridge directly to central Seville. Bus C2, in the other direction, returns to central Seville via Triana.

EXCURSIONS FROM SEVILLE

GRANADA

Granada, in particular the Moorish palaces that constitute the world-famous Alhambra, has always been the top excursion venue for Costa del Sol holiday-makers, but the long and tiring route from Seville necessitated an overnight stay. Now, with the new highway, completed in 1990, motorists can make the 160-mile journey in less than three hours. Nevertheless, a day trip does not enable the visitor to view adequately any more than the Alhambra and the Royal Chapel the Ferdinand and Isabella. To see Granada Cathedral and the picturesque Albaicín and Sacromonte quarters, together with the numerous Renaissance, Baroque and Mudéjar churches, necessitates an overnight stay or a return journey.

When the Moors were expelled from Granada in 1492, Seville was compared to it, unflatteringly, as a 'straw hut'. The same does not apply today, as most of Granada's picturesque lower city was swept away in the nineteenth century, only selected buildings of note being preserved. Seville's overall colour and charm is not repeated and, apart from the pulsatingly hot summer months, Andulusia's capital is a more appealing city in which to stay for any length of time.

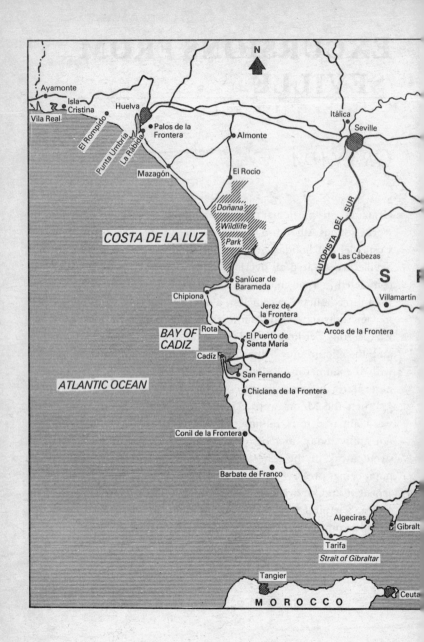

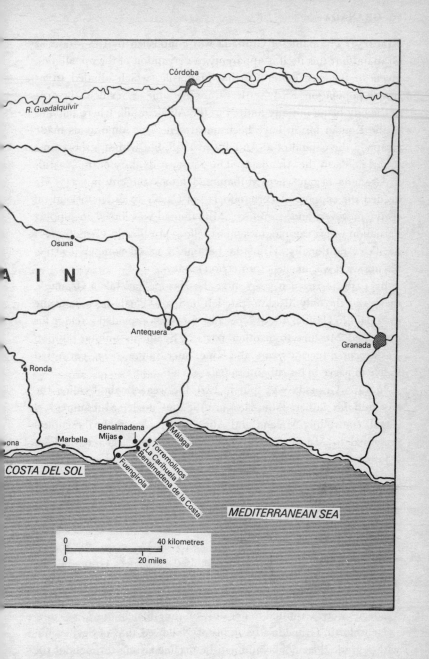

Córdoba

R. Guadalquivir

Osuna

A I N

Antequera

Granada

Ronda

Benalmadena
Mijas

Marbella

Málaga

Torremolinos
La Carihuela
Benalmadena de la Costa

ona

COSTA DEL SOL

Fuengirola

MEDITERRANEAN SEA

0	40 kilometres
0	20 miles

History   The name of Granada was established by the Moors as Granata, but this itself is apparently a corruption of the appellation given to the city under Carthaginian rule, which alluded to its Jewish population. Early settlers were the same as Seville's, the area of the city being initially limited to the Albaicín hill, where remains of the Roman forum have been unearthed. The Almoravids made Granada the capital of al-Andalus in 1148, but within a short time it had fallen to the Almohads. The 250-year dynasty of the Nasrids in Granada began when Muhammad I took the city in 1237. He needed the support of Fernando III of Castile in order to fend off rivals, however, and, in return, Muhammad was forced to support Fernando in his campaigns against fellow-Muslims in Córdoba and Seville. Additionally, Granada became a vassal state of Castile, paying what was in effect 'protection money'.

By 1248, just eleven years after the Nasrids had taken Granada, theirs was the only Muslim state left in Spain. Partly because of the dues paid to Castile, but also because Granada provided a refuge for unwanted Muslims from other parts of Spain, its unique position was accepted for 250 years, the King, later Sultan, being permitted to live in peace in his Alhambra palace.

In 1482 Granada was split in two, the weak Boabdil ruling the city and his father, Abu Hassan Ali, and uncle, Muhammad el Zagal, controlling Málaga and Almería. By 1490, only the capital remained in Muslim hands, but it was under siege and fell on 2 January 1492 without offering resistance. Ferdinand and Isabella granted Boabdil an estate in the Alpujarra mountains and he is alleged to have wept as he gazed on his beloved city for the last time, earning the unsympathetic comment from his mother: 'You do well to weep like a woman for what you could not defend as a man.'

The Catholic Monarchs had promised to respect Granada's Islamic religion, but their word was not kept. Eighty thousand books in Arabic were burned, mosques were converted to churches and the Mudéjars were permitted to live only on the Albaicín hill.

Henceforth, Granada's basic history followed that of Seville, but with a gradual economic and artistic decline lasting throughout the sixteenth century. Granada's Golden Age, in the seventeenth century, focused on the Baroque style, and some of the most splendid churches in Spain were built there at this time, those of La Cartuja monastery and San Juan de Dios hospital being particularly outstanding.

The occupancy of Granada by Napoleon's troops in 1810 caused a great deal of damage, particularly within the Alhambra, where there was a garrison, but Wellington liberated the city in September 1812. Praiseworthy restoration of the Alhambra and other Moorish remnants in the nineteenth century, encouraged by the Romantic movement, was counterbalanced by the covering of the Darro river, the destruction of the ancient city wall and gates, and the laying out of the dreary Gran Vía de Colón, for which many important structures were demolished.

The low-lying centre of Granada is basically modern, although interspersed with historic buildings, particularly churches. North of the Gran Vía de Colón, the adjoining hillside areas of Albaicín and Sacromonte, with its famous gypsy caves, were fortunately spared and provide the most attractive, albeit tiring, areas of the city in which to stroll. Palm trees, cobbled streets and whitewashed houses and churches retain the atmosphere of Moorish Granada and the views, of course, are stupendous.

THE ALHAMBRA
Open daily, summer 09.30–19.45, winter 09.30–17.15.
Admission charge.

Undoubtedly one of the great architectural wonders of the world, visitors to Seville should make every attempt to arrange an excursion to this magical complex of palaces, set against the permanently snow-capped peaks of the Sierra Nevada's highest mountains. If Seville's Alcázar has impressed, then the Alhambra will be a knockout!

As with all major 'sights', the greatest mitigation of a tourist's enjoyment is a surfeit of other tourists, and the Alhambra, for all its size, can be overrun at peak times. I was fortunate to make my last visit early in January, when, in spite of a warm day, there were few visitors; but winters in Granada can be icy cold and not everyone will be willing to take that risk. During 'the season', it may be

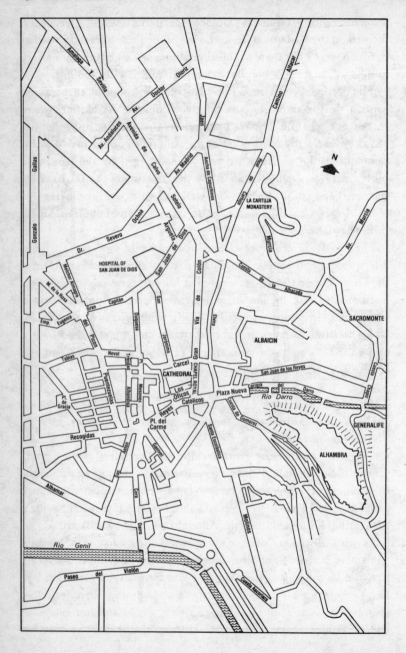

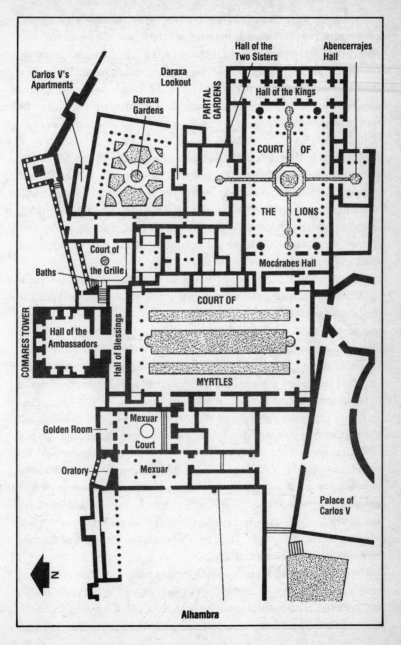

Carlos V's
Apartments

Daraxa
Gardens

Daraxa
Lookout

Hall of the
Two Sisters

Abencerrajes
Hall

PARTAL GARDENS

Hall of the Kings

COURT   OF

THE   LIONS

Court of
the Grille

Baths

Mocárabes Hall

COMARES TOWER

Hall of the
Ambassadors

Hall of Blessings

COURT OF

MYRTLES

Golden Room

Mexuar
Court

Oratory

Mexuar

Palace of
Carlos V

N

Alhambra

preferable to visit the constituent parts of the complex in reverse order, arriving early and making straight for the gardens and Generalife. The two museums within the Carlos V Palace are rarely crowded, and they might be seen next on returning to the palace area. During the lunch period, most of the coach parties will have been transported to a restaurant and the famous patios will then be less congested.

History The Islamic, and most important, parts of the Alhambra were all built during the 250-year rule of Granada by the Nasrid dynasty, 1237–1492. Work was begun by Muhammad I, who transferred his court here from an existing palace, set on the Albaicín hill on the opposite side of the Darro river. The advantage of the new site was its superior defensive position, most of the steep escarpment being impossible for attackers to scale.

A fortress had stood nearby from time immemorial, and the existing Vermilion Towers are said to date from the Roman or even the Phoenician occupation. The name 'Alhambra' derives from a corruption of *al Qual'ah al-Hamra* (the Red Fort), the name given to the fortress in the ninth century because of the red bricks from which it was built. This appellation was revived when, it is said, Muhammad I insisted that work on building the Alhambra continued during the night, illuminated by the red glow of torches.

One of the great surprises of the Alhambra is that it exists at all. It was customary throughout Islam, due partly to superstition, partly to vanity, for a new ruler to completely destroy the palace of his predecessor, Seville's Alcázar being a good example of this. Various reasons have been suggested why successive Nasrid rulers preferred remodelling the exteriors to wholesale demolition: the hillside area was restricted, potentially hostile Christian kingdoms prevented a move to a less defensible site and there was a shortage of finance throughout the fifteenth century.

After Muhammad I, the most important builders at the Alhambra were Yusuf I (1333–54) and his son, Muhammad V (1354–91), who was restored to the throne with the aid of the Christian Pedro I. None of them, however, seem to have expected their palaces to last, the flimsiest products – plaster, timber and tiles – being employed as facing materials. Stone was reserved for mosques and colleges, which were built to withstand the ravages of time.

Fortunately for posterity, the Moors had developed a plaster of exceptional strength, lacking the usual characteristic of brittleness; this set like stone and could be carved in a similar way. Virtually all the filigree carving within the Alhambra is in plaster or wood, most of it original.

Ceramic tiles within the palaces are less authentic, most having been replaced by modern copies.

Although surrounded by Christian states for virtually their entire existence, the Nasrids upheld traditional Muslim architectural conservatism, the Gothic style passing them by as though it had never existed.

Apart from decorative themes, Arabic calligraphy in particular, Islamic palaces differed fundamentally from their Christian counterparts: there are no defined axes, rooms are built around open patios, single-storey pavilions with high ceilings are preferred to multi-storey structures, columns are slender, possibly in imitation of tent poles, and water, a rare desert commodity, is displayed with abandon in pools, cascades and fountains. When Boabdil surrendered to the Catholic Monarchs in 1492, the Alhambra remained intact; it had fallen to the threat of force, not through bombardment.

Surprisingly, the ascetic Ferdinand and Isabella, fervently Roman Catholic to the point of mania, seemed to be content to live in the demonstrably Islamic palaces, making the minimum of changes. As might be expected, it was the iconoclastic Emperor Carlos V who did most damage, dumping his heavy Renaissance palace beside the delicate Courtyard of the Lions.

Spanish monarchs continued to stay at the Alhambra until the eighteenth century, Philip V being, briefly, its last royal occupant. Henceforth decline set in, and the Alhambra narrowly escaped demolition in 1812, when Napoleon's garrison, retreating from Granada, blew up some of the defensive wall and towers. Apparently, gunpowder had been ignited that would have blown the whole complex sky-high, but a Spanish corporal bravely extinguished the fuse.

Decay was halted when the Romantic movement, inspired by Victor Hugo, Alexander Dumas and Washington Irving, led to its rehabilitation; in 1870 it was declared a national monument.

Miraculously, the Alhambra has survived, virtually intact, as the supreme example of Islamic architecture in Spain. Although built towards the end of the 800 years of Muslim rule it appears to summarize the entire period, combining strength, radiance and melancholy. One can still echo the words of Carlos V: 'Ill-fated the man who lost all this.'

Access The most convenient approach to the Alhambra for the majority of visitors is from Plaza Nueva, a long, rectangular square created over the Darro river, which now flows beneath it. From the south of this *plaza* the Cuesta de Gomerez winds uphill. It should be remembered that the area in the vicinity of the Alhambra was originally kept clear of high trees, as these would have provided cover for attackers. Instead, aromatic shrubs covered the slopes. Most of these had disappeared by the early nineteenth century, and the terrain was bare. Surprisingly, it was the Duke of Wellington who arranged for elm trees to be shipped from England.

The entrance to the Alhambra grounds is marked by the **Puerta de las Granadas** (Gateway of the Granadas), a Renaissance structure displaying the arms of Carlos V and erected in 1536 to replace the Moorish original.

Immediately right, perched on a high spur, are the **Bermejas Towers**, dating from 1240, the Alhambra's oldest fortification. The structure replaced several predecessors: a watchtower is believed to have stood at this point even before the Moors arrived.

The road continues, but it is pleasanter to follow the upper path. Passed on the left is a fountain, the **Pilar de Carlos V**, made by *Nicolao de Corte* in 1545.

Ascend the steps that follow, turn left and proceed to the **Puerta de la Justicia** (Gateway of Justice), which marks the entrance to the palaces. Built in 1348 by Sultan Yusuf, it was here that judgements were made to settle petty grievances.

The open hand of Fatima on the keystone of the arch represents the five requirements of the Islamic faith. A key above the inner archway is a reference to the Prophet Muhammad's power to unlock the gates of paradise. The door, including its fittings, is original. A dog-leg turn up a ramp provides the usual form of entrance to a Moorish palace, preventing as it does a straightforward surge by attackers.

Tickets are purchased from the office, approached by steps, right. To the left of the ticket office stands the **Puerta del Vino** (Wine Gateway), its name indicating that this once served as the Alhambra's wine cellar. Although there are references to Muhammad V, the gateway is an earlier structure.

A plaque beside it commemorates the French composer Claude Debussy who, although he never visited the Alhambra, wrote a piano piece dedicated to the gateway, based on a postcard he received. Beyond the Puerta del Vino, the now open **Plaza de los Aljibes** (Square of the Cisterns) was originally filled with additional gateways and fortifications. These were cleared in 1494 for the construction of two rainwater cisterns, in case the aqueduct was severed in time of siege: both are now covered.

Overlooking the south-east side of the *plaza* is the Renaissance palace of Carlos V, to be described later.

Ahead lies the Alcazaba fortress, which occupies the western plateau of the site, formerly accommodating its military establishment. The present fortress, built in the mid thirteenth century, is surrounded by great walls and towers, but only basements survive of the barracks that once stood within.

At the far end, steps lead up to the delightful **Jardín de los Adarves**, laid out in the seventeenth century; its flowers and bushes are renowned for their scent, the backdrop of snowy mountains adding drama to the scene. The short **Torre de la Polvera**, right, is inscribed with the famous words of Izaca: 'There is nothing so terrible in life as to be blind in Granada.'

Steps, left, descend to the **Torre de la Vela**, which provides the finest views from the Alhambra of the city and the Sierra Nevada. The tower's great bell, installed by the Catholic Monarchs, once served as an 'alarm clock', its chimes notifying the farmers below that it was time to water their crops.

Arrows guide the visitor to the **Puerta de las Armas**, originally the Alhambra's main entrance. It has the same twisted passageway as the Puerta de la Justicia, and for the same defensive reasons.

Signs indicate the **Palacios Nazaries** (Nasrid Palaces), the most important section of the Alhambra. They occupy the central, higher plateau of the hill on which the complex is built.

As in all Nasrid palaces, legal and official matters of importance were dealt with in the **Mexuar**. Constructed for Ismael I, the present building was remodelled by Muhammad V. The hall was converted to a chapel by Philip V in 1629, and motifs of the Christian kings now merge with the Nasrid décor in a confusing but endearing way.

Extending from the end of the hall is a richly-decorated **oratory**, with its Mecca-facing *mihrab* (Muslim prayer niche).

On the east side of the hall, the **Patio del Mexuar** was created by Philip V in conjunction with the Mexuar's conversion to a chapel.

To its north stands the **Cuarto Dorado** (Golden Room) where the Christian governors of the Alhambra lived. Its ceiling was made for the Catholic Monarchs.

After his marriage, Carlos V occupied the apartments on the east side.

Facing the Cuarto Dorado is the façade that fronts Yusuf I's **Colmares Palace**. It was built by his son Muhammad V and apparently served as the inspiration for the façade of Pedro's palace at the Alcázar in Seville. This is one of the most important structures within the Alhambra, the carved eaves being exceptional.

In the centre of the Patio del Mexuar, the fountain's basin is a modern replacement, the original being transferred to the Daraxa gardens in 1945.

A passage leads eastward to the official section of the palace, where important visitors were received.

The **Patio de los Arrayanes** (Court of Myrtles) gains its name from the hedges of myrtle on two sides of the long fish pond that takes up most of the area.

On its north side rises the castellated **Torre de Comares**, the highest watchtower in the defensive wall of the Alhambra. This was incorporated into the Comares Palace of Yusuf I but predates it. The origin of the name Comares is disputed: it may refer to builders from the nearby town of Comares, or to the Spanish word for Moorish stained-glass windows, *comarías*.

Fronting this tower is a portico with an extraordinary arcade, the columns of which appear far too delicate to support their load.

The portico leads to the **Sala de la Barca**, *barca* being a corruption of the Arabic for 'divine blessing'. The cupola ceiling of cedar is a splendid reproduction of the original, destroyed by fire in 1890.

This rectangular hall served as an antechamber to the **Salón de Embajadores** (Ambassadors' Hall), which is approached from its north side. There, as the name indicates, foreign ambassadors were received; these would, of course, have included representatives from the other Spanish kingdoms, all of which were Christian by the time the hall was built. Created within the existing Torre de Comares, no other room in the palace surpasses its extravagant decoration, plasterwork being painted in well-preserved primary colours, which the Moors believed to have mystical connotations. The cupola ceiling, although high, is well lit from large, deeply recessed windows.

In the central recess, facing the entrance, stood the royal throne.

Return to the Court of Myrtles and proceed clockwise. Ahead, a similar portico on the south side originally fronted apartments that were demolished for the construction of Carlos V's palace. Before this is reached, a doorway, left, on the east side, conducts the visitor to the private area of the palace, to which few were invited.

This section is known as the *harem*, which indicates domesticity, not sexual depravity as much western literature suggests.

Immediately entered is the **Mocarabes Hall**, its name referring to the original cupola, which was replaced by the present Baroque ceiling.

Ahead lies the Alhambra's most famous courtyard.

Patio de los Leones (Court of the Lions) Although relatively small, the Court of the Lions, built by Muhammad V, is regarded as one of the world's most sublime architectural feats. Here is demonstrated the synthesis of Moorish artistic genius, combining sky, light, water and intricate carving, each element being given equal status and density.

Faced with such magic, detailed analysis seems almost indecent. Suffice it to point out that the capitals to each column differ in design and that, because they depict life, the lions supporting the alabaster basin of the fountain that gives the patio its name are believed to have been added by Christians. These lions have a rather despondent mien, and as Théophile Gautier remarked in 1842, don't really look like lions at all.

Observers may have noted that west Muslim art, like Jewish art, is normally non-representational, depending on abstract or stylized patterns and calligraphy. The Koran does not expressly forbid the depiction of living forms, but the traditional view has been that as only Allah can create life, it is wrong to impersonate his work. A wish to preclude any form of idolatry may also have had an initial influence, bearing in mind that Islam evolved in a pagan region.

Proceeding anti-clockwise, the **Sala de los Abencerrajes** is lit from sixteen windows. According to tradition, it was here that the last ruler of Granada, Boabdil, executed members of the Abencerrajes family as they entered. He had learned that their leader had been intimate with his consort. As might be expected, the brown marks on the fountain's bowl are said to be the bloodstains from their severed heads, which were thrown into it.

The outstanding domed ceiling is original.

Approached from the east end of the courtyard is the **Sala de los Reyes** (Hall of the Kings), subdivided into three rooms. The 'Kings' referred to are painted on leather, fixed to the cupolas of the rear alcoves. They may represent the early Nasrid rulers, but this is uncertain, indeed their very existence here is a mystery. Moorish antipathy to depicting lifelike forms has already been referred to, and the artists were almost certainly Christians. Experts have confirmed that the paintings are fourteenth-century and betray an Italian influence.

Many consider that the **Sala de las Dos Hermanas** (Hall of the Two Sisters) is the most beautiful room in the Alhambra: its stalactite ceiling is certainly peerless. The name refers to the two white marble slabs set in the pavement. It is a large hall, and records confirm that it was set aside for the sultana and her attendants, which may account for the incredible sumptuousness of the décor. Originally, when the Arabic lettering that decorates the walls was outlined in gold and the paintwork fresh, the effect would have been even more overwhelming.

Some have judged the calligraphy, the text of poems by *ibn Zamrak*, to be the best cursive Arabic in existence. Other texts within the Alhambra include verses from the Koran, religious homilies and more poems, generally praising the Nasrid rulers and the architects of the palace.

Lying behind this hall is the **Sala de los Ajimeces**, with similar décor. Its name refers to the windows, divided by a mullion or mullions, and known as *ajimez*; the type was probably developed by the Visigoths long before the Moorish invasions.

These windows look out from a central niche over the Daraxa gardens but, before the obstructing Palace of Carlos V was built, views also encompassed the surrounding hills.

A passage leads to a small courtyard, from where the **baños** (baths) may be entered; however, there is nothing of great interest to see.

Gardens of the Alhambra A gentle slope forms the eastern section of the hill. Only two ruined houses and a small mosque now remain of the royal city that once stood here; this is known to have included shops, baths, a university and a great mosque.

Muhammad III built the great Alhambra mosque on this slope in 1308, and it was while at prayer within that Sultan Yusuf was assassinated in 1354. Remarkably, its main building, which evidently possessed an exquisite interior, survived the occupancy of the Christian Monarchs and Carlos V virtually unscathed, but Napoleon's troops demolished it in 1812.

Most of the area covered by the lost city is now laid out as gardens, all dating from the Christian era; the Moors had preferred small patios and views of open country to extensive gardens. Two of the most important gardens, the **Daraxa** and the **Partal**, adjoin the north-west section of the palaces complex. The latter includes a portico (*partal*), all that survives from a lost palace.

Signs lead visitors to the Generalife summer palace, which is a fifteen- to twenty-minute walk away, lying north-east of the Alhambra on its own hill.

Many of the Alhambra's twenty-two watchtowers will be passed *en route*, all of them now possessing Spanish names, and a complete tour of the ramparts may be made. Much destruction was caused by Napoleon's retreating troops who blew up part of the defences.

Near the Puerta de la Justicia, a seventeenth-century brick tower, formerly the **San Francisco Convent**, has been converted to a *parador*: accommodation must be booked well in advance.

The Generalife   Sited somewhat higher than the Alhambra, the palace of the Generalife became a royal residence during the summer months. It is now the venue for the annual International Festival of Music and Dance.

The route followed from the Alhambra is a delight, passing, as it does, a series of gardens.

Those expecting a conventional palace will discover, instead, a complex of gardens and patios, separated by pavilions and arcades. In fact the name Generalife derives from *Yannat al-arif* (Garden of the Architect).

Dating from the mid thirteenth century, remodelling took place some fifty years later, when the lookout tower was added. Extensions for the Catholic Monarchs were made in the sixteenth century.

The arcaded **Patio de la Acequia** (Channel Patio), so named because of its open aqueduct, provides the north entrance, immediately signifying the importance of water to the palace. The upper storey of the entry pavilion may be viewed.

The north-east pavilion, opposite, was enlarged shortly after the capture of Granada in 1492.

Views to the north, over the river Darro, are gained from a lookout balcony that lies behind the north-west arcade.

Approached by stairs, the **Patio de los Cipreses** is a walled garden, with flowers and ancient cypress trees, beneath one of which Zoraya, consort of Boabdil, is reputed to have met her Abencerraje lover, thus leading to the massacre of the family already referred to. The gallery was built for Philip III.

La Escalera del Agua (Water Stairway) is another water garden of rare beauty within the Generalife.

The **Silla del Moro** (Seat of the Moor) watchtower is approached from a path that winds uphill, passing a nineteenth-century mirador.

A return to the Alhambra may, if time permits, include visits to its two most important post-Muslim additions, both constructed to the south.

Santa María de la Alhambra occupies the site of the patio of the great mosque. It was begun in the late sixteenth century to extravagant designs by *Juan de Herrera*; however, budgets were exceeded and *Juan de Orea*, who completed the building, was forced to simplify the church.

An aisleless **nave** is separated from its chapels by pilasters.

The basin of the baptismal font was re-used from a Moorish fountain.

Juan López de Almagro designed the high altar's reredos in 1671, incorporating sculptures by *Pedro de Mena*.

There is absolutely nothing wrong with the **Palacio de Carlos V**, Spain's finest Italian Renaissance building, except that it shouldn't be here at all. Carlos V could hardly be called sensitive, siting his ultra-solid palace at an angle where the delicate Moorish courts of the lions and the myrtles link. Fortunately, the intimate nature of the Islamic structures prevents the huge building from intruding once they have been entered.

Apartments to the south of the Court of the Myrtles, damaged by a fire, were demolished for the palace, but most of it was built on the site of a cemetery attached to the mosque. The architect, *Pedro Machuca*, was a follower of Michelangelo, and the palace, his only work to survive, is more Italian in style than any other important building in Spain. *Luis Machuca*, the architect's son, continued the work, but there were frequent suspensions, caused by rioting Moors, who were taxed to pay for the palace, and by a series of earthquakes, and completion did not take place until 1940 (and the patio never did receive its projected dome).

Facing the Puerta de los Aljibes, the portal is decorated with carvings by *Juan de Orca*, who worked on them while completing the adjacent church, and *Antonio de Leval*. Reliefs above are by *Juan de Mijares*.

The great central **patio** is circular, the capitals of its two arcades being Doric and Ionic respectively.

Sculptures by *Nicolao de Corte* decorate the portal facing the Puerta de la Justicia.

Approached from the south end of the Patio de los Arrayanes is the **Museum of Hispano Muslim Art** (Arte Hispano Musulmán). Open Monday to Saturday 10.00–14.00. Admission charge.

This is a fascinating museum, where Grenadine artefacts from the tenth century are exhibited. The emphasis is on the Nasrid dynasty.

Of outstanding interest are Nasrid paintings from the fourteenth and fifteenth centuries (**Hall III**), original, unrestored ceramic tiles from the Alhambra (**Hall VII**) and, above all, the Jarrón de la Alhambra (Alhambra vase), made in the fourteenth century for the Alhambra (**Hall VIII**).

Also situated within the palace is the **Fine Arts Museum** (Bellas Artes). Open Tuesday to Sunday 10.00–14.00. Admission charge. The museum features Grenadine art from the fifteenth century – both sculpture and paintings by the greatest artists who worked in the region.

The picturesque arch from San Gil, a church that once stood in Granada's Plaza Nueva, provides the entrance to Hall II. Artists to note in particular include: *Sánchez Cotán*, *Alonso Cano*, *Pedro de Mena* and *Pedro Bozanegra*, all of whom lived in the seventeenth century, the Golden Age of Grenadine art.

GRANADA CATHEDRAL
Open daily 10.30–13.00 and 16.00–19.00, winter 15.30–18.00. Admission free.

Those with restricted time should bear in mind that although the famous Royal Chapel, with the tombs of Ferdinand and Isabella, adjoins the cathedral, it may be approached only via a separate entrance, to the south-east. The cathedral cannot be considered one of Spain's greatest, but its west façade by *Alonso Cano*, and portals and chancel by *Diego de Siloé* are exceptional. Founded in 1492, Granada Cathedral was first sited, successively, within two former mosques. The present building was commissioned in 1518 from *Enrique Egas*, aided by *Juan Gil de Hontañón*.

The cathedral was originally designed in Gothic style, but *Diego de Siloé* took over in 1528, making wholesale Renaissance alterations. A series of architects then worked on the building until its completion in 1703.

Exterior *Alonso Cano*, painter, sculptor and architect, the last great artist of the Granada School, designed the west front in 1667, abandoning Siloé's plans: Cano evolved a highly personal Classicism which, in spite of its simplicity, achieves a satisfying vigour.

The north tower was only half-built, and its proposed matching south tower entirely dispensed with.

Above the central portal is an *Annunciation* medallion by *José Risueno*.

Flanking the same entrance are figures of St Peter and St Paul by *Verdiguier*.

The north façade, fronting Calle de la Cárcel Baja, displays two outstanding portals by *Siloé*, the second, the **Puerta del Perdón** (Gate of Forgiveness), being regarded as exceptional.

Interior Stonework, painted white, creates a cold atmosphere. It is immediately apparent that although the Renaissance style dominates, the exceptional height and plan, with inner and outer arcades, are Gothic in concept.

Most of the chapels lack outstanding features but, in the last north chapel before the curve of the apse begins, the **Capilla de Nuestra Señora de Antigua** incorporates an outstanding Baroque reredos by *Cornejo*, 1716. It is believed that its fifteenth-century Virgin was brought to Granada by the Catholic Monarchs. The apsidal **chancel** is a major Renaissance work, unusual for the great height of its roof and rounded-headed arch.

Figures of Ferdinand and Isabella at prayer were added, *c.* 1675, to the balconies adjoining the marble pulpits. They are the work of **Pedro de Mena** and **Medrano** respectively.

Above them are busts of Adam and Eve by **Alonso Cano**, who also painted the scenes from *The Life of the Virgin* between the **sanctuary**'s upper row of pilasters, in 1664.

Choir stalls, made in the sixteenth century, originally occupied the more usual position in the centre of the nave.

On the south side of the apse, following the Puerta del Colegio, is the entrance to the cathedral's **sacristy**.

An eighteenth-century addition to the cathedral, the present sacristy possesses two outstanding treasures against its east wall: a masterly *Crucifixion*, carved by **Montañés**, and, in the display case below, an exquisite *Immaculate Conception* by **Cano**. The Virgin appears to hold the onlooker in a sympathetic gaze from all angles. Facing the Nuestra Señora de la Antigua Chapel, on the south side, is the **Santiago Altar**. Its figure, *St James on Horseback*, is by **Pedro de Mena**.

Above this, the painting of *La Virgen de los Perdones* (Virgin of Forgiveness) was presented to Isabella I by Pope Innocent VIII in 1491.

Enrique Egas, the cathedral's first architect, designed the portal to the Royal Chapel, which follows, in late Gothic style; it no longer provides access. Although of no great importance in its own right, the **Jesús de Nazarene Altar**, in the next bay, made in 1722, serves as a frame for important paintings by **Ribera**, **Cano** and **El Greco**.

The sarcophagus of Bishop Jaime Forch lies in the most westerly of the south chapels, which he provided: the **Capilla de San Miguel.** It is an exuberant neo-Baroque work.

A small **museum**, adjoining the tower on the north-west corner, includes Flemish tapestries depicting *The Life of Constantine*, and the great silver monstrance presented by Isabella I.

St John as a Child, one of several paintings in the cathedral's collection, is by **Alonso Cano**, who worked from a studio in the tower.

To enter the Royal Chapel it is necessary to leave from the cathedral and follow Calle de los Oficios east, passing the south side of the cathedral.

ROYAL CHAPEL (CAPILLA REAL) *Enrique Egas*
1505–17
Calle de los Oficios.
   *Open summer 11.00–13.00 and 16.00–19.00, winter 10.30–13.00
and 15.30–18.00.*
   Admission charge.

Once more entered from the Lonja after a period of restoration, the
chapel, built by *Enrique Egas* in 1522, serves as a memorial to the
Catholic Monarchs and their immediate family, but it no longer
contains their remains.

Egas was commissioned to design the building in 1505. Isabella I
had died the previous year, followed by Ferdinand in 1516, and
their bodies lay in the convent of San Francisco, within the Alhambra, until this chapel was ready to receive them in 1521.

Interior   The late-Gothic chapel is aisleless, and roofed by a rib
vault. A choir projects over the west end of the **nave**, which is
divided from the chancel by a Plateresque grille, made in 1520.

A frieze of Gothic lettering around the chapel describes its
purpose.

Four sepulchral monuments, similar in style, dominate the
chapel.

To the south of the altar lie the recumbent figures of Ferdinand
and Isabella with, at their feet, a lion and a lioness respectively – a
useful aid to identification, as both monuments are similar in appearance. The serenity of their expressions in death disguises the
monarchs' suffering in life, caused by the early death of their son
and the madness of their daughter. It should be borne in mind that
Isabella 'wore the trousers', Ferdinand never effectively being more
than 'King Consort' in Castile.

Isabella was apparently a sympathetic woman of great intelligence
and vision: witness her support of Columbus against her husband
and most of the court. However, even allowing for the times, the
Catholic Monarchs' enthusiasm for the horrors of the Inquisition
must place them among the great monsters of history, their religious
intolerance paving the way for Spain's gradual decline, through the

loss of many of its most gifted inhabitants, the Jews and the Moors.

A Florentine, **Domenico Fancelli**, carved the piece, of Carrara marble, at his Genoa studio in 1517. His side reliefs are outstanding.

To the north of the altar lie the figures of Ferdinand and Isabella's daughter, Joan the Mad, and her husband, Philip the Fair, the work of **Bartolomé Ordóñez**, 1520.

Descend steps, east of the monuments, to a small **crypt**. Here are displayed two lead coffins, which enclosed the remains of the Catholic Monarchs until Napoleon's troops threw them out as part of their desecration of the chapel in 1812.

The sumptuous reredos of the high altar was carved by **Felipe Vigarny** in 1522. It incorporates a scene depicting *St John the Evangelist being Boiled in Oil*; however, there is no evidence that this event occurred, St John apparently being the one disciple of Jesus to escape martyrdom and live to a grand old age.

Against the north wall of the **chancel**, a reredos features a fifteenth-century triptych of the Passion by the Dutch painter **Dierick Bouts**.

From the south side, opposite, a door leads to the **sacristy** of the chapel, now virtually a museum and art gallery.

The crown and sceptre of Isabella, and the sword of Ferdinand, with its handle of gold, are displayed in the central glass case.

Paintings exhibited are part of Isabella's collection, all of which was donated to this cathedral. Outstanding works by **Memling**, **Bouts** and **Botticelli** are included, the most important being identified by the names of their painters.

A door from the west end of the Royal Chapel leads to the square **Iglesia del Sagrario.**

It is impossible during a one-day visit to view adequately more than the Alhambra, the Royal Chapel and possibly the cathedral, but, if an overnight stay is to be made, a visit (possibly by taxi) to the hilltop esplanade of the **Church of San Nicolás** in the Albaicín will be next in importance for most visitors, as it is from here that the world-famous view, encompassing the Alhambra and the permanently snow-capped Sierra Nevada mountains, is gained.

The **Albaicín** still preserves two minarets, emphasizing its Moorish appearance.

Two of Granada's many interesting churches, **La Cartuja**, with its overwhelming sacristy, and **San Juan de Dios**, displaying a Churrigueresque reredos, are a delight for Baroque enthusiasts.

RESTAURANTS
Los Manueles, 2 Calle Zaragoza.

Los Manueles has been established for seventy-five years and will serve speedy *tapas* or a full meal. Grenadine specialities such as *tortilla sacromonte*, made with brains, and *jamón de Trevélez* (mountain ham) will tempt the gourmet. A ceramic plaque above the entrance to a functions room records that Juan Carlos dined here in 1982. Notwithstanding, prices are most reasonable.

Aldebarán, 10 Calle San Anton (closed Sunday evening and Monday).

Also centrally situated, this restaurant is somewhat grander, *tapas* being limited to the first-floor bar area. The food is very innovative, with the accent on delicate sauces, and the menu changes regularly. The Spanish love of combining fish and meat is often exhibited, an example being chicken and crayfish in a light creamy sauce.

CÓRDOBA

Situated approximately 90 miles from Seville, Córdoba makes an easy day-trip excursion although, like Granada, there is a great deal of interest to see that warrants a longer stay. Primarily, of course, it is Córdoba's former mosque that attracts the visitor – the great Mezquita. Those arriving at the station or bus terminal will find it convenient to approach the mosque via the old Jewish quarter, afterwards visiting the renowned Callejón de las Flores and Plaza del Potro. If time permits, the Alcázar, south of the mosque, will be next in importance on most agendas.

Córdoba is the city of the quintessential Andalusian patio, and many flower-bedecked examples will be seen.

History Although it was an important city in Carthaginian and Roman times (both Senecas were born in Córdoba), it was the establishment here of Baghdad's emirate in 719 that laid the foundations of Córdoba's greatness. Abdul Rahman I, the only Umayyad to escape his family's slaughter by the Abbasids in Syria, asserted independence in 756, and in 926 Abdul Rahman III proclaimed an independent caliphate. Under the Moors, Córdoba became the greatest city in Europe, being the first true metropolis to be created on the continent since ancient Rome. Uniquely, it possessed a public water supply and drainage, the major thoroughfares even being illuminated at night. There are believed to have been around 200,000 buildings within the city walls, including numerous mosques and baths. Schools and libraries encouraged learning and, throughout the tenth century, Córdoba was the cultural centre of the world, with Muslim, Christian and Jew living in harmony.

The Umayyads were deposed in 1031, thus ending both the caliphate and Andalusian unity, and the region dissolved into small kingdoms, known as *taifas*, Córdoba falling under the jurisdiction of Seville. At the same time, the feuding Christian states united under St Fernando, and the Reconquest of the remaining Muslim kingdoms in Iberia began. In 1236, after strong resistance, Córdoba fell to St Fernando, and later served as the base of the Catholic Monarchs throughout their long siege of Granada. Gradually the important Moorish buildings disappeared as mosques were demolished or converted to Christian churches, beginning with the great mosque.

There has been little expansion outside the tenth-century walls, and modern industrialization appears to have bypassed the city; even the coming of the railway has made little visual impact, the station being sited discreetly to the north. Even more surprising, and unlike Granada, no new thoroughfares have been permitted to plough through the ancient core. What remains, therefore, is a small-scale city, still dominated by gleaming white 'Moorish' style homes, ancient churches and, above all, the huge Mezquita.

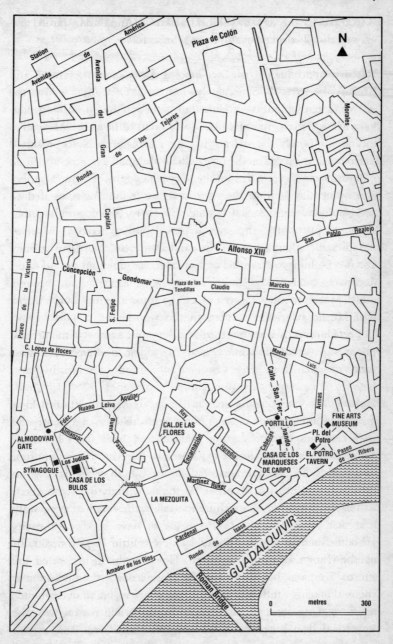

CÓRDOBA MOSQUE/CATHEDRAL (LA MEZQUITA)

Open daily, summer 10.30–13.30 and 16.00–19.00, winter 10.30–13.30 and 15.30–17.30.

Admission charge, but free during Mass.

It should be stressed immediately that the former Aljama mosque has been, in its entirety, a Christian cathedral for more than 750 years. Nevertheless, the building is still referred to as the Mezquita (the mosque), only the sixteenth-century choir and chancel erected within being regarded as the true cathedral.

Dating from the eighth century, Córdoba's great mosque was the most influential Muslim building in Spain, establishing, as it did, the Caliphate style that was to dominate Ibero/Islamic architecture. Although European, the mosque rivals other western Muslim examples, including those at Cairo and Damascus. Nearby Morocco possesses nothing comparable and, in any case, does not permit non-Muslims to enter its mosques.

The Mezquita's roofed area of 23,400 square metres makes it the third largest religious building in the world, and a polychrome 'forest' of structural columns supports the roofs. The exquisite prayer wall survives from the tenth century, boasting the finest Byzantine work in Spain.

History Having taken Córdoba *c.* 740, the Moors established a mosque within a section of the Visigothic church of San Vicente, the city's most important, sharing the building with the Christians. Within fifty years, due to the expansion of the Moorish population, the building had become too small to serve both religions and the Christians were paid to vacate it. At the same time, they were given permission to rebuild other churches that the Moors had previously destroyed.

Abdul Rahman I began to build a new mosque in 785, demolishing the church as work progressed. However, he incorporated the external west wall of San Vicente for reasons of speed and economy. This wall, facing south-west, established the orientation of the building throughout its long history and is the prime reason why the prayer wall does not precisely face towards Mecca as is usual. Abdul

Rahman II extended the building southward in 833, but Al Hakam II pushed the prayer wall back even further in 961–76, to the edge of the river, increasing the size of the mosque by half.

It was Hisham II's powerful vizier, Al Mansour, however, who was responsible for the final dimensions of the building – his eastward extension in 987 proved to be the greatest of all, increasing the mosque's size once more by half.

On St Fernando's capture of Córdoba in 1236, one of his first acts was to consecrate the mosque to Christianity.

His son, Alfonso X, created a chancel, together with a sacristy that was to become a royal mausoleum, at the point where Al Hakam II's extension had begun. In the fifteenth century this was extended by a nave when some Moorish columns were demolished.

But it was the controversial decision to build a much larger, cruciform structure in the centre of the mosque that caused most destruction, thirty-six columns being lost. This parallels in many ways the situation at Granada's Alhambra, where Carlos V's Renaissance palace unsympathetically intrudes on another Moorish masterpiece. Once again Carlos was the culprit, although this time he gave approval to the clergy's scheme rather than instigating it. Some historians have alleged that Carlos regretted approving the project, but with his iconoclastic record, this seems to be highly dubious.

Begun in 1523, the cathedral, which eventually burst through the roof of the mosque, was structurally complete by 1599, although work continued on it until 1776.

Early in the seventeenth century, the minaret was enclosed by the present tower.

Exterior The rectangular area of the mosque is immediately bounded by four streets, from which little more than the protective wall and its entrances can be seen.

Calle del Carreval Herrero, on the north side, passes the face of the tower, in the north-west corner. In 951, Abdul Rahman III rebuilt an earlier minaret and the structure provided the inspiration for Seville's Giralda as well as minarets at Marrakesh and Rabat in

Morocco. By 1593 this was on the point of collapse, and ***Hernán Ruiz the Elder*** encased it within the present Baroque tower. His work was completed by 1618, but the figure of St Raphael by ***Pedro Paz***, which surmounts the tower, was not erected until 1664.

An anti-clockwise tour of the walls of the Mezquita now begins in Calle de Torrijos, skirting the west façade. Due to its many decorative entrances, the west wall of the mosque is of greatest interest.

First passed is the **Postigo de Leche** (Milk Gate), which refers to the foundling infants deposited here by poor mothers so that they could be cared for in the nearby orphanage. Its design is Gothic.

Walls throughout are castellated with stepped battlements, a typical Moorish feature but first recorded in Ancient (pre-Muslim) Persia. The **Puerta de los Deanes** (Doorway of the Deans) follows. Islamic in design but with some later amendments, the doorway gives access to the south-west corner of the courtyard.

Now follows the section that may incorporate the external west wall of the Visigothic church, known to have been re-used by Abdul Rahman I.

The next doorway, **Puerta de San Esteban** (St Stephen's Doorway), was an important side entrance to the first mosque and known as Bab al Uzara (Vizier's Doorway). Entirely Islamic in design, it is, although somewhat modified, the oldest example to survive; the flanking windows are false.

The buttress that follows marks the beginning of Abdul Rahman II's exteriors, its wall being the oldest unaltered stretch now visible. Christian decorative features have been added to the horseshoe arch of the **Puerta de San Miguel** (St Michael's Doorway), believed to have given direct access from the caliph's palace, via a concealed passage.

To the right, the buttress marks the start of Al Hakam II's extension, which includes three more doorways, all similar in design to the Puerta de San Esteban, although the **Puerta de la Paloma** (Doorway of the Dove) was given Gothic features in the fifteenth century.

Many visitors will now wish to continue southward to view the Mezquita from the bridge.

The **Puerta del Puente** (Bridge Gate), at the approach to the bridge, formerly provided the entrance to Córdoba from the bridge through the city wall. The structure was originally Roman, and was rebuilt by the Moors in 766, but the present gateway is entirely sixteenth-century work, being designed by *Hernán Ruiz the Younger*, as a Classical triumphal arch, to honour Philip II. It was completed in 1589.

Only the Roman foundations remain of the **Puente Romano** (Roman Bridge). Some Muslim rebuilding work is evident, but much of the bridge was demolished to halt the Christian armies at the Reconquest. Restoration was not completed until the reign of Enrique II in the fourteenth century.

The figure of St Raphael on the parapet was added in 1651.

From this bridge, much of the cathedral's superstructure, rising through the roof of the mosque, appears in view: in the foreground the polygonal roof of the vestry and, behind this, the pitched roof of the choir and the polygonal roof of the crossing surmounting the south wall of the chancel. In the background rises the tower.

Return to Calle del Cardenal González, which skirts the south wall of the Mezquita.

As this wall formed the *qibla* of the mosque, there are no portals. The first bays incorporate round-headed recesses.

Extending slightly is the wall of the *mihrab*.

A plain section indicates the position of the vestry.

This is followed by regularly buttressed bays, the second of which marks the earlier extremity of Al Hakam II's extension; the remainder represents the width of Al Mansour's work.

Calle del Magistral González Francés conducts the visitor past the east façade of the building, all of it enclosing Al Mansour's extension. Doorways were re-used from the earlier east wall.

The **Puerta de Santa Catalina** marks the beginning of the courtyard wall. Although remodelled in 1573, most of the doorway retains its Plateresque detailing.

Returning to Calle del Cardenal Herrero, a much-venerated altar, dedicated to the **Virgen de los Faroles** (Our Lady of the Lamps), is decorated with a copy of a modern painting by the local artist *Julio Romero de Torres*.

The **Caño Gordo** doorway leads to the courtyard, but the main entrance is the **Puerta del Perdón** (Doorway of Forgiveness). Its large porch formerly accommodated the Ecclesiastic Tribunal.

Although an Islamic structure, fourteenth-century Mudéjar altera-tions predominate. All mosques include a courtyard (*es-sahn*) contain-ing a fountain for ritual washing before the interior (*chami*) is entered. Córdoba's courtyard originally received shade from a variety of trees, but in the Renaissance period the Christians replaced these with more formal orange trees, hence the name, as at Seville Cath-edral, **Patio de los Naranjos**.

None of the ablutions fountains survive, the present examples being purely decorative.

Unlike Seville, no later construction has altered the dimensions or basic appearance of this courtyard. However, it is believed that the aisles and nave of the mosque were originally open to it, the Chris-tians subsequently walling them up to create chapels.

Apart from this, the north façade of the mosque was rebuilt by Abdul Rahman III in the tenth century. His work included the main entrance, although the original eighth-century arch of Abdul Rahman I was incorporated. It is known as the **Puerta de las Palmas** (Doorway of the Palms) or **Benediciones** (Blessings), and the latter name commemorates the blessing given to the Christian armies that assembled here before commencing their siege of Granada.

Interior It is surprisingly easy to get lost among the columns that stretch like palm-trees in all directions, most of them equidistant. For the sake of orientation, it is simpler to assume that the chancel of the centrally-placed cathedral faces due east, rather than north-east, as it does, and similarly, that the distant prayer wall faces south rather than south-east. All directions are given, therefore, on this basis.

By continuing directly ahead, keeping initially to the right of the cathedral's choir, and then turning left, the sections of the mosque are seen in chronological order. The choir and chancel of the cathedral are best regarded as a separate entity.

From the entrance, a nave which originally led without interruption to the *qibla* is distinguished by a greater distance between its columns than that of the many aisles. This marks the centre of the original mosque of Abdul Rahman I, and affinities with Umayyad work in Syria and Jerusalem have been noted.

Sidi ben Ayub, the first architect appointed, was apparently instructed that speed was of the essence, as he made use of existing columns and cupolas, both from the Visigothic church, which was gradually demolished as work progressed, and earlier, Roman examples. Some columns may have been left in their earlier positions, as four rows were already standing, forming the inner and outer aisles of St Vincent.

Close inspection will reveal that several columns are buried in the floor and others are raised on plinths, indicative of their differing heights and sources.

As has been noted, the west wall of the church was also re-used.

With these economies, the rectangular building was completed within twelve months of its commencement in 785.

Five aisles flanked each side of the nave of this early mosque; the eight aisles further west all represent Al Mansour's tenth-century extension. A series of individual roofs, rather than a monolith, was built to cover the structure. Ceilings were of timber, and their coffered panels were brightly decorated. All were replaced, however, in the eighteenth century by Baroque cupolas. Their present original style dates from the modern restoration work of *Velázquez Bosco*.

To support these roofs, an ingenious two-tier system of round-headed arches was employed to spread the load (the more efficient, pointed Gothic arch had not yet been invented). There was no precedent for this in the Arab world, and it is believed that the inspiration came from the Roman aqueduct at Mérida, where two tiers of arches had been similarly constructed from alternate stone and brick sections.

At Córdoba, the lower arch is horseshoe-shaped, an important feature of Caliphate architecture.

The north wall of the cathedral aligns with the original south wall of the first mosque.

From this point ahead, up to the north wall of the Villaviciosa Chapel, stretches the short extension of Abdul Rahman II, 833–48. Eighty more columns were required and, once again, existing reserves provided them, including those of white marble from the Roman amphitheatre at Mérida.

The capitals are varied, coming from Roman and Visigothic sources, plus eleven Islamic examples especially commissioned.

Al Hakam II demolished the *macsura* (private chapel), added to this extension by Muhammad I, and most of the *qibla* that it faced, but the base of the latter may still be seen directly ahead. All this was, of course, connected with the extension made by Al Hakam II in 961–76, which provided the existing *qibla*, with its outstanding *mihrab* and *macsura*.

Immediately south of the base of the former *qibla*, work began on constructing a cathedral in the fifteenth century. Three rows of columns from five aisles and the west side of the nave were demolished, and walls were erected. However, the project was never completed and its walls were eventually removed.

Al Hakam II's extension is approached via the **Villaviciosa** or **del Lucernario Chapel**. Built in the thirteenth century by Alfonso X as the sanctuary, its decoration is outstanding Mudéjar work.

Alfonso also built a sacristy to its east, which later became a royal pantheon, Fernando IV being buried here in 1312 and Alfonso XI in 1371. Enrique II rebuilt the pantheon, now known as the Royal Chapel, in the fourteenth century. Its Mudéjar style blends well with its surroundings. By the time Al Hakam's extension was built all sources of existing structural material appear to have dried up – completely new columns, of blue Córdoba marble, bearing Corinthian capitals, alternate with columns of pink Carbra marble and Composite capitals.

It is at the south end, however, that the great glory of the Mezquita is revealed, focusing on the *mihrab*, the third in the mosque to be built. The area must be illuminated for its *Arabian Nights* magnificence to be fully appreciated, and it may be necessary to await the arrival of a tour party that has made the necessary arrangements for this to be done.

Fronting the *mihrab* is Al Hakam's private *macsura*, roofed by three cupolas. Ribs interconnect, possibly inspiring the Gothic rib vault, although, unlike the latter, they do not meet in the centre.

Mosaic work throughout is Byzantine, its craftsmen and materials being supplied by the Emperor Nicephorus of Byzantium, at the behest of Al Hakam.

Flanking the *mihrab* and supporting its horseshoe arch are pairs of Roman columns and capitals, re-used from Abdul Rahman II's *mihrab*.

Its 'shell' cupola was carved from one piece of solid marble.

An opening, left, connects the *mihrab* with the Baroque **sacristy**, formerly the chapterhouse, which now accommodates the treasury, where a silver monstrance, by *Enrique de Arfe*, 1518, and an ivory crucifix, by *Alonso Cano*, are the prime exhibits.

Two bays further east begins the extension of Al Mansour. Work commenced in 987, and it is said that such was Al Mansour's enthusiasm that the great vizier laboured on the project himself.

A section of the eastern wall of Al Hakam II's extension, now dilapidated, has been re-erected, right.

Al Mansour's eight-aisle extension, effectively increasing the previous mosque by half, had to be built to the east, as the courtyard to the north, the river Guadalquivir to the south, and the caliph's palace to the west effectively precluded any alternative. Fortunately, the exceptional *mihrab* was left in its existing position, although the extension meant that it was now sited off-centre, unusual in a mosque.

There were no innovations of importance in Al Mansour's extension, even the earlier doorways being re-used; however, the horseshoe arches have developed a shallow point, which immediately identifies the area.

Once more, columns and capitals were specially made and match those of Al Hakam II's extension.

Cathedral A decision was made by Córdoba's ecclesiastical authorities in 1523 to build a cathedral within the former mosque. The municipal leaders strongly objected, but Carlos V came down in the project's favour and **Hernán Ruíz the Elder** was appointed architect. On his death in 1547, work continued under the direction of his son, **Hernán Ruíz the Younger**. However, the cathedral took 234 years to complete, and the work of various architects, in several styles, is apparent.

The height of the cathedral, its pointed sanctuary arch and the rib vaults of the sanctuary and crossing betray the Gothic conception of the original architect.

Juan de Ochoa constructed the dome above the crossing in 1599; its plasterwork, by *Gutierrez Garrido*, is Italian in style.

Pedro Duque Cornejo came from Seville to carve the 105 exceptional choir stalls, and was aged eighty by the time of their completion in 1784.

The high altar's Classical reredos, by *Alonso Matías*, is a seventeenth-century piece, incorporating paintings by *Antonio Palomino* and carvings by *Pedro de Paz*.

Both pulpits are attributed to *Verdiguier*.

JEWISH QUARTER

A pleasant walk southward from the station or bus terminal, in the direction of the mosque, follows the gardens that border the entire west flank of the city.

At the half-way point, the **Puerta de Almodovar**, left, gives access to the former Jewish quarter. Built in the fourteenth century, this picturesque Mudéjar gateway in the city wall retains its horse-shoe arch.

From here an impressive length of the wall stretches southward.

Within the gateway, Calle Maimónides continues south, leading to Calle de los Judios, where the only part of an ancient **synagogue** to have survived in Andalusia may be found. (It is open free of charge, 10.00–14.00 and 18.00–20.00, Sunday 10.00–13.30.) The building does not date from the Arab occupation, but was built in 1315 (confirmed by a Hebrew inscription). After Ferdinand and Isabella proscribed the Jewish religion, it served many purposes, including that of a rabies hospital.

The prayer hall, all that remains, has lost most of the original Mudéjar decor and Hebrew texts. Its gallery was reserved for women.

The timber ceiling is a replica, but the clerestory windows, providing soft lighting, are original.

Continuing towards the Mezquita, the bullfighting museum is found within the fifteenth-century **Casa de las Bulas** (*bulas* refers to papal bulls, not bullfighting, and is a linguistic coincidence), overlooking the Plaza de las Bulas. (Open 09.30–13.30 and 17.00–20.00. Closed Monday and Saturday. Admission charge.)

Although the museum does not form part of a bullring, it is the most comprehensive of its type in Spain outside Madrid. Of particular interest to *aficionados* is the large collection of documents dating from the seventeenth century, before the present ritual of the *corrida* was established.

Bloodstained costumes, and the skin of the bull that killed the great matador Manolete, will appeal to those with gruesome tastes. Manolete's bloodstained shirt, however, is in Madrid.

Leaving the museum, right, the **Capilla de San Bartolomé** is approached. Believed to have been built in the thirteenth century, soon after Córdoba had fallen to St Fernando, the chapel is fronted by a small patio.

The rib-vaulted, aisleless building is decorated with outstanding fourteenth-century plasterwork.

A doorway and the ceramic pavement are Mudéjar. Frequent signs lead the visitor through the maze of streets eastward to the Mezquita.

CALLEJÓN DE LAS FLORES AND PLAZA DEL POTRO

High on any visitor's agenda is the **Callejón de las Flores** (Alleyway of Flowers), Córdoba's most photographed street, lying north of the mosque. Virtually every house displays window-boxes bursting with geraniums for most of the year.

Leading from this street, right, is Calle Velázquez Bosco, where **Arab baths** have been preserved within a modern development; they are not, however, as impressive as Granada's.

Leading northward from the north corner of the Mezquita, Calle

Encarnación joins Calle Rey Heredia, which conducts the visitor to a concentrated section of interest.

The **Arco del Portillo** is a reminder that a Moorish wall, through which the gate gave access, formerly divided the city between Almedina and Ajerquia. To the south, in Calle Cabezar, stands the fifteenth-century **Casa de los Marqueses de Carpio**, built around a Gothic tower on the site of a Roman structure, some of the walls of which survive to the rear.

Patios retain Mudéjar work, but have been greatly altered.

Continuing eastward, crossing Calle San Fernando, streets lead to the **Plaza del Potro**, a Córdoban landmark, its name referring to the foal that decorates the *plaza*'s fountain.

Founded by the Catholic Monarchs, the former **Hospital de la Caridad** occupies the entire east side of the *plaza*. Its main façade is modern, although designed to complement that of the hospital's Plateresque church.

The complex now accommodates two museums.

The **Bellas Artes Museum** concentrates on the seventeenth-century Córdoban School of painting. (Open Tuesday to Sunday 10.00–14.00 and 18.00–20.00 (not Sunday p.m.). Admission charge to non-Spaniards.)

The **Julio Romero de Torres Museum** displays the early twentieth-century works and possessions of the painter Romero de Torres, who was born in the mid eighteenth-century house (of specialist interest only).

Facing this, on the opposite side of the *plaza*, stands the **Posada del Potro**, an ancient inn mentioned by Cervantes in *Don Quixote*. Recently restored, this building now incorporates a cultural centre.

The remaining (north-west) side of the *plaza* is fronted by the Baroque façade of the church of the **San Francisco Convent**, founded in the thirteenth century by St Fernando. The medieval cloister survives.

Carvings by *Pedro de Mena* and paintings by *Valdés Leal* embellish the church.

If time permits, return to the south corner of the Mezquita and continue ahead, passing the eighteenth-century column erected by

Verdiquer in homage to the Archangel St Raphael, to reach Calle Amador de los Rios and the remains of Córdoba's Alcázar, with its delightful gardens.

ALCÁZAR DE LOS REYES CRISTIANOS
Open 09.30–13.30 and 17.00–20.00, winter 16.00–19.00.
Admission charge to non-Spaniards.

This Alcázar dates from the Reconquest, the Moorish Alcázar having stood on the site of what is now the bishop's palace, facing the mosque.

Alfonso X built a chapel dedicated to San Eustaquio (Eustace) in the thirteenth century, and Alfonso XI built a fortress around it in 1382. Mudéjar remodelling took place in the following century, when the fortress was adapted to a palace; the Moorish-style gardens date from this period.

The Catholic Monarchs resided in the Alcázar for only a short time, prior to the fall of Granada, in spite of the name by which the palace is now known.

There were originally four corner towers, but the east tower was demolished in 1850. Visitors enter via the square **Torre de los Leones** (Tower of Lions); its hall is the original Capilla de San Eustaquio.

From the tower's upper walkway, the octagonal keep, **Torre del Homenaje**, is reached. The circular **Torre del Rio** (Tower of the River), also known as **Torre de los Jardines** (Tower of the Gardens), may not be entered. It was here that victims of the Inquisition were imprisoned in the sixteenth century, and may also, possibly, have been the prison of Granada's last sultan, Boabdil, who is known to have been incarcerated somewhere in the fortress.

Archaeological finds exhibited in the Alcázar, all discovered in Córdoba province, include a carved Roman sarcophagus, Roman armour and, in the Baroque **Salón de los Mosaicos**, exceptional mosaic pavements from the first century. Also of interest are the fifteenth-century **Royal Baths**, laid out in the Moorish manner (below the Salón de los Mosaicos), and the **Royal Stables** (Caballerizas Reales), constructed in 1570.

The gardens are bounded to the south by the finest existing stretch of the tenth-century city wall, punctuated by the **Puerta de Sevilla**.

Those spending more than a day in Córdoba will find additional features of interest in the upper part of the town. Highlights include the **Archaeological Museum**, housed in the Renaissance Paez Palace, designed by *Hernán Ruiz the Younger*, **San Pablo Church**, little changed from the thirteenth century, **San Nicolás**, with Mudéjar decoration, and **San Lorenzo**, renowned for its rose window.

RESTAURANTS
El Caballo Rojo, 28 Calle Cardenal Herrero 47 53 75. Open daily for lunch and dinner (from 20.30). One of Andalusia's outstanding restaurants, El Caballo Rojo faces the entry to the Mezquita. Emphasis is on regional food, particularly the revival of traditional dishes. Soups, including a delicious almond *gazpacho*, are outstanding, as is the Córdoban speciality of oxtail.

El Blasón, Calle Zorrilla (ask for the Gran Teatro, which it adjoins) 48 06 24. Open daily for lunch and dinner (from 20.00). Try to reserve a table in the atmospheric nineteenth-century room. Owned by El Caballo Rojo, the food here is more international in flavour but very innovative, with unusual combinations. Salmon is a speciality. Order your meal over a drink in the attractive patio bar on the ground floor.

ITÁLICA

Site open Tuesday to Saturday 09.00–18.00, Sunday 9.00–15.00.

Admission free.

Every July, the International Dance Festival takes place in the amphitheatre.

Just six miles from Seville lie the ruins of the Roman city of Itálica. Most of the antiquities excavated have been removed to museums, Seville's Archaeological Museum in particular, but some important mosaic pavements remain. Of outstanding interest is the great amphitheatre.

Buses leave the Calle Reyes Católicos end of Avenida Marqués de Paradas every thirty minutes, in the direction of Santiponce; alight at the terminus for the excavations, a journey of fifteen to twenty minutes. Visitors are given a free plan of the site.

Itálica, named in recognition of the Italian peninsula, was founded by Scipio Africanus in 206 BC. Initially it served as a resting camp for legionnaires from the Peninsula campaign and the second Punic war, but soon developed into an important town. Trajan and probably Hadrian, future emperors who ruled successively from 98 to 138 AD, were born at Itálica, the latter giving it the official name Colonia Aelia Augusta. In 144 AD, the consul Lucius Mummius distributed trophies acquired from Corinth among the citizens, which is why Greek statues have been discovered on the site. It is also indicative of the importance of the town.

The Vandals and the Suebi successively took Itálica in the fifth century, and in 531 Teudis, a Christian, became the first Visigothic King of Iberia, establishing the court in Seville. From then on Itálica was deserted, gradually falling into ruins. Ignored by the Moors, the existence of Itálica was never forgotten and eventually the Christians from Seville, particularly during the Renaissance period, plundered the site for mosaic pavements and sculptures. Examples may be seen in the House of Pilate and the House of the Countess of Lebrija, in addition to the Archaeological Museum. Excavations began in earnest in the nineteenth century, revealing the amphitheatre and great baths; further work revealed the lower levels of some of the houses.

From the entrance, the **amphitheatre** lies directly ahead, and it is best viewed initially from its lower level. Built during the second century, in a natural hollow, Itálica's amphitheatre could accommodate around 25,000 spectators, the lower tiers being reserved for important families. It is elliptical in shape, and only the Colosseum in

Rome and the Pozzuoli arena are believed to have been larger. Ten doors gave access, and the most important has been restored.

At basement level was installed equipment to service the various events. There are no records, but presumably the usual Roman entertainments of chariot-racing, gladiator contests, animal-baiting and much worse took place. An elephant tusk discovered here is exhibited in the Patio de los Naranjos of Seville Cathedral.

It is not permitted to climb the tiers, but the upper, more spectacular level may be reached from the path that climbs up to it from outside the arena. The great blocks of stone once formed part of the now totally ruined façade of the amphitheatre. Upper tiers of seating have suffered more from the ravages of time than those below. A return towards the entrance to Itálica leads to the approach path to the remains of the town.

Visitors enter through the ancient wall at the north end of the main street, always known by the Romans as **Cardo**. Here, the thoroughfare is twice the width of that in Pompeii. Remains of houses survive only in the northern sector of the town; they are believed to have been built for the aristocracy during the reign of Hadrian. Presumably the other quarters of Itálica were reserved for the proletariat, their flimsier houses having left no trace. Features of interest are indicated by the Spanish names given to the ruins of the once splendid houses that they adorned. Most lie to the left of Cardo and are indicated in sequence on the plan by the numbers 8–13. Excavations continue and some areas will not be accessible.

Casa de la Exedra (8)   Facing the entrance is the ruined vestibule that gives the house its name.

Casa de Neptúno (9)   Named from the *Triumph of Neptune* mosaic.

Casa de los Pájaros (10)   The dwelling has been partly reconstructed and an exceptional mosaic of birds (*pájaros*) forms the pavement to a patio.

Casa de Hilas (11)   A grand house built around several patios, each with mosaics and fountains.

At the south end of Cardo, to the right, are the remains of the forum. Returning northward, the third street, left, leads to the **Casa**

del Planetario (7), with the most interesting pavement still in position. This depicts the busts of the seven Roman gods that represent the planets and have inspired the names of the days of the week.

Continuing westward, passing two side streets, the great **baths** are reached. Hadrian would not permit mixed bathing, and the baths for men are to the right and centre, those for women to the left. Hot and cold baths were provided for both sexes.

A smaller public **baths** and the **theatre** are currently being excavated in Santiponce village, but are not expected to be open to the public for some time.

Buses returning to Seville leave just past the service station on the near side of the road.

Between Itálica and Seville stands the former Cistercian monastery of **San Isidoro del Campo**, a Gothic masterpiece founded by *Alonso Pérez de Guzmán* in 1301. The complex is being restored as a *parador* and may not be visited until it has been opened.

Costa de la Luz

Stretching southward to Tarifa from Ayamonte, the small town that faces the Portuguese border, the Costa de la Luz (Coast of Light) is still, amazingly, one of Europe's best-kept 'secret' holiday regions. The climate, particularly its sunshine hours, is Mediterranean, but with a soft Atlantic breeze tempering the summer heat. Far surpassing those of Andalusia's Mediterranean coast, however, are the beaches of fine golden sand and the delightful, unspoiled towns and villages that intersperse the coastline. This is where the well-heeled Sevillanos spend as much of the summer as they can, average temperatures generally being at least 10°F lower on the coast than in the scorching interior.

Many of the architectural features noted in Seville – wrought-iron work, fountains and ceramic tiles – are repeated along this coast, the undistinguished, uniformly white houses and multi-storey blocks of the Mediterranean resorts being little in evidence. The expansion of Jerez and Seville airports in 1991 must now put this coastline in grave danger from the developers; however, it is bisected by the Doñana wildlife park, within which no buildings or road construction are permitted, and this may prove to be its saviour. Moreover, Spain has surely learnt its lesson from the appalling coastal developments of the recent past, developments that are now being deserted by tourists in droves, as they favour more agreeable venues.

From Seville, the visitor must go either to the northern part of the coast around Huelva, or to the southern section around Cádiz, as there is no road link between them without making a return to Seville. Buses serve most resorts, those to the Huelva region leaving from the Damas bus station, near the old Córdoba railway terminus. All Costa de la Luz destinations, from Sanlúcar de Barrameda southward, are reached by vehicles that leave from the central bus station. Those without their own cars will probably find the southern section preferable, as public transport is better and the towns offer more variety.

THE HUELVA COAST

Ayamonte, looking across the river Guadiana to Portugal's Algarve, is an attractive, ancient town, with Roman and Arab remains. It possesses a *parador* with a stunning view, a harbour, and the magnificent sand beach of Isla Canela. A new bridge now provides easier access to and from the Algarve, at the Portuguese border town of Vila Real.

From Ayamonte eastward the scenery is very flat, and most developments are modern, without much interest. However, **El Rompido** is a long-established fishing village, fronted by three miles of sand dunes. This is followed by **Punta Umbria**, a more obvious 'resort' that is untypical of the coastline.

Huelva is a large town with interesting features, but few will wish to spend much time there. Just outside Huelva, to the east, is the historic former port of **Palos de la Frontera**, from which Columbus sailed on his first historic voyage. A great monument commemorates the explorer in nearby **La Rábida**, where the monastery in which he stayed prior to setting sail is preserved.

The road continues southward to the disappointing 'hotel town' of **Mazagón**, on the edge of the **Doñana National Park**, which was created in 1969 to conserve Europe's largest wildlife sanctuary, now covering 76,000 hectares. Inhabitants include the praying mantis, tarantula spider, giant black bumble-bee (harmless), Montpelier snake (up to seven feet long) and giant ocellated lizard. Soaring above may be the griffon vulture, golden eagle and Spanish imperial eagle. A great sandy beach fronts the entire coastline of the park, uninterrupted by highways or buildings. The road veers northward to **El Rocío** and **Almonte**, terminal point of the springtime Romería del Rocío, and continues to Seville.

THE CÁDIZ COAST, JEREZ AND ARCOS

Lying slightly inland from this coast are the delightful towns of **Arcos de la Frontera** and the better-known Jerez de la Frontera. The former is dramatically perched on a steep rock spur, rising above the river Guadalete. Views towards the coast from Plaza del Cabildo, the main square, are memorable.

The castle and churches of **Santa María** and **San Pedro**, with their defensive walls, give Arcos a medieval aspect.

Much of the domestic architecture of **Jerez de la Frontera**, neglected by most tourists, is reminiscent of Seville, just sixty miles distant. While possessing no great 'sights', Jerez is an attractive town, with excellent *tapas* bars. The great sixteenth-century

Collegiate church of **Santa María**, the 'cathedral' of Jerez, is approached from Plaza de la Encarnación by a great flight of steps. **Santiago** and **San Miguel** churches both have outstanding Isabelline portals, whereas **San Dionisio** is Mudéjar.

All visitors, rightly, of course, connect this town with sherry, which was the original pronunciation of its name, formerly spelt Xeres. Visits may be made to most *bodegas* in the morning, Monday to Friday, where the unique manufacturing process of sherry is explained and sampling hospitably encouraged. The *bodegas* of Pedro Domecq and Sandeman are particularly welcoming and centrally situated. Near the Sandeman *bodega* is the **Riding School**, where outstanding equestrian displays take place on Thursdays.

Buses from Seville transport passengers direct to **Sanlúcar de Barrameda**, a large but picturesque town built around traditional *plazas* on two levels. The upper, Barrio Alto, overlooking the sea, is where Sanlúcar originated, and it is here that most of the historic buildings are to be found. They include **Santiago Castle**, the fourteenth-century church of **Nuestra Señora de la O**, with its Mudéjar portal, the Baroque **La Merced** church and the **Palace of the Counts of Niebla**. The lower, Barrio Bajo, occupies flat land, once under water, and it appears that the sea is still retreating, as the old town is now half a mile from the beaches. Not to be missed is the church of **La Trinidad**, with its Mudéjar ceiling and tomb of the Governor of Castile. The beach itself is magnificent and uncommercialized. Towards the river Guadalquivir, a fishermen's seafront quarter offers many *tapas* bars, where the speciality, of course, is shellfish, fresh from the sea. A dry *manzanilla*, the local, sherry-type wine, is the normal accompaniment. Foreign tourists are rare here, and are made very welcome.

Ferries ply across the river from the fishermen's beach to the deserted sand dunes of the **Doñana National Park**, where, even in mid-August, solitude is to be found. Remember, there are absolutely no facilities.

A coastal bus from Sanlúcar proceeds to **Chipiona**, with its famous lighthouse. This town also has wonderful beaches and is definitely a resort, with the advantages and disadvantages that this entails. Its rubbish dump, sited beside the beach to the north, is a surprising 'amenity'.

Some buses continue to **Rota**, many people's favourite base on this coast. Facing the Bay of Cádiz, Rota benefits from a warm Caribbean current that creates higher sea temperatures than those on the Costa del Sol. I have not seen a more picturesque resort in southern Spain. The ancient fishing town's medieval walls and fourteenth-century castle overlooking the port seem almost too good to be true. Behind, a series of theatrical *plazas*, linked by archways, adds to the charm; surprisingly, no sense of unreality intrudes. Modern hotels and apartment blocks have been built, but these are kept well away from the town centre.

Many visitors are surprised to learn that there is an American naval base just outside Rota, because nothing is visible; the occasional presence of the extremely well-behaved sailors for many years has ensured a lively bar and restaurant scene. An added bonus is that English is widely spoken, a rarity in small Andalusian towns.

Southward, the road follows the Bay of Cádiz, mostly comprising golden beaches and pine woods. As the delightful town of **El Puerto de Santa María** is approached, its nearby sandy beaches of **Fuentebravia**, **Vista Hermosa** and **La Puntilla** reflect the wealth of the area, with their luxury developments.

El Puerto de Santa María is worth visiting in its own right. Sherry is made here as well as at Jerez, and much of the town's wealth is based on this wine, most of which is shipped from the port.

Merchants involved in trade with America established their base at El Puerto from the sixteenth century, and this accounts for the many aristocratic mansions that have survived. The **Castle of San Marcos** retains Visigothic features and incorporates a thirteenth-century church. **San Francisco Church** is sixteenth-century, and there are several monastic buildings, including the exceptional **La Victoria**, with its Gothic façade and cloister.

Cádiz is built on an island, linked to the mainland by a causeway to the south and a new bridge to the east which is much less congested. Considering its exceptional site, sandy beach and ancient history, Cádiz should be an appealing city, but somehow it misses out. The approach to the ancient core is tedious and most of the streets are narrow, following a monotonous grid pattern, with few of the expected marine vistas being revealed.

The Phoenicians appear to have founded Cádiz, as Gadir, *c.* 1000 BC, and it is, therefore, the oldest city in the western world. Cádiz acquired great wealth from its brief monopoly position in the eighteenth century as Spain's trading port with America, but when this was lost it suffered a decline. The British have seen to it that little of the ancient city survives, bombardments by Essex and Howard in 1596 and Nelson in 1800 being particularly destructive.

Remains of *Vauban*'s Napoleonic wall, with its **Puertas de Tierra** (Land Gates), give access to the oldest quarter, the Barrio Populo, centred around the cathedral. Here the streets follow their medieval winding pattern and this sector of the city, on the south side of the narrow neck of the isthmus, is the most attractive.

The Baroque **Cádiz Cathedral**, with its gleaming ceramic dome, is the city's most important building; it was designed by *Vicente Aro*, and built from 1720–1838.

Much of the cathedral's early eighteenth-century chancel came from Seville's La Cartuja monastery.

In the crypt is buried *Manuel de Falla*, the composer (1876–1946), who was born and died in Cádiz. The **Treasury** displays outstanding pieces, including a processional cross by *Enrique de Arfe*, the Corpus Christi monstrance and the 'Million' monstrance, which reputedly includes a million jewels.

Santa Cruz Church, to the east, was the original cathedral of Cádiz. Founded in 1262, most of the building was destroyed in the 1596 bombardment.

A Gothic arch to the portal and a rib vault to the baptistery are all that survive.

Baroque reredoses within include sculptures by *Alonso Martínez*.

Further west is the late seventeenth-century **Oratory of St Philip Neri**. The Spanish Cortes sat here in 1812 to debate the State's Constitution.

Murillo's painting of *The Immaculate Conception* is the feature of the high altar's reredos.

From Cádiz the main road continues southward to Tarifa via **Chiclana de la Frontera**, with the great beach of **Playa de la Barrosa** four miles distant.

Further superb beaches at **Conil de la Frontera** and **Barbate de Franco** are reached from side roads.

Surf-boarders make a beeline for **Tarifa**, due to the almost constant winds that blow through the Straits of Gibraltar and virtually guarantee good surfing. The town has an ancient history, being founded by the Moors on top of a Roman port in the eighth century.

Tarifa's castle dates from the Muslim period; within this fortress, the church of **Santa María** incorporates Roman columns and is built on the site of the mosque.

Although Tarifa marks the official end of the Costa de la Luz, golden sand beaches continue as far as **Algeciras**, the ferry port for Tangier and Ceuta. From its bay are gained the best views of Gibraltar.

COSTA DEL SOL

Due to its warm, sunny climate and protective backdrop of mountains, this entirely Mediterranean coast, stretching north-eastward from Tarifa to just past Almería, has been developed over a thirty-year period to become the most popular in Europe. On approaching its coastline from other parts of Andalusia, the visitor may be forgiven for thinking that an invisible border has been crossed between Spain and an international no-man's-land of skyscraper apartment blocks, flashing signs, discos, hamburger stalls and *pizzerías*. Many establishments are owned by foreigners, and just about every national cuisine is on offer – except Spanish. Supply has now overtaken demand, and it was estimated in 1991 that at least 50 per cent of all British-owned commercial and domestic properties were up for sale. Nevertheless, there remains the ever-present summer sunshine and, with the notable exception of the Marbella region, prices are still reasonable.

Developments stretch along the entire coastline, but the centres of Estepona, Marbella, Fuengirola and Torremolinos retain the greatest appeal, particularly for the British. There are no golden sands on the Costa del Sol – all are grey, and therefore less attractive than those of the Costa de la Luz.

Estepona and Marbella are both old-established towns, with attractive centres that lie behind the beachside developments. A fishing port adds to **Estepona**'s sense of greater reality, and the town has always had a strong appeal for the British.

Marbella is really a world of its own, French Riviera prices reflecting its popularity with the international set. The old town, lying well back, where your actual Spaniard still lives, is probably the most appealing of all those to be found in the coastal resorts, and here prices in the *tapas* bars remain fairly Spanish. A trip should be made to the famous **Puerto Banus** yacht marina nearby, to observe Spain's most luxurious and expensive venue, where the beautiful people mingle with fugitive hoodlums.

In the low mountains behind Marbella lies **Ronda**, one of the most spectacularly sited towns in Spain. Its approach road is less hair-raising than heretofore, but still full of excitement. Ronda is split into a 'new' and an old town, linked by a bridge that spans a steep ravine. The modern rules of bullfighting were established in Ronda by the Romero family, and its bullring, built in 1785, may be visited.

Further north, **Fuengirola** has long been a British enclave, attracting retired couples who, in each other's company, manage to avoid the loneliness experienced by so many expatriates living in more remote or non-British locations. Naturally, English pubs, tea-rooms and book-shops proliferate. Someone has evidently stipulated a maximum height for the beachfront buildings and, of course, each block reaches that height exactly, creating an unappealing cliff-face of concrete. Because of this, Fuengirola has one of the least appealing beaches on the coast. Immediately behind it is **Mijas**, which although now rather touristy, remains an attractive hillside village.

A train from Fuengirola station connects the coastal towns that lie further north, terminating at Málaga centre after stopping immediately outside the airport. **Benalmadena Costa** has become an appealing resort, with a new yacht marina and delightful sea-front promenade. Restrictively, only a narrow strip of land exists between the beach and the main highway, and behind this, the terrain is very steep. A few miles inland is the old town of **Benalmadena**, an attractive, peaceful spot.

The promenade continues northward to **La Carihuela**, until quite recently a picturesque fishermen's quarter but now a mile-long stretch of bars and restaurants. Vivacity and the low-rise nature of the buildings retain a strong appeal, with prices of the properties in the village at the rear being some of the highest on the coast. In 1990 the promenade was extended from La Carihuela around the headland to Torremolinos, the Costa's oldest established resort.

Very international, **Torremolinos**, is seedy, noisy and run-down, with only vestiges of its ancient village centre surviving. In addition, the beach is a steep climb from the town itself. Why then does it still attract so many, in all age groups? Probably the liveliness of Torremolinos all the year round is its greatest appeal and, although the town is large, concentration on the hilltop site creates a sense of a defined community. Hotels, restaurants and bar prices are some of the lowest on the coast, and property, for those seeking a *pied-à-terre* in the sun, is currently on offer for a song.

In spite of its climate, **Málaga** has always struck me as a grey town, to be avoided unless on a shopping spree. Work continues on the south tower of its **cathedral**, begun in the sixteenth century but, like the city, lacking any features of exceptional interest.

Málaga's sea-front promenade is attractive but can be dangerous at night.

Buses and trains connect the city directly with Seville, Córdoba and Granada.

GIBRALTAR AND TANGIER

Many visitors to southern Spain, particularly those from England, take the opportunity to spend a day on one of the last surviving

British colonies and to sample the closest Muslim country to western Europe.

GIBRALTAR

Gibraltar's airport is the most convenient arrival point for the Costa del Sol's southern resorts. Taxis congregate on the Spanish side of the adjacent border, and buses from La Linea bus station, a fifteen-minute walk away, journey along the coast towards Málaga, or in the other direction to Cádiz. There are also services to Jerez and Seville, although it is usually necessary to change buses at Algeciras.

It must be said that Gibraltar, British by treaty since 1713, is a great disappointment to many, and certainly a stay at the rock's overpriced hotels should be avoided if possible. **Main Street**'s early nineteenth-century buildings, with Spanish touches, are attractive, but elsewhere the urban scene is dominated by hideous barracks and cheap housing blocks connected with Gibraltar's long naval history.

A shopping spree in Main Street (shops close most of the afternoon) should concentrate on spirits, cigars, cigarettes and clothing. As the town is a duty-free port, other items such as perfumes, electronic goods and cameras should also be good buys, but ensure that you know the UK price before purchasing. Most shops are Indian-owned and bargaining is expected. *Caveat* very much *emptor!*

A cable-car to the peak is exhilarating, and views over the mountains of the Costa del Sol, particularly towards sunset, are memorable. A walk down should ensure an encounter with the famous apes, the only wild examples in Europe. Nobody knows where they came from – they certainly don't exist in Morocco.

Some visitors may also wish to see Gibraltar's caves, discovered during excavations of tunnels during the Second World War; they are not exceptional, however.

Perhaps the biggest let-down in Gibraltar is the sheer bad value for money and an unprofessional, take-it-or-leave-it attitude. **The Rock** is a superb luxury hotel that cannot be recommended too highly, but the lower-grade establishments leave much to be desired, particularly when compared with their Spanish counterparts a few miles away. Reasonably priced rooms just do not exist. Food, in most establishments, is generally terrible, of the chicken (tasteless broiler) and chips variety, and the pubs, which specialize in keg beer, do not seem to have heard that alcohol is duty-free in Gibraltar: a scotch, for example, will cost little less than in England. This greed spreads to the banks, which, in my experience, are unique in charging for cashing Eurocheques. Remember to take sufficient sterling, which in Gibraltar is on a par with the Gibraltar pound; however, when leaving make sure that you have no Gibraltar money, as it is exchanged elsewhere at a lower rate than sterling.

Motorists should fill up in Gibraltar before leaving, to take advantage of the cheap petrol: all service stations close by 21.00.

TANGIER

For many tourists, Tangier will represent the only direct contact that they will ever make with either the third world or a Muslim country. Most will find it invigoratingly different from the conventional European holiday resort.

Morocco, at the time of writing, does not require a visa from UK passport holders, nor are there any unusual formalities, apart from completing an immigration card. Ferries regularly ply across the Straits from Algeciras (two and a half hours), and most will find this the best method of access. Moroccan money (*dirhams*) should be purchased on the boat. Land is constantly in view, and the voyage is full of interest, particularly when the ferry skirts the Moroccan coastline of mountains and sandy bays (all deserted and ripe for eventual development – it is probably the western Mediterranean's finest unspoiled stretch).

In summer, there are also limited catamaran services from Gibraltar, and flights from Gibraltar airport to Tangier take just twenty minutes. As might be expected, however, being Gibraltar, the trip is one of the most expensive for its distance in the world and, an additional disadvantage, no luggage may be left at the airport, even for a short while.

A catamaran service direct from Seville to Tangier, via the Guadalquivir river and the Costa de la Luz, was inaugurated in 1990. A check should be made to confirm that this apparently wonderful trip, interrupted by the Gulf War, has been revived.

Being a busy port, and with its comparatively recent history of international control, Tangier is not really typical of Morocco, both Spanish and French influence being in evidence. The low hill overlooking the harbour is where the picturesque *medina* and *kasbah* are to be found, and most tourists immediately make for it. Confronted by tourists, a Moroccan who does not fall into the limited category of wealthy tends to become the most tenacious hustler in the world, and will try to sell anything conceivable (and inconceivable). It is best to completely ignore all offers and smilingly indicate that your only language is Serbo-Croat. Any sign of interest and you are lost. Most of the hustlers are basically harmless and good-natured, but there are some nastier specimens of the genre who hang around the port, and a quick escape from this area should be made. Search immediately for a blue 'Petit Taxi' (the large 'Grand Taxis', usually Mercedes, are more expensive) and proceed to the **Hotel El Minzah** – not because you are staying there but because any rip-off demands by the taxi driver can be sorted out with the aid of the friendly doormen. Pay an absolute maximum of five *dirhams* for the short trip.

A walk downhill passes the **Grand Socco** (Large Square) and then, through an archway, the narrow streets of the picturesque *medina* unwind. Look for the stall that sells home-made nougat, one of Tangier's best buys.

Directly ahead is the appealing **Petit Socco**, a good spot for a coffee or a Moroccan mint tea (very sweet). To the left is the labyrinthine *souk* (market), where you will be the world's most popular person. Never pay more than a third of the asking price – walk away in contempt, whatever 'bargain' is reached, in order to gain a final reduction. Most goods on sale, however, although perfectly acceptable in their native land, are hardly suitable in a European or an American home. What will you actually do with that kaftan, berber rug, *tajine* (stewing pot) or engraved brass plate when you get it back? Ladies enamoured of chunky jewellery may find some of the silverware attractive, particularly the earrings, and there can be bargains. For men, the European-style leatherware – wallets, briefcases, etc. – embroidered with a fake Cartier double C monogram are excellent value. They are well-made and cost much less than their European equivalents, but bargain in several shops before buying. Clothing, however cheap, should not be purchased, as it will invariably fall to pieces in a short time.

Surmounting the hill, the **kasbah**, incorporating the former royal palace, provides great vistas.

On returning to the Hotel El Minzah, one of Morocco's finest, continue uphill to the **Café de Paris**, still the city's most popular terrace for a late afternoon tea or coffee (English tea is available). **Boulevard Pasteur** stretches eastward from the Café de Paris and is Tangier's main drag, entirely European in its architecture. A superb view of the Straits of Gibraltar is gained from the boulevard's nearby terrace.

Mosques, of course, abound in Tangier but they are of little architectural interest externally and Morocco, uniquely among North African countries, does not permit non-Muslims to enter them.

Probably the best town-centre daytime bar is **Chez Rubis** (English spoken), which also serves excellent steaks. Very cheap and good Moroccan food is available most of the day at the **Agadir** restaurant, run by two charming brothers, in a side street running uphill from the Boulevard Pasteur, facing the Café de Paris.

Tangier has a superb summer climate, but it faces north and loses the sun early in the winter months. Lively but noisy beach bars – try **Emma's BBC Bar** – operate from mid-May to mid-October. The sandy crescent of beach is one of the finest in the world and a great rarity, as maritime cities are usually restricted to a deep-water harbour.

ARCHITECTURAL TERMS

Aisle   Parallel areas subdivided by arcades.

Ajimez   Windows divided into lights by colonettes. Probably developed by the Visigoths.

Altar   Table of stone at which Mass is celebrated in a church or chapel. The most important altar, generally situated at the east end, is known as the high altar.

Altar frontal   Covering of the front of the altar facing the worshippers.

Altar rail   Low structure protecting the area in which the high altar stands.

Ambulatory   Passageway in a church formed by continuing the aisles behind the sanctuary.

Apeadero   Waiting area for transport.

Apse   Semi-circular or polygonal extension to a building.

Architrave   Internal or external moulding surrounding an opening.

Archivolts   Inner bands of an arch, tracing its curve.

Ashlar   Large blocks of smoothed stone laid in level courses.

Atrium   Roofed courtyard of a building.

Attic   Low top storey of a building.

Baldacchino   Dome-shaped cover to a high altar, revived in the Baroque period.

Baroque   Exuberant development of the Classical style.

Barrel or tunnel vault   A curved roof.

Bay   Compartment of a building divided by repeated elements.

Bay window   A straight-sided window projecting at ground level.

Boss   Ornamental projection covering the intersection of ribs in a roof.

Buttress   Structure attached to a wall to counter an outward thrust.

Capital   Top section of a column or pilaster, usually carved in the distinctive style of a Classical order.

Castellated Battlemented parapet. Usually stepped Moorish or Mudéjar work in Andalusia.

Chapter house Meeting area for the clerical hierarchy.

Churrigueresque Spanish development of the Baroque style to its ultimate exuberance, particularly ornamentation, in the first half of the eighteenth century.

Cladding Material added to provide an external surface.

Classical Styles following those of ancient Greece or Rome.

Clerestory An upper range of windows, usually in a church, designed to increase the natural light.

Cloister Covered arcaded passageway, usually four-sided, beside the main nave of a monastic church.

Coffering Recessed ceiling panelling.

Convent A complex housing a monastic community, male or female.

Corbel Wall bracket, generally of stone.

Corinthian Greek Classical order. Columns are slender and their capitals are intricately decorated with carved leaves and small spiral scrolls (volutes).

Cornice A projecting decorative feature running horizontally at high level.

Crossing Where the nave, transepts and chancel intersect in a church.

Cufic A stylized form of Arabic lettering.

Cupola Small domed roof, often surmounting a turret.

Cusp Decorative feature of Gothic tracery. The intersection of foils (or lobes) forms a pointed projection.

Dado Lower section of wall, often tiled in Spain.

Doric Greek Classical order, the oldest and sturdiest. The capitals of Doric columns are virtually undecorated.

Dormer window Window protruding from a sloping roof.

Eave Horizontal edge of a roof overhanging the wall.

Fanlight Oblong or semi-circular window above a door.

Finial Decorative terminal to a structure, e.g. spire or gable.

Flamboyant Waved lines of tracery producing a flame-like effect.

Fluted Vertical grooving.

Flying buttress   Archlike structure that transfers weight from the wall.

Fresco   Painting on a freshly plastered wall to obtain greater permanence.

Gable   Upper section of wall at each end of a building.

Gallery   Upper level storey, always open on one side, and usually arcaded. Alternatively, a long room for displaying works of art.

Gargoyle   Decorative protruding spouts that drain rainwater from roofs. Often carved as beasts or demons in Gothic buildings.

Gothic   Architectural style from twelfth to sixteenth centuries employing the pointed arch; *see* Isabelline.

Gothic Revival   Attempt to reproduce the Gothic style.

Grisaille   Grey monochrome decoration.

Ionic   Greek Classical order. Columns are slenderer than those in the Doric order and capitals are decorated at corners with spiral scrolls (volutes).

Isabelline   Gothic architecture *c.* 1480–1510, incorporating carved decoration. Follows approximately the reign of Isabella I. Limited to Spain.

Keystone   Central stone at the apex of an arch or where the ribs of a vault intersect. Frequently elongated to form a boss.

Light   Section of a window filled with glass.

Lintel   Horizontal section of stone or timber spanning an opening to distribute the weight that it bears.

Lobe   Petal shape formed by Gothic tracery.

Misericord   'Mercy' seat provided by a shallow surface for resting purposes that protrudes horizontally when the seat itself is tipped up. Supporting brackets are often richly carved with various subjects, not always religious. Generally in the form of Gothic choir stalls.

Modernism (or Modernisme)   Architecturally, not a style but the application of functional planning and new structural techniques, combined with craft materials. Gothic Revivalism had an early influence on the appearance of the buildings, but styles became eclectic. Evolved in the 1880s in Catalonia, the movement began to peter out *c.* 1914. Few examples are found in Seville.

Moulding Decorative addition to a projecting feature, such as a cornice, door frame, etc.

Mudéjar A continuation of the Moorish style, by Moorish craftsmen who remained after the gradual Christian Reconquest of Spain.

Nave Body of the church housing the congregation.

Oratory Small private chapel.

Order Classical architecture where the design and proportions of the columns and entablatures are standardized.

Oriel window Window projecting as a bay but at an upper level.

Patio Paved area within a building, open to the sky. Roman in origin and popularized by the Moors.

Pier Solid structure supporting a great load.

Pilaster Shallow, flat column attached to a wall.

Pinnacle Vertical decorative feature surmounting a Gothic structure.

Plateresque Renaissance architecture with filigree carving in the manner of silversmiths (*plata* = silver). Early sixteenth-century and limited to Spain. Moorish, Gothic and Renaissance themes were included.

Portal Important doorway.

Portico Classical porch of columns supporting a roof, usually pedimented.

Quoin stones Dressed stones fitted externally at the angles of a wall to give added strength.

Renaissance Rebirth of Classical architecture as evolved in Italy in the fifteenth century. Replaced by Mannerism and Baroque from the mid sixteenth century.

Reredos Decorative structure, usually standing behind the altar in a church or chapel. Generally made of wood but occasionally of stone. On the Continent, confusingly referred to as a retable.

Rib Protruding band supporting a vault. Occasionally purely decorative.

Rococo Last phase of the Baroque style in the mid eighteenth century, with widespread use of detailed ornamentation.

Romanesque Style of architecture featuring semi-circular arches.

Popular from the ninth century to *c.* 1250. Few examples are found in Andalusia.

Rose window   Circular window used in Gothic architecture. Its tracery pattern resembles a rose. Introduced in the mid thirteenth century.

Rustication   Use of stonework on the exterior of a building to give an impression of strength. The jointing is always deep.

Sacristy   Room in a church for storage of sacred vessels and vestments. Generally used for robing. Also known as a vestry.

Sanctuary   Area reserved for the clergy, in which the high altar stands.

Sarcophagus   Carved coffin.

Sebka   Decorative brickwork developed by the Almohads, e.g. on the Giralda.

Terracotta   Unglazed earthenware used as tiles and decorative features.

Tracery   Intersecting bars that create a decorative pattern in Gothic architecture.

Transept   The area that runs on either side of the crossing of a large church, normally north and south, forming the cruciform (cross) plan. Rarely extends from the external walls of the church on the Continent, as it does in England.

Transitional   The merging of Gothic with Romanesque architecture, e.g. Santa Ana Church in Triana.

Triforium   Blind passage that runs above the roof of an aisle within a church.

Trompe l'œil   Painting that 'tricks the eye' into believing it is three-dimensional work.

Trophy   Decorative sculptured arms or armour.

Tuscan   Classical order. Roman adaptation of the Greek Doric.

Tympanum   Semi-circular or triangular space between the lintel of an opening and the arch above it.

Vault   An arched structure forming a roof.

Vestibule   Entrance hall or anteroom.

Visigothic   Adaptation of Roman architecture by the Visigoths (in Seville, sixth to seventh century).

FOOD AND DRINK IN SEVILLE

Spanish food is little known outside the Iberian peninsula, partly because it varies greatly from region to region and partly because authenticity depends to a high degree on products that are difficult to find elsewhere. It is generally agreed that the best cooking exists in the northern regions of the country, particularly their mountainous areas, which is where foreign visitors rarely go. Most tourists, of course, keep to the sunny Mediterranean resorts and here, particularly in the hotels, food tends to be 'international', the only indication that the diner is in Spain being the presence of the ubiquitous *paella* and *gazpacho*.

Centuries of widespread poverty, and the lack of a restaurant tradition, are probably responsible for the accusation that Andalusia has the least distinctive of all the regional cuisines, but while this is generally true, it does not mean that one cannot eat extremely well in Seville. The basic raw materials – meat, fish and vegetables – are almost always of a very high standard and, as elsewhere in Spain, the charcuterie is unbeatable. Health enthusiasts will be pleased to learn that the most common sauce that accompanies dishes is made by frying garlic in pure olive oil, often with the addition of fresh tomatoes: the modern doctor's prescription for avoiding heart attacks.

An Arab influence can be traced in the Andalusian preference for very sweet biscuits and cakes, often made with honey, egg yolks and ground almonds, and a few enterprising restaurants are attempting to revive Mozarab dishes, but it cannot be said that the more common specialities to be found in Seville have an obvious Arab connection. In fact, Catalonia, which was occupied by the Moors only for a very short period, offers far more dishes that combine fruit and nuts with meat and fish, regarded as a typically Arab feature. The famous *gazpacho*, once believed to be an Arab inheritance, now appears to have Jewish antecedents.

Throughout Spain, regional, sometimes even provincial, boundaries tend to act as 'cuisine enclosures'. In Seville, for example, the superb Jamón Real *bodega* proclaims that it 'imports' produce from Extremadura – the region that adjoins Andalusia to the north! Do not expect, as a general rule, to find specialities from other Spanish regions in the city.

Breakfast (*Desayuno*)

In Andalusia, the usual Continental favourites – croissants and bread – are supplemented by toasted rolls (*tostadas*) accompanied by either butter, jam, spicy sausage-spread (*sobrasada*), *pâté* or various flavours of pork dripping. It is common for help-yourself bowls of these spreads to be left on the bar counter; no one minds if you select different flavours for the two slices. *Churros*, a favourite throughout Spain, are sold in many establishments, not all of them *churrerías*; these deep-fried tubes of dough may be sugared, but many prefer to dunk them in a cup of hot, very thick chocolate. As most breakfast establishments are also *tapas* bars, it is normally easy to order eggs and ham, for example, if preferred. Visitors used to English bacon do not generally find the Spanish version an acceptable substitute, as it is very fatty and strong-flavoured.

Tapas

Andalusia's great gift to the culinary world, and now most fashionable in Britain, *tapas* is simply a very small portion of any dish that the bar has prepared: it is usually accompanied by a glass of wine. There are more than 3,000 bars in Seville, the majority of which serve *tapas* in some form – from a humble dish of olives to an expensive *ración* (larger helping) of cured ham. *Tapa*, literally meaning lid, is believed to have evolved from the Seville custom of placing a small dish over a glass of wine to protect it from dust and nautically-minded insects. On the dish would be placed a morsel of bread, ham, cheese, etc. This has gradually evolved into an art-form, whereby almost 100 varieties of snacks are offered in some bars – the long menu usually being hand-written on a board. Consumption of *tapas* begins around 11.30, but it is not always clear where breakfast ends and *tapas* begins. In any case, it continues throughout the day.

Due to its proximity to both the Atlantic and the Mediterranean, and the excellence of its mountain hams, Seville's *tapas* tends to be dominated by seafood and charcuterie, neither of which are cheap, a lengthy tasting session often costing more than a three-course meal in a restaurant. Spaniards like to make a bar tour, sampling a different *tapa* in each one visited. Obviously, weight-watchers who indulge will generally find that at least one formal meal per day is best eliminated. Many of Seville's restaurants also have *tapas* bars, sometimes, but not always, in different sections from the set tables: the menu is often identical, only the size of portions varying.

The long vocabulary that follows this section includes most items found in Seville, although more specialities and local expressions may still be encountered.

Lunch (*Comida*)

Tapas aside, the Sevillano would never dream of sitting down to a three-course lunch before 14.00, and often later. On Sunday, it is expected to last through the entire afternoon. The capacity or purse of many visitors will frequently mean that *tapas* will replace the usual lunch.

Dinner (*Cena*)

Regular dependence on *tapas* throughout the day as a main meal replacement will eventually pall, and a conventional dinner then proves welcome. For a city of its size, 'pure' restaurants are remarkably few, particularly when compared with the vast selection in Madrid and Barcelona. As may be imagined, it is the commercial area of Los Remedios where most are to be found, entirely due to the business meal trade. Los Remedios holds scant interest for tourists, but the odd excursion for dinner is easily made by bus or taxi, Sevillanos never begin dinner before 22.00.

Specialities (Especialidades)

Seville's culinary specialities may be eaten as *tapas*, *raciones* or part of a main meal. Look out for: *gazpacho*, cold soup; *rabo (or cola) de toro*, oxtail; *jamón Jabugo*, supreme cured ham; *pescaíto frito*, fried seafood, prepared in specialist establishments; *aceitas*, huge green olives from Seville, claimed to be the world's finest – *a la Sevilla* refers to any dish prepared with these olives; *huevas a la flamenca* – eggs with diced ham, *chorizo*, asparagus and peas; *cocido*, a meat and vegetable stew; *menudos*, tripe prepared with *chorizo* and *morcilla*; *riñones al jerez*, kidneys braised in sherry. In Seville's *tapas* bars it is normal to offer *picos* – short, dry bread sticks, like stunted grissini. Not everyone likes them, and bread (*pan*) may be ordered if preferred. Cheese-lovers will generally have a thin time in Andalusia, little being available apart from Manchego, a ewes' milk cheese of varying tangyness that is found all over Spain. Cabrales, made from goats' milk, is reminiscent of Roquefort and excellent either cold or hot; however, only the better establishments sell it.

Desserts are rarely of interest outside the higher-grade restaurants, crème caramel (*flan*), fresh fruit and yoghurt being the usual 'selection' offered.

A word about hams

The Sevillano will discuss the merits of cured hams as a Frenchman will wines, and the subject is surprisingly complicated, with its own terminology. Hams are cured in brine and then hung, sometimes for many years, until perfection is reached. From their superficial appearance, one imagines that they are hard and dry, but in fact the surface is soft and slightly sticky to the touch. Cured ham is known as *serrano*, the best coming from mountain breeds (*ibérico*). The most highly regarded animal has a strain of wild boar's blood and its trotters are black, hence the name *pata negra*. As Winnie the Pooh fans know, Piglets prefer haycorns, and the best-tasting pigs are fed exclusively on acorns (*bellotas*). In the adjacent province of Huelva's mountain village of Jabugo, the famous hams of that name are produced and Spaniards boast, with some justification, that they are the finest in the world. So valuable are these hams that would-be buyers must use, with the utmost care, an ivory tool to test their quality, watched by the eagle eye of the producer – drying out has to be avoided at all costs.

The sine qua non is, therefore, *jamón Jabugo de bellota* and its price will vary with grade and age. A minimum of 1,600 *pesetas* will be demanded in a *tapas* bar or restaurant for a *ración*. Always be sure that the cut ham has a glistening oiliness and is marbled with fat, otherwise it will be too dry and lack the succulence that is its hallmark. The best Jabugo requires virtually no movement of the jaws – it will melt on the tongue.

Drink

Wine As with food, most Spanish wines keep to their own areas of production. Exceptions are Rioja, from the north, Valdepeñas from La Mancha and, of course, sherry from Jerez or Puerto de Santa María. Up-market bars will also be able to supply the sparkling *cava* from Catalonia.

English visitors, used to drinking sherry only as an aperitif, are surprised to find that in Andalusia where it is far less alcoholic, sherry is a normal accompaniment to a meal, particularly seafood. Most popular is *fino*, due to its dryness. Sweet, particularly cream, sherry is rarely drunk in Spain, being regarded as an idiosyncratic foreign aberration. *Manzanilla* is similar to sherry, but comes from the coastal vineyards of Sanlúcar de Barrameda and has a slight tang of the sea. *Manzanilla* is also a type of tea – therefore, be sure in a bar to specify *manzanilla vino*, as barmen assume that all English-speaking visitors perpetually drink tea. Also from Sanlúcar is a recently developed, rather flinty white wine, Castillo de San Diego, which is a particularly good accompaniment to the local shellfish.

Beer Spanish continental-type lager is always available, draught or bottled, and some of the more expensive bars also hold a range of foreign beers, including British. Many regard Seville's Cruzcampo beer as the best in Andalusia.

Spirits, liqueurs and aperitifs Virtually all overseas brands, apart from scotch, are made in Spain, no matter what the label may at first glance imply. This dates back to the Franco period when, short of overseas currency, the Spanish forbade the import of foreign goods, forcing their manufacturers either to set up production units in Spain or forgo the market. The results were rarely a success, possibly due to variations in the water. A blind testing of most well-known brands of gin, white rum or vodka would leave many visitors foxed as to what spirit they were drinking, let alone the brand. However, Negrita is a very drinkable rum, of medium colour, and the better bars now stock the higher-priced Tanqueray gin, imported from England, which is, for easily guessed reasons, indistinguishable from the Gordon's gin that is made in the UK.

French and Italian brands of liqueurs and aperitifs suffer a similar fate, generally being slightly sweeter and lacking the character of the original. Campari (made in Barcelona) is, however, a fairly good impersonation. Even sherry (Jerez or Xeres), undoubtedly a Spanish drink, often appears to be made to a lower alcoholic strength than the exported version – it is, however, more acceptable in this form as an accompaniment to food.

Brandy As *cava* is not champagne, brandy is not cognac, but in all fairness it has never pretended to be. In general, Spanish brandies are heavy and tend to sweetness, some from the south even developing a thick caramelized flavour. Lovers of French brandy will probably prefer a 103 (*ciento tres*) or the Torres range. It is common in a bar to ask for a '*carajillo*', which involves pouring a generous slug of brandy into black coffee. A combination of brandy and anisette in equal measures is a *sol y sombra* (sun and shadow).

Alcoholic long drinks Ask a foreigner what he knows about Spanish drinks and he will probably mention *Sangria*, which originated in the Costa Brava. Consisting basically of orange juice, red wine and brandy, care is generally taken to ensure that tourist versions are not too overwhelming.

Non-alcoholic long drinks In summer, the Spanish soft drink specialities suddenly appear, having been replaced in the cooler months by hot chocolate and coffee. Try *horchata*, a sweet milk-shake based on ground tiger-nuts (*chufas*) and served just below freezing point. It is delicious, thirst-quenching and incredibly high in calories. Weight-watchers are probably better advised to concentrate on *granizadas* made from fruit syrups or coffee, drunk with a straw through crushed ice. As is general in continental Europe, soft drinks are much better than their British equivalents, tastes are more natural and artificial sweeteners unknown.

Hot drinks 'English' tea is available in most supermarkets, but the importance of using boiling water immediately is not always appreciated by caterers. Coffee is pretty uniform – always *espresso*, as in France, but at least flavoursome. Nowhere are instant varieties offered. Hot chocolate is usually very thick, sometimes almost like a hot chocolate mousse. Spaniards like to dip their breakfast *churros* (long crisp strips of deep-fried dough) in the chocolate.

Restaurants and bars

The selection of restaurants and bars that follows should not be considered to be exhaustive. Most are a personal choice, but some have been included based on recommendations. During 1992, pavilions at Expo will incorporate restaurants and there will be a unique opportunity to sample a variety of national cuisines. Restaurants in Seville are widely spread, and emphasis in this book is given to those that are centrally located. Few economy restaurants exist, their place in Seville being taken by the *tapas* bars, some of which provide separate tables at the rear.

Tapas bars of note tend to congregate in certain areas, the most important being around Calle San Eloy, Plaza de Alfafa, the Calle Antonia Diáz and Calle Arfe intersection (my personal favourite), Calle Mateos Gago and the streets that run into it, and the Triana side of Isabel II bridge.

Restaurants
Luxury – 6,000 *pesetas* and over
All restaurants in this grade should be booked well in advance from April to October 1992, when opening periods may well be extended. Few normally open for lunch before 13.30 or for dinner before 20.30.

The restaurants and bars that follow are indicated on the maps, when applicable, by their number, preceded by R.

1 Albahaca (La) (map page 95) 12 Plaza Santa Cruz (422 07 14). Not Sunday. Meals are served in a series of delightful small rooms with period decor. La Albahaca is renowned for innovative food, with unusual combinations. A seasonally varied menu is offered, now fractionally more international than heretofore.

Specialities: a definitive *caldito sevillano con guarnición*, lamb with thyme, and all desserts, particularly the bitter oranges in gelatine, made from freshly picked fruit growing in the square outside.

2 Burladero (El), Hotel Colón (map 218–19) 1 Calle Canalejas (422 55 25). Not Sunday. First-class international food with Spanish touches. Sadly, the popular 'tasting' menu is no more.

3 Dorada (La) (not on map) 6 Virgen de Aguasantas (445 51 00). Not Sunday. The most famous of the Los Remedios restaurants, La Dorada, specializing in sea-food, now has off-shoots in Madrid, Barcelona and Paris. Fish is beautifully prepared and of the highest standard. The vast L-shaped room appears rather clinical, in spite of the ship's lanterns and sailor-boy costumes of the waiters.

Specialities: fish baked in a salt crust – there is no salty flavour – including gilt-head (*dorada*), bass and sole, exceptional *gazpacho*, caramelized baked apple.

4 Egaña Oriza (map pages 120–21) 41 Calle San Fernando (422 72 54). Not lunch, weekends or August. Another restaurant created within an old mansion. The emphasis here is on Basque dishes, particularly sea-food.

Specialities: crayfish, *gazpacho*, hake with clams, game in season.

5 Itálica, Hotel Alfonso XIII (map pages 120–21) Calle San Fernando (422 28 50). As may be expected, a beautiful dining-room in which international food is served.

Specialities: steaks served in many ways.

6 San Marco (map pages 218–19) 6 Calle Cuna (421 24 40). Not Monday or August. Set in an eighteenth-century mansion, San Marco offers, in spite of its Italian name, a range of international and *nouvelle cuisine* dishes and is currently the highest rated of its type in Seville.

Specialities: pheasant ravioli with *foie gras*, duck with Seville olives, mouth-watering desserts.

Expensive – 4,000–6,000 *pesetas*

7 Bailén 34 (map pages 140–41) 34 Calle Bailén (422 52 81). Closed Sunday, August and Saturday p.m. in July. Andalusian dishes are prepared with authenticity. Bailén is renowned for the quality of its meat.

Speciality: *rabo de toro*.

8 Corral del Agua (map page 95) 6 Callejón del Agua (22 48 41). Not Sunday or January and February. Under the same management as La Albahaca, this fairly new (1987) restaurant serves exquisite food, whenever possible in its romantic, flower-bedecked patio, which retains a well and a fountain. Wonderful at lunchtime if the sun is not too hot.

Specialities: ice-cold *ajo blanco con pasas* (white *gazpacho* made with garlic, cream, almonds and vinegar, sprinkled with raisins), chicken 'grandmother' style, an outstanding *tocino de cielo* dessert.

9 Don Raimundo (Mesón) (map pages 166–7) 26 Calle Argote de Molina (422 33 55). Not Sunday p.m. Seville's prettiest restaurant, decorated with antiques. The place to come for traditional Andalusian dishes, which Don Raimundo has specialized in reviving.

Specialities: game in season, soups, various desserts based on dried fruits, nuts, honey and cream.

10 Figon del Cabildo (map pages 140–41) 19 Calle Arfe (422 01 17). Not Sunday or July or August. Basic Spanish and international food in an 'up-market *taverna*'. Excellent quality meat and fish.

11 Rio Grande (map pages 236–7) s/n Calle Betis (427 83 71 or 427 39 36). Sensational views from Triana's riverside to the Tower of Gold are unbeatable by day, or at night when all is illuminated. Terrace and dining-room. Apart from the famous setting, the food maintains a high standard and includes most local favourites.

Specialities: hake with tiny eels, fried fish.

Economical – below 4,000 *pesetas*

12 Casa Robles (map pages 166–7) 58 Calle Alvarez Quintero (421

31 50). Concentrates on Andalusian dishes served in a small restaurant approached from the *tapas* bar.

13 Tenorio (Mesón el) (map page 95) 9 Calle Mateos Gago (421 40 30). Lively interior and Andalusian food. Portions rather small.

Specialities: *regaña*, a large, thin crispbread, served to accompany all dishes in place of bread, Andalusian stew.

Bars (mostly *tapas* bars, but including *bodegas* (off-licences) and fried fish specialists)

14 Alfafa (map pages 166–7) Plaza de Alfafa/Calle Candilejo corner. One of the many *tapas* bars around Plaza de Alfafa. Excellent Andalusian cooking – particularly the *menudos* (tripe).

15 Alicantina (La) (map pages 166–7) 2 Plaza del Salvador. Beside El Salvador church, this is a popular, fairly modern *tapas* bar. The Russian salad is famous – but not cheap.

16 Aviles (Juan García) (map page 95) 20 Calle Mateos Gago. Not Monday. Very limited *tapas* – ham, olives, etc. The great attraction is the intimacy and antique sheen of the ancient counter.

17 Bacalao (El) (map pages 166–7) 15 Plaza Ponce de León. Understandably, from its name, the bar specializes in salt cod dishes – almost fifty varieties are prepared.

18 Caracoles (Los) also known as **Casa Antonio** (map pages 166–7) 15 Calle Pérez Galdós. Not Wednesday. Again, as the name implies, the bar's *tapas* specializes – this time in snails.

19 Entre Cárceles (Bodega) (map pages 166–7) 2 Calle Manuel Cortina. Open evenings only. Bullfight and *feria* posters give a very 'Spanish' atmosphere. It is interesting to observe the 1940s posters, confirming that, almost uniquely, the Iberian peninsula was having fun while the rest of Europe was engaged in bloody warfare. On offer is Fino Imperiál, one of the most delicious and expensive sherries produced. Raid the piggy-bank to taste one – resembling an *amontillado*, to me it is the essence of Christmas. Very few *tapas* are offered.

20 Estrella 3 (map pages 166–7) Calle Estrella. Not Sunday. Discreetly sited in one of Seville's most complicated labyrinths, this is worth any amount of effort to find. Don't worry, the 1950 vintage bakelite radio has not worked for years – it is just décor. Low ceilings, a ceramic dado and the general air of venerability makes the Estrella exceptional, but it also serves some of the most innovative *tapas* in the city – even providing *churros*. Try the delicious, home-made vegetable or fish *pâtés*, and green peppers stùffed with tuna fish. After a few sherries, one of the ancient columns may appear to be leaning – it does.

21 Giralda (map page 95) 2 Calle Mateos Gago. Pastiche Mudéjar décor gives an *Arabian Nights* atmosphere to this bar, which also incorporates some genuine features from original Moorish baths. Few establishments can match the wide range of *tapas*, seventy-five varieties sometimes being on offer.

22 Hijos de E. Morales (map pages 140–41) 11 Calle García de Vinuesa. Delightfully dilapidated. In spite of its central position no food whatsoever is available. Comprising two large bars, one almost taken over by barrels, this is the nearest *bodega* in Seville to a nineteenth-century time-warp.

23 Jamón Real (map pages 140–41) 5 Calle Lope de Arenas. Not Tuesday. I am being honourably masochistic in divulging the excellence of Jamón Real – although small, it is my favourite *tapas* bar in Seville. Uniquely in the city, produce is 'imported' from the adjoining mountainous region of Extremadura, and much of it, particularly the cheese, is far superior to Andalusian equivalents. Try to go with a Spanish friend who speaks English – or find one quickly in the bar, as the charming and very sympathetic owner and her son speak only Spanish. Food available is listed all over the place – small posters, blackboards, display cards, and it is not too clear what is being served over the counter or what is available to take away only. If on the menu, *lechón ibérico al horno*, baked sucking pig, is a must – right up to Segovia standards. Also ask for *morcilla* or *chorizo blanco* (i.e. made without blood and very delicate). Virtually all the food comes from small farmers (*artesanos*), and the hand-produced results speak for themselves. Exceptional is the *torta de credo*, goat's-milk cheese, with a ripe *brie* texture; *queso del casar*, alternatively, is firmer and slightly sweet. The list of gourmet delights seems endless.

24 Kiosko de las Flores (map pages 236–7) (nestles beside Isabel II bridge on the Triana side). Not Monday. Seville's most famous fried-fish establishment. A vast range of sea-food is fried in the finest olive oil, each delicate morsel lightly coated with batter. It has been suggested that the battered English fish, of fish and chips fame, was inspired by this speciality, shippers of wine from Jerez returning with the recipe. A half portion is sufficient for most, and this is available at the bar only – those sitting at tables outside must order a whole portion per person. The value is tremendous, whitebait (*chanquetes*) and prawns (*gambas*) being the most popular. No bread or butter is provided, only *picos*. Surprisingly, beer seems a more popular accompaniment than wine, possibly due to the slight saltiness of the food.

25 Moro (Mesón del) (map page 95) 4 Calle Mesón del Moro. Evenings only. The chief interest of the bar is the remains of Moorish baths, said to have been built by Mudéjars in 1491. Particularly lively at weekends.

26 Patio (El) (map pages 140–41) 9 Calle San Eloy. One of the best of the lively *tapas* bars in Calle San Eloy; most of them are very popular with youngsters.

27 Pez de Espada (Bodega) (map pages 140–41) 8 Calle Hernando Colón. A large fried-fish establishment with a wide range. Try the dish of mixed varieties.

28 Rincón Gallego del Pulpo (map pages 140–41) 21 Calle Harinas. Specialities from Galicia are the main attraction. One of Spain's great dishes is *pulpo a la gallego* (octopus, marinated with red pepper and garlic). It is served hot, accompanied by boiled potatoes, either as a *tapa* or a *ración*. Also offered is home-made *torta de Santiago* – a cake with a slightly lemon flavour, quite heavy but with crisp edges, and the whole dusted with icing sugar.

29 Rinconcillo (El) (map pages 166–7) Calle Girona/Calle Alhóndiga. Seville's oldest bar, built in 1670. It was here that, according to tradition, *tapas* evolved. See page 216 for architectural details. The Jabugo ham is invariably delicious.

30 Robles (Casa) (map pages 166–7) 58 Calle Alvarez Quintero. Centrally situated, the *tapas* bar is as important to the establishment as its restaurant. Excellent *charcuterie* is served in a smart atmosphere. See also restaurant 12.

31 Román (Casa) (map page 95) 1 Plaza de los Venerables. A remodelled ancient tavern in the heart of the Santa Cruz quarter, Casa Román is renowned for its Jabugo ham, supplied by Sánchez Romero Carvajal, a famous producer.

32 Santa Cruz (Bodega) (map page 95) 1 Calle de Rodrigo Caro. Incredibly popular, particularly with youngsters at night, it is hard to find better value *tapas* in Seville; the size of the portions is remarkably large. A godsend to those on a limited budget!

33 Serranito (Mesón) (map pages 140–41) 11 Calle Antonia Diáz. Ceramic tiles and photographs of bullfighters make this a popular venue. Food is varied and top quality. Unusually, there is a printed menu to study at leisure, a boon for foreigners.

34 Serranito (Mesón) (map pages 140–41) 9 Calle Alfonso XII. Sister establishment to the above. A completely tiled, street-facing terrace is an added attraction.

35 Sevilla Jabugo 1 (Mesón) (map pages 140–41) 5 Calle Arfe. This is a large, rather smart *tapas* bar, where the accent is on Jabugo ham from Sánchez Romero Carvajal, which can also be purchased to take away. Preferential service appears to be given to regulars.

36 Triana (Bodega) (map pages 236–7) 5 Pagés del Corro. Closed Saturday p.m. *Tapas* specializes in rabbit and kid.

FOOD VOCABULARY

Acedía	*small sole*	Ajo blanco	*white garlic*
Aceite	*oil*		*gazpacho*
Aceituna	*olive*	Albaricoque	*apricot*
Achicoria	*endive*	Albóndigas	*meat balls*
Adobo	*marinated in*	Alcachofas	*artichokes*
	vinegar	Alcaparras	*capers*
Aguacate	*avocado pear*	Aliñados	*garnished*
Ahumada	*smoked*	Allioli	*garlic mayonnaise*
Ajillo	*garlic*	Almejas	*clams*
Ajo	*garlic*	Almendras	*almonds*
		Alubias	*kidney beans*

Amarga	bitter	Cabrillas	type of snail
Anchoas	anchovies	Cabrito	kid
Anguila	eel	Calabacín	courgette
Apio	celery	Calamares	squid
Arenque	herring	Caldereta	stew
Arroz	rice	Caldo gallego	a light soup;
Atún	tunny		generally inspired
Atún mechado	tunny minced		cabbage water
	with bacon and	Callos	tripe
	garlic, served	Camarones	tiny shrimps
	with a wine	Caña	stew
	sauce	Canaillas	spiky shellfish
Avellana	hazelnut	Cangrejo	crab or crayfish
Aves	poultry	Cangrejo de	seawater crayfish
Azafrán	saffron rice	mar	
Bacalao	dried and salted	Cangrejo de rio	freshwater
	cod		crayfish
Bacalao fresco	fresh cod	Caracoles	snails
Bellotas	acorn-fed	Carne	meat
Berberecho	cockles	Casera (a la)	home-made
Berenjena	aubergine	Castaña	chestnut
Besugo	sea bream	Cebolla	onion
Bistec	steak	Centollo	spider crab
Bocadillo	sandwich	Cerdo	pork
Bocas rusas	crabs' claws	Cereza	cherry
Bogavante	lobster	Chacinas	pork sausage meat
Bonito	striped tunny	Champiñon	mushroom
Boquerónes	fresh anchovies	Chaquetes	whitebait
Caballa	mackerel	Chipirones	baby squid
Caballito	fried bread	Chirimoya	custard apple
Cabrales	blue goat's-milk	Chocos	cuttlefish
	cheese from	Chorizo	spicy sausage,
	Asturias, with a		eaten cold, or hot
	strong flavour;		in stews:
	probably the most		sometimes made
	characterful		with chillis and
	Spanish cheese		then very fiery
	generally	Chuletas	chops
	available	Churrasco	barbecued meat

Churros	*fried batter in thin tubes, a popular breakfast*	Espárragos trigueros	*wild asparagus fried with garlic*
Cigalas	*small crayfish, 'Mediterranean prawns'*	Espinacas	*spinach*
		Estofado	*braised*
		Fabada (Asturiana)	*casserole of butter beans, pork, chorizo and spicy black pudding*
Ciruela	*plum or prune*		
Cocido	*meat stew with vegetables*		
		Fabes	*broad beans*
Cocido a la sevillana	*as above but meat is fried with eggs and potatoes*	Fiambres	*slices of cold meat*
		Filete	*fillet (meat)*
		Flan	*crème caramel*
Coco	*coconut*	Frambuesa	*raspberry*
Cola de toro	*oxtail*	Freidurías	*fried and battered seafood*
Conejo	*rabbit*		
Coquinas	*clams*	Fresa	*strawberry*
Corazón	*heart*	Frio	*cold*
Cordero	*lamb*	Frito	*fried*
Cordoníz	*quail*	Fritura Sevillana	*mixed fried fish*
Criadillas	*sweetbreads*		
Dátil	*date*	Gallo campero	*large, free-range chicken*
Dorada	*gilt-head (fish)*		
Embutido	*varied sausages*	Gamba	*prawn*
Emparedado	*grilled roll with a filling*	Garbanzos	*chick-peas*
		Gazpacho	*iced soup: usually of tomato, cucumber, olive oil, vinegar, garlic, pimento and croûtons*
Eneldo	*dill*		
Ensalada	*salad (variada – mixed, sin tomates – green)*		
		Guarnición	*garnished*
Entreméses variados	*hors d'oeuvre*	Guarrito	*piglet*
		Guisado	*stewed*
Escabeche	*marinade of oil, paprika, vinegar and herbs usually for preserving fish or poultry*	Guisantes	*peas*
		Habas	*broad beans*
		Habichuelas	*green beans*
		Hamburguesa	*hamburger*
		Helado	*ice-cream*
Espárragos	*asparagus*	Higado	*liver*

Higos	*fig*	Lima	*lime*
Hinojo	*fennel*	Limón	*lemon*
Horno (al)	*baked*	Lomo	*loin*
Huevas	*fish roe*	Lubina	*sea bass*
Huevos	*eggs: duro –*	Manchego	*ewe's-milk*
	hard, escalfado		*cheese: varies in*
	– poached, frito –		*strength and*
	fried, revuelto –		*texture with*
	scrambled		*age*
Huevos a la	*fried eggs with*	Manta	*cover*
Valenciana	*peas, tomato,*	Manteca	*pork dripping*
	chorizo,	Mantequilla	*butter*
	asparagus, red	Manzana	*apple*
	pepper, diced ham	Mariscos	*seafood*
Huevos al nido	*eggs on a 'nest' of*	Mechada	*filled with egg*
	fried potatoes		*and garlic*
Hurta	*type of bream*	Mejillones	*mussels*
Ibérico	*mountain breed of*	Melocotón	*peach*
	pig	Melva	*fish like tunny*
Jamón	*ham*	Menestra	*casserole*
Jamón en dulce	*boiled ham*	Menudos	*tripe stewed with*
(or York)			*chorizo*
Jamón Jabugo	*the best serrano*	Merluza	*hake*
	ham, from the	Miel	*honey*
	Huelva region	Mojama	*dried tunny*
Jamón serrano	*lean, dry-cured*	Montadito	*served on pieces of*
	ham		*bread*
Judía	*bean*	Morcilla	*spicy blood*
Judía verde	*green bean*		*pudding*
Langosta	*spiny lobster or*	Morcón	*blood sausage*
	large crayfish	Mostaza	*mustard*
Langostino	*large prawn*	Naranja	*orange*
Leche	*milk*	Nata	*whipped cream*
Lechón	*suckling pig*	Navajas	*razor shell (looks*
Lechuga	*lettuce*		*like crab sticks)*
Legumbres	*vegetables*	Oliva	*olive*
Lenguado	*sole*	Ostion	*large Cadíz Bay*
Lentejas	*lentils*		*oyster*
Liebre	*hare*	Ostra	*oyster*

Paella	*saffron rice, cooked with fish, chicken, shellfish and vegetables*	Pijotas	*whiting*
		Pimienta	*pepper*
		Piña	*pineapple*
		Pinchito	*kebab*
Paella de mariscos	*paella made with seafood only*	Pinchos morunos	*small kebabs*
Pajaritos	*tiny birds*	Pisto	*stewed vegetables*
Palitos de queso	*cheese straws*	Plancha (a la)	*grilled on a hot plate*
Pan	*bread*		
Parrilla (a la)	*grilled*	Plátano	*banana*
Pasas	*raisins*	Platos combinados	*dish of several components at an inclusive price*
Pastas	*biscuits*		
Pastel	*cake*		
Pata	*trotter*	Poco hecho	*rare, e.g. steak*
Pata negre	*black trotters (pig)*	Pollo	*chicken*
		Pollo asado	*roast chicken*
Patatas	*potatoes*	Polvorónes	*shortbread*
Patatas fritas	*fried potatoes (chips)*	Pomelo	*grapefruit*
		Postres	*desserts*
Pato	*duck*	Potaje	*dish*
Pavías	*small pieces fried with egg*	Pringa	*bread dipped and toasted*
Pavo	*turkey*	Pulpito	*baby octopus*
Pedroches	*ewe's-milk cheese from Córdoba*	Pulpo	*octopus*
		Puntas	*tips (ends)*
Pepinillo	*gherkin*	Puntillitas	*type of small squid*
Pepino	*cucumber*		
Pepito	*long sandwich*	Puré de patatas	*mashed potatoes*
Pera	*pear*	Queso	*cheese*
Percebes	*barnacles, taste like salty shrimps*	Rábano	*radish*
		Rabo de toro	*oxtail*
Perdiz	*partridge*	Rape	*monkfish*
Pescado	*fish*	Raya	*skate*
Pescaíto frito	*assorted fried fish in batter*	Rebozados	*fried in breadcrumbs*
Pez espada	*swordfish*	Repollo	*cabbage*
Picada	*minced meat*	Riñones	*kidneys*
Picos	*breadsticks*	Rodaballo	*turbot*
Pierna	*leg*	Romana (a la)	*fried in batter*

Sal	*salt*	Tortilla	*omelette French*
Salchicha	*pork sausage*	Francesa	*style, soft textured*
Salchichón	*hard, salami-type*	Trucha	*trout*
	sausage, eaten	Turrón	*nougat*
	cold	Uva	*grape*
Salmonete	*red mullet*	Vapor (al)	*steamed*
Salpicón	*chopped meat,*	Venera	*scallop*
	eggs, anchovies	Verde	*green*
	and onions	Vinagre	*vinegar*
Salsa	*sauce*	Yema	*egg yolk*
Salteado	*sautéed*	Zumo de fruta	*fruit juice*
San Jacobo	*veal, pork or ham*		
	fried with cheese		
	and breadcrumbs	**Restaurant queries and**	
Sepia	*cuttlefish*	**requests**	
Serranito de la	*cured ham fried*	Ashtray	*cenicero*
casa	*with bread and*	Beer	*cerveza*
	green peppers	Bill	*cuenta*
Sesos	*brains*	Bread	*pan*
Sobrasada	*type of chorizo*	Butter	*mantequilla*
	spread	Cheese	*queso*
Solo	*on its own*	Coffee – black	*café solo*
Solomillo	*sirloin steak*	Coffee – white	*café con leche*
Sopa	*soup*	Cold	*frio*
Sopa de ajo	*soup of garlic,*	Cream	*nata*
	paprika, bread	Credit card	*tarseta de crédito*
Taquitos	*small pieces*	Cup	*taza*
Ternera	*veal*	Drinks	*bebidas*
Tocino	*fatty, strong-*	Dry	*seco*
	flavoured bacon	Fork	*tenedor*
Tomillo	*thyme*	Glass (for water	*vaso*
Toro de lidia	*fighting bull*	or beer)	
Tortilla	*plain omelette*	Glass (for	*copa*
Tortilla	*'Spanish'*	wine)	
Española	*omelette, with*	Hot	*caliente*
	onions and	(temperature)	
	potatoes, firm	Hot (flavour)	*picante*
	textured, eaten hot	Ice	*hielo*
	or cold	Ice-cream	*helados*
		Knife	*cuchillo*

Lemon	*limón*	Spoon	*cuchara*
Medium	*regular or mediano*	Sugar	*azúcar*
		Sweet	*dulce*
Menu	*carta*	Tea	*té*
Mustard	*mostaza*	Traveller's cheques	*cheques de viajes*
Neat	*solo*		
Nothing	*nada*	Vinegar	*vinagre*
Oil	*aceite*	Waiter	*camarero*
Pepper (condiment)	*pimienta*	Water (tap)	*agua corriente (or del grifo)*
Plate	*plato*	Water (gassy mineral)	*agua con gas*
Rare	*poco hecho*		
Roll	*panecillo*	Water (flat mineral)	*agua sin gas*
Salad	*ensalada*		
Salt	*sal*	Well done	*muy (or bien) hecho*
Sandwich	*bocadillo*		
Serviette	*servilleta*	Wine (white)	*vino blanco*
Set menu	*menú del dia*	Wine (red)	*vino tinto*
Speciality	*especialidad*	Wine (*rosé*)	*vino rosado*

INDEX

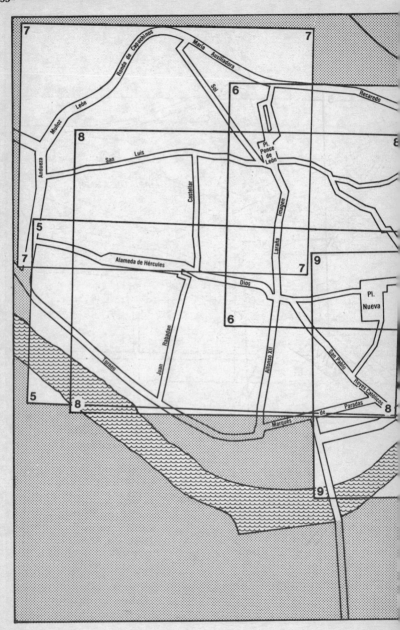

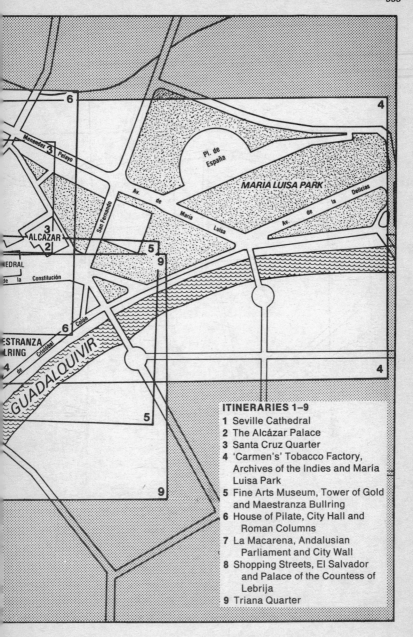

ITINERARIES 1-9

1 Seville Cathedral
2 The Alcázar Palace
3 Santa Cruz Quarter
4 'Carmen's' Tobacco Factory, Archives of the Indies and María Luisa Park
5 Fine Arts Museum, Tower of Gold and Maestranza Bullring
6 House of Pilate, City Hall and Roman Columns
7 La Macarena, Andalusian Parliament and City Wall
8 Shopping Streets, El Salvador and Palace of the Countess of Lebrija
9 Triana Quarter

FOR THE BEST IN PAPERBACKS, LOOK FOR THE 🐧

In every corner of the world, on every subject under the sun, Penguin represents quality and variety – the very best in publishing today.

For complete information about books available from Penguin – including Puffins, Penguin Classics and Arkana – and how to order them, write to us at the appropriate address below. Please note that for copyright reasons the selection of books varies from country to country.

In the United Kingdom: Please write to *Dept E.P., Penguin Books Ltd, Harmondsworth, Middlesex, UB7 0DA.*

If you have any difficulty in obtaining a title, please send your order with the correct money, plus ten per cent for postage and packaging, to *PO Box No 11, West Drayton, Middlesex*

In the United States: Please write to *Dept BA, Penguin, 299 Murray Hill Parkway, East Rutherford, New Jersey 07073*

In Canada: Please write to *Penguin Books Canada Ltd, 2801 John Street, Markham, Ontario L3R 1B4*

In Australia: Please write to the *Marketing Department, Penguin Books Australia Ltd, P.O. Box 257, Ringwood, Victoria 3134*

In New Zealand: Please write to the *Marketing Department, Penguin Books (NZ) Ltd, Private Bag, Takapuna, Auckland 9*

In India: Please write to *Penguin Overseas Ltd, 706 Eros Apartments, 56 Nehru Place, New Delhi, 110019*

In the Netherlands: Please write to *Penguin Books Netherlands B.V., Postbus 3507, 1001 AH, Amsterdam*

In West Germany: Please write to *Penguin Books Ltd, Friedrichstrasse 10–12, D–6000 Frankfurt/Main 1*

In Spain: Please write to *Alhambra Longman S.A., Fernandez de la Hoz 9, E–28010 Madrid*

In Italy: Please write to *Penguin Italia s.r.l., Via Como 4, 1-20096 Pioltello (Milano)*

In France: Please write to *Penguin Books Ltd, 39 Rue de Montmorency, F-75003 Paris*

In Japan: Please write to *Longman Penguin Japan Co Ltd, Yamaguchi Building, 2–12–9 Kanda Jimbocho, Chiyoda-Ku, Tokyo 101*

A CHOICE OF PENGUINS

The Time Out London Guide
The Time Out Paris Guide
The Time Out New York Guide

Compiled by *Time Out* magazine – with twenty years' experience of providing information about events and entertainment – these guides are different: witty, humorous and thoroughly readable. Jam-packed with information, the Time Out guides will show you a good time in the *real* London, Paris or New York.

Raw #2   Edited by Art Spiegelman and Françoise Mouly

Raw returns with an all-new collection of avant-garde American, European and Japanese commix – and a new chapter of *Maus*. '*Raw* ... indicates how far comics have come from their early, invincible innocence' – *Newsweek*

I: The Philosophy and Psychology of Personal Identity   Jonathan Glover

From cases of split brains and multiple personalities to the importance of memory and recognition by others, the author of *Causing Death* and *Saving Lives* tackles the vital and vexed questions of personal identity. 'Fascinating' – Anthony Storr

War and Peace   Leo Tolstoy

This massive chronicle portrays Russian life during and after the Napoleonic War. Few would dispute its claim to be regarded as the greatest novel in any language.

The Penguin Guide to Ancient Egypt   W. J. Murnane

This unique and authoritative guide describes the ancient sites and monuments of Egypt, and places them within the context of their time and within the realities of the present day.

Plants from the Past   David Stuart and James Sutherland

As soon as it is planted, even the most modern garden can be full of history, whether overflowing with flowers domesticated by the early civilizations of Mesopotamia or with plants collected in the Himalayas for Victorian millionaires.

A CHOICE OF PENGUINS

Ginsberg: A Biography   Barry Miles

The definitive life of one of this century's most colourful poets. 'A life so dramatic, so dangerous, so committed to hard-volume truth, that his survival is a miracle, his kindness, wisdom and modesty a blessing' – *The Times*. 'Read it to the end' – Michael Horovitz

The End of Nature   Bill McKibben

'An environmental blockbuster ... an extraordinary book, combining an impressive body of scientific detail with the lightest of literary and philosophical touches' – *Daily Telegraph*. 'Even for those who have been living and breathing green issues for the last twenty years this will be a powerful and very disturbing book' – Jonathon Porritt

Coleridge: Early Visions   Richard Holmes

'Dazzling ... Holmes has not merely reinterpreted Coleridge; he has recreated him, and his biography has the aura of fiction, the shimmer of an authentic portrait ... a biography like few I have ever read' – *Guardian*.

The Speeches of Winston Churchill   David Cannadine (ed.)

The most eloquent statesman of his time, Winston Churchill used language as his most powerful weapon. These orations, spanning fifty years, show him gradually honing his rhetoric until, with spectacular effect, 'he mobilized the English language, and sent it into battle'.

A Green Manifesto for the 1990s   Penny Kemp and Derek Wall

Written by two leading members of the Green Party, this manifesto sets out a new political agenda not only for the 1990s but for the twenty-first century.

Heat Treatment   Justin Wintle

On unorthodox tour in the melting-pot of the Far East, Justin Wintle discovered that the women's intentions left little to the imagination and that the food destroyed his digestive system. As fears of massive cockroaches and of catching AIDS reduced him to a state of persistent hysteria, he learned the full extent of the Orient's extremes.

A CHOICE OF PENGUINS

Return to the Marshes   Gavin Young

His remarkable portrait of the remote and beautiful world of the Marsh Arabs, whose centuries-old existence is now threatened with extinction by twentieth-century warfare.

The Big Red Train Ride   Eric Newby

From Moscow to the Pacific on the Trans-Siberian Railway is an eight-day journey of nearly six thousand miles through seven time zones. In 1977 Eric Newby set out with his wife, an official guide and a photographer on this journey.

Warhol   Victor Bockris

'This is the kind of book I like: it tells me the things I want to know about the artist, what he ate, what he wore, who he knew (in his case ... everybody), at what time he went to bed and with whom, and, most important of all, his work habits' – *Independent*

1001 Ways to Save the Planet   Bernadette Vallely

There are 1001 changes that *everyone* can make in their lives *today* to bring about a greener environment – whether at home or at work, on holiday or away on business. Action that you can take *now*, and that you won't find too difficult to take. This practical guide shows you how.

Bitter Fame   Anne Stevenson
A Life of Sylvia Plath

'A sobering and salutary attempt to estimate what Plath was, what she achieved and what it cost her ... This is the only portrait which answers Ted Hughes's image of the poet as Ariel, not the ethereal bright pure roving sprite, but Ariel trapped in Prospero's pine and raging to be free' – *Sunday Telegraph*

The Venetian Empire   Jan Morris

For six centuries the Republic of Venice was a maritime empire of coasts, islands and fortresses. Jan Morris reconstructs this glittering dominion in the form of a sea voyage along the historic Venetian trade routes from Venice itself to Greece, Crete and Cyprus.

A CHOICE OF PENGUINS

Riding the Iron Rooster   Paul Theroux

An eye-opening and entertaining account of travels in old and new China, from the author of *The Great Railway Bazaar*. 'Mr Theroux cannot write badly … in the course of a year there was almost no train in the vast Chinese rail network on which he did not travel' – Ludovic Kennedy

The Life of Graham Greene   Norman Sherry
Volume One 1904–1939

'Probably the best biography ever of a living author' – Philip French in the *Listener*. Graham Greene has always maintained a discreet distance from his reading public. This volume reconstructs his first thirty-five years to create one of the most revealing literary biographies of the decade.

The Chinese   David Bonavia

'I can think of no other work which so urbanely and entertainingly succeeds in introducing the general Western reader to China' – *Sunday Telegraph*

All the Wrong Places   James Fenton

Who else but James Fenton could have played a Bach prelude on the presidential piano – and stolen one of Imelda's towels – on the very day Marcos left his palace in Manila? 'He is the most professional of amateur war correspondents, a true though unusual journo, top of the trade. When he arrives in town, prudent dictators pack their bags and quit' – *The Times*

Voices of the Old Sea   Norman Lewis

'Limpidly and lovingly, Norman Lewis has caught the helpless, unwitting, often foolish, but always hopeful village in its dying summers, and saved the tragedy with sublime comedy' – *Observer*

Ninety-Two Days   Evelyn Waugh

With characteristic honesty, Evelyn Waugh here debunks the romantic notions attached to rough travelling. His journey in Guiana and Brazil is difficult, dangerous and extremely uncomfortable, and his account of it is witty and unquestionably compelling.

FOR THE BEST IN PAPERBACKS, LOOK FOR THE

A CHOICE OF PENGUINS

The Russian Album Michael Ignatieff

Michael Ignatieff movingly comes to terms with the meaning of his own family's memories and histories, in a book that is both an extraordinary account of the search for roots and a dramatic and poignant chronicle of four generations of a Russian family.

Beyond the Blue Horizon Alexander Frater

The romance and excitement of the legendary Imperial Airways East-bound Empire service – the world's longest and most adventurous scheduled air route – relived fifty years later in one of the most original travel books of the decade. 'The find of the year' – *Today*

Getting to Know the General Graham Greene

'In August 1981 my bag was packed for my fifth visit to Panama when the news came to me over the telephone of the death of General Omar Torrijos Herrera, my friend and host...' 'Vigorous, deeply felt, at times funny, and for Greene surprisingly frank' – *Sunday Times*

The Time of My Life Denis Healey

'Denis Healey's memoirs have been rightly hailed for their intelligence, wit and charm ... *The Time of My Life* should be read, certainly for pleasure, but also for profit ... he bestrides the post-war world, a Colossus of a kind' – *Independent*

Arabian Sands Wilfred Thesiger

'In the tradition of Burton, Doughty, Lawrence, Philby and Thomas, it is, very likely, the book about Arabia to end all books about Arabia' – *Daily Telegraph*

Adieux: A Farewell to Sartre Simone de Beauvoir

A devastatingly frank account of the last years of Sartre's life, and his death, by the woman who for more than half a century shared that life. 'A true labour of love, there is about it a touching sadness, a mingling of the personal with the impersonal and timeless which Sartre himself would surely have liked and understood' – *Listener*

A CHOICE OF PENGUINS

Brian Epstein: The Man Who Made the Beatles   Ray Coleman

'An excellent biography of Brian Epstein, the lonely, gifted man whose artistic faith and bond with the Beatles never wavered – and whose recognition of genius created a cultural era, even though it destroyed him' – *Mail on Sunday*

A Thief in the Night   John Cornwell

A veil of suspicion and secrecy surrounds the last hours of Pope John Paul I, whose thirty-three day reign ended in a reported heart attack on the night of 28 September 1978. Award-winning crime writer John Cornwell was invited by the Vatican to investigate. 'The best detective story you will ever read' – *Daily Mail*

Among the Russians   Colin Thubron

One man's solitary journey by car across Russia provides an enthralling and revealing account of the habits and idiosyncrasies of a fascinating people. 'He sees things with the freshness of an innocent and the erudition of a scholar' – *Daily Telegraph*

Higher than Hope   Fatima Meer

The authorized biography of Nelson Mandela. 'An astonishing read ... the most complete, authoritative and moving tribute thus far' – *Time Out*

Stones of Aran: Pilgrimage   Tim Robinson

Árainn is the largest of the three Aran Islands, and one of the world's oldest landscapes. This 'wholly irresistible' (*Observer*) and uncategorizable book charts a sunwise journey around its coast – and explores an open secret, teasing out the paradoxes of a terrain at once bare and densely inscribed.

Bernard Shaw   Michael Holroyd
Volume I 1856–1898: The Search for Love

'In every sense, a spectacular piece of work ... A feat of style as much as of research, which will surely make it a flamboyant new landmark in modern English life-writing' – Richard Holmes in *The Times*

A CHOICE OF PENGUINS

The Assassination of Federico García Lorca   Ian Gibson

Lorca's 'crime' was his antipathy to pomposity, conformity and intolerance. His punishment was murder. Ian Gibson – author of the acclaimed new biography of Lorca – reveals the truth about his death and the atmosphere in Spain that allowed it to happen.

Between the Woods and the Water   Patrick Leigh Fermor

Patrick Leigh Fermor continues his celebrated account – begun in *A Time of Gifts* – of his journey on foot from the Hook of Holland to Constantinople. 'Even better than everyone says it is' – Peter Levi. 'Indescribably rich and beautiful' – *Guardian*

The Time Out Film Guide   Edited by Tom Milne

The definitive, up-to-the-minute directory of 9,000 films – world cinema from classics and silent epics to reissues and the latest releases – assessed by two decades of *Time Out* reviewers. 'In my opinion the best and most comprehensive' – Barry Norman

Metamagical Themas   Douglas R. Hofstadter

This astonishing sequel to the bestselling, Pulitzer Prize-winning *Gödel, Escher, Bach* swarms with 'extraordinary ideas, brilliant fables, deep philosophical questions and Carrollian word play' – Martin Gardner

Into the Heart of Borneo   Redmond O'Hanlon

'Perceptive, hilarious and at the same time a serious natural-history journey into one of the last remaining unspoilt paradises' – *New Statesman*. 'Consistently exciting, often funny and erudite without ever being overwhelming' – *Punch*

When the Wind Blows   Raymond Briggs

'A visual parable against nuclear war: all the more chilling for being in the form of a strip cartoon' – *Sunday Times*. 'The most eloquent anti-Bomb statement you are likely to read' – *Daily Mail*

THE PENGUIN TRAVEL LIBRARY – A SELECTION

Hindoo Holiday J. R. Ackerley

The Flight of Ikaros Kevin Andrews

The Innocent Anthropologist Nigel Barley

A Curious Life for a Lady Pat Barr

First Russia, Then Tibet Robert Byron

Granite Island Dorothy Carrington

An Indian Summer James Cameron

Siren Land Norman Douglas

Brazilian Adventure Peter Fleming

The Hill of Devi E. M. Forster

Too Late to Turn Back Barbara Greene

Pattern of Islands Arthur Grimble

Writings from Japan Lafcadio Hearn

A Little Tour in France Henry James

Mornings in Mexico D. H. Lawrence

The Stones of Florence and **Venice Observed** Mary McCarthy

They Went to Portugal Rose Macaulay

The Colossus of Maroussi Henry Miller

Calcutta Geoffrey Moorhouse

Spain Jan Morris

The Big Red Train Ride Eric Newby

The Other Nile Charlie Pye-Smith

The Marsh Arabs Wilfred Thesiger

Journey into Cyprus Colin Thubron

Ninety-Two Days Evelyn Waugh

Maiden Voyage Denton Welch